ANXIETY AND
MOOD DISORDERS
FOLLOWING TRAUMATIC
BRAIN INJURY

Brain Injuries Series
Published and distributed by Karnac Books

Orders:
Tel: +44 (0)20 7431 1075; Fax: +44 (0)20 7435 9076
E-mail: shop@karnacbooks.com
www.karnac books.com

ANXIETY AND MOOD DISORDERS FOLLOWING TRAUMATIC BRAIN INJURY

Clinical Assessment and Psychotherapy

Rudi Coetzer

KARNAC

First published in 2010 by
Karnac Books Ltd
118 Finchley Road, London NW3 5HT

British Library Cataloguing in Publication Data

A C.I.P. for this book is available from the British Library

ISBN 978 1 85575 647 2

Edited, designed and produced by The Studio Publishing Services Ltd
www.publishingservicesuk.co.uk
e-mail: studio@publishingservicesuk.co.uk

www.karnacbooks.com

CONTENTS

ACKNOWLEDGEMENTS

As is the case with most academic works, it is impossible to mention everyone who directly or indirectly shaped this book. First and foremost, I would like to thank Dr Ceri Bowen, who approached me at the right time and was a huge source of encouragement throughout the project. Before that, several people over many years influenced my thinking on the topics covered in this book. I am especially grateful for a thorough and rigorous covering of psychopathology and psychotherapy by several lecturers during my clinical training. This has always proved invaluable. My first clinical neuropsychology post, at Tygerberg Hospital/University of Stellenbosch Medical School, was particularly formative, and I remain grateful to all those I worked with there. Over more recent years, my colleagues at the North Wales Brain Injury Service and Bangor University made me aware of how difficult it is to disentangle the psychological, environmental, and biological factors contributing to emotional difficulties after brain injury. And all these colleagues were never short on humour, even after very long and trying days at the unit where we work. I am, of course, also hugely indebted to the patients from whom I learnt so much and who kindly consented to their cases being written up for inclusion in this book. Finally, my gratitude to those close to me, who did not appear to be too perturbed by my obvious distraction while writing this book.

ABOUT THE AUTHOR

Dr Rudi Coetzer is a Consultant Neuropsychologist employed full-time as a clinician by the Betsi Cadwaladr University Health Board (NHS) in North Wales. He is a visiting lecturer at Bangor University and a Practitioner Full Member of the Division of Neuropsychology (British Psychological Society). Dr Coetzer has been Head of the North Wales Brain Injury Service since the inception of the Service during 1998. Prior to his current post, he helped to develop and worked in a neuropsychiatry and neuropsychology clinic of a large university teaching hospital. He has almost two decades of clinical experience in working with brain-injured persons. During the late 1990s, Dr Coetzer and colleagues developed the North Wales Brain Injury Service, a community-based neuro-rehabilitation service for persons with acquired brain injury. In addition to service development, he has a special interest in psychotherapy as an approach to the rehabilitation of adults with acquired brain injury.

For all the remarkable, special people with brain injury I have met.

SERIES EDITOR'S FOREWORD

Rudi Coetzer is an emerging author. In this, his second book, he brings an eloquent voice and a well organized approach to the neglected topic of the assessment and management of anxiety and mood disorders following traumatic brain injury. Beginning with the pathophysiology, incidence, and prevalence of traumatic brain injury, Dr Coetzer covers a number of key areas such as the clinical presentation, assessment, and psychological approaches to management, before discussing in detail a number of specific disorders. This includes major depression, panic disorder, and phobias, as well as some of the rarer forms.

This is a very well written text with a developing argument that revolves around a number of central themes. First, it takes a close look at how much models of psychotherapy and psychological therapy can be adapted to brain injury populations, and does this by analysing both the emerging literature and also case study material taken from his clinical practice. Second, while starting out from the *DSM-IV* category system as a means of "signposting" the reader, the limitations of such a system are fully acknowledged (e.g., issues of aetiology; the non-specific nature of many symptoms, etc). Third, it details how symptoms related to traumatic brain injury themselves can complicate issues of diagnosis (e.g., fatigue, confusion, poor memory). Fourth, the principle concern of Dr Coetzer is to ensure that this vulnerable group of people receive the help they need and that the incidence of anxiety and other mood disorders in the population is fully recognized. In particular, I see the sections on guidance about "differential diagnosis" and "strategies and themes" as unique strengths of the book. As a demonstration of his breadth of knowledge, Dr Coetzer comprehensively reviews a range of treatments, including psychoanalytic and psychodynamic psychotherapy, cognitive–behavioural therapy, behaviour activation and therapy, anxiety management, relaxation techniques, reassurance and psychoeducation, mindfulness, counselling for grief and loss, combined psychotherapy with cognitive rehabilitation, and family therapy. Overall, this is a stimulating read for clinician and researcher alike.

Ceri Bowen, Putney
December 2009

PREFACE

There are many truly excellent texts addressing the cognitive impairment, behavioural difficulties and cognitive rehabilitation of persons after traumatic brain injury. Few textbooks however exclusively address the most common emotional difficulties or mental health problems that can have such an adverse effect on rehabilitation and outcome after brain injury. The primary intention of this book is to cover the clinical assessment and psychological management of mood and anxiety disorders after traumatic brain injury. *The Diagnostic and Statistical Manual of Mental Disorders, 4th Edition* (*DSM-IV*) (American Psychiatric Association, 1994) classification system is used throughout this book to provide the diagnostic underpinnings to discuss the hugely complex area of anxiety and mood disorders after traumatic brain injury. While *DSM-V* is expected to be published in the near future, clearly the research and case reports on mental disorders after traumatic brain injury up to this point are based on the current or earlier versions of the *DSM*. Furthermore, there is likely to be a considerable time lag before *DSM-V*-based studies on mood and anxiety disorders after traumatic brain injury begin to emerge.

There are, of course, many different mental health difficulties associated with traumatic brain injury. Some are perhaps controversial, others are more frequently reported or, indeed, better researched. There are other forms of acquired brain injury, such as stroke, that result in mental health difficulties also. Nevertheless, this book focuses solely on anxiety and mood problems after traumatic brain injury for three specific reasons. These reasons are as follows. First, anxiety and depression are the most common emotional difficulties after traumatic brain injury. Second, traumatic brain injury is not directly related to a systemic or progressive disease process; it almost always follows an undesired and unexpected event and, as such, has the potential, in addition to physical injury, to result in significant psychological issues. Third, anxiety and mood disorders perhaps lend themselves more to psychological formulation and interventions, which, with regard to treatment approaches, is the focus of this book also. It is, of course, recognized that pharmacological approaches to anxiety and depression after traumatic brain injury are at least as important as psychological interventions. However, a review of pharmacological approaches to the management of emotional difficulties after traumatic brain injury is clearly beyond the scope of this book. Several excellent texts covering this topic exist, and the reader is advised to consult these where appropriate. In addition to pharmacological approaches, there are, of course, also other crucial rehabilitation interventions for this population that are not covered here: for example, occupational therapy, physiotherapy, and speech and language therapy.

This book provides an introduction to anxiety and mood disorders after traumatic brain injury and a psychological perspective on their evolution and management. It is aimed at a range of professionals in training (or those responsible for providing training in psychopathology, neuropsychology, and psychotherapy), or newly qualified practitioners who may have an interest in working with patients who present with anxiety or depression, commonly seen in post-acute brain injury rehabilitation settings. This is an introductory text, and it is assumed that the reader would not necessarily yet have had extensive clinical exposure to, or academic training in, either psychiatric diagnostic systems or traumatic brain injury. As far as is possible, clinical aspects of anxiety and depression after traumatic brain injury have been emphasized. Case reports from my caseload or the literature are used to illustrate some of the issues related to the diagnosis and psychological management of anxiety or mood problems associated with traumatic brain injury. This book deals only with moderate to severe traumatic brain injury. Of course, mild traumatic brain injury, post-concussion disorder, or, indeed, other forms of acquired brain injury (for example, stroke), can and do result in anxiety and mood disorders also, but, as already pointed out, these are not addressed in this book.

With regard to the organization of the text, the core chapters (1–12) in the book follow a structure that can potentially be utilized to form the basis of a lecture series on traumatic brain injury, emotional sequelae, and psychotherapy approaches to rehabilitation. The first chapter in this book deals with both the pathophysiology and incidence/prevalence of traumatic brain injury. Chapters Two and Three address the clinical presentation and assessment of mood and anxiety disorders following traumatic brain injury. Chapter Four provides a brief overview of psychological therapy thought to be effective in general for anxiety and mood disorders. The remainder of the chapters cover mood and anxiety disorders after traumatic brain injury. Each of these chapters is structured as follows. First, a definition of the mood or anxiety disorder covered in the chapter is provided, following *DSM-IV* (American Psychiatric Association, 1994) diagnostic criteria. This is followed by a discussion of diagnostic dilemmas when diagnosing these specific disorders in the presence of traumatic brain injury. A review of the specific disorder after traumatic brain injury is then provided, before proceeding to a case report to illustrate some of the points covered earlier in the chapter. Finally, a brief overview of psychological approaches to management and themes likely to present during psychological therapy is provided. Each chapter concludes with a brief summary of the main points covered in the chapter. The final core chapter (Chapter Twelve) briefly reviews anxiety and mood disorders in special populations. The book concludes with a short summary chapter (Chapter Thirteen).

Rudi Coetzer
North Wales, UK
January 2010

CHAPTER ONE

Traumatic brain injury

Introduction

To some extent, traumatic brain injury is like the proverbial elephant in the room. In most countries of the world, the problems stemming from traumatic brain injury are well known and present significant challenges to policy makers, healthcare systems, providers of social care and clinicians. It is probably one of the most challenging healthcare problems of our time. More people today survive a traumatic brain injury than ever before, leading to an increasing demand on limited healthcare resources. While the numbers of people with traumatic brain injury may not be as enormous as some chronic illnesses for example, the problems patients experience are perhaps encapsulated in the complex and chronic difficulty following traumatic brain injury. Severe traumatic brain injury results in a wide range of impairments that almost always lead to significant disability. These impairments may be physical, cognitive, emotional, behavioural, and social, or, in many cases, a combination of these. The complex disability usually associated with traumatic brain injury does not always fit neatly into existing systems of service provision and, as a result, often pose significant challenges to providers of both health and social care.

Clearly, then, in view of the complex disability that often follows traumatic brain injury, it should become obvious to us that patients' needs on many occasions cannot be fully met by a single provider of healthcare. As a result, patients may fall through the net and be left with extremely limited support over the long term. Traumatic brain injury and its presentation to this day continue to be poorly understood by many, including healthcare professionals. One of the potentially confusing areas is what actually constitutes a traumatic brain injury. It is important to note that not all injuries to the head necessarily result in a traumatic brain injury. Furthermore, it is important to note that this book addresses only moderate to severe traumatic brain injury. It does not address the distinctly different and complex areas encompassed by, for example, mild traumatic brain injury or post-concussion disorders. In this chapter, a brief overview of the nature of traumatic brain injury, as well as its incidence and prevalence, is provided. The reader needing access to more detailed information regarding neuro-anatomy may wish to consult a text such as that of Crossman and Neary (2000), for example.

Pathophysiology

Before proceeding to a more in-depth discussion of the pathophysiology of traumatic brain injury, it is necessary for us to consider a few general points about the topic. A traumatic brain injury does not really constitute a single, discreet event. During traumatic brain injury the brain is actually injured twice, initially as a result of physical force and subsequently because of biochemical and other changes. In view of this fact, traumatic brain injury is commonly divided into primary and secondary injuries. The primary injury is the direct result of mechanical force, meaning the actual blow to the head resulting in severe acceleration, severe deceleration, or, in some cases, both. The secondary injury to the brain results from complex biochemical changes. These follow almost immediately after the initial mechanical injury. Clearly, the direct effects of the primary injury are irreversible from the moment it happens. In contrast, some of the secondary effects can sometimes be prevented or minimized by medical or surgical intervention.

The forces applied to a person's head during traumatic brain injury may manifest themselves differently with regard to the actual physical damage caused. Hence, at the very first level of classification or describing the damage caused by an injury, traumatic brain injuries are often classified as either an open or a closed head injury. By definition, this means that during an open head injury the brain comes into contact with the outer environment, whereas during a closed head injury it does not. Thus, in the event of an open head injury, the skull and coverings of the brain have been pierced by the injury (or the object causing the injury, for example, a hammer or bullet), thus exposing the brain. Because of this, open head injuries tend to carry a higher risk of infection than closed head injuries. Certain types of open head injuries result in more focal damage to the brain: for example, gunshot wounds or stab wounds to the head. In contrast, closed head injuries tend to result in more diffuse injury to the brain. Some of the important differences between the primary and secondary injury are discussed next.

The primary injury

As pointed out above, the primary injury to the brain is the direct result of force being applied to the head: for example, a blow to the head with an object like a hammer, cricket bat, or similar object. The substantial energy associated with these forces is transmitted to the head and then, if and when a brain injury occurs, the brain itself. This transmission of energy generally results in localized force being applied to the head or skull, as well as a sudden acceleration of the head. In other cases, the primary injury may result from the person's head hitting a stationary or fixed object: for example, during a motor vehicle accident or a fall from a significant height. In these cases, the result is a sudden deceleration of the person's head. Under certain conditions, both acceleration and deceleration or repeated transfer of energy can take place, such as might occur during high-speed both-end motor vehicle accidents.

In the individual case, it is, of course, not always possible to distinguish between all the different forces occurring during a head injury. In many cases, externally applied force can result in complex combinations of forces transmitted to the brain. Furthermore, under other circumstances the head is rotated suddenly, often leading to a more diffuse transmission of force. An example of this might occur when a motor vehicle travelling at high speed rolls over several times. In some cases, the transmission of force is more repeated or sustained. Although relatively rare, an example of this would be the cumulative injuries sustained over time by a boxer. However, in most cases the basic mechanisms of injury remain the same. The energy or momentum associated with these forces is ultimately transmitted to the vulnerable, soft brain tissue of the person. It should be noted, though, that injury to areas other than actual brain tissue also occurs sometimes. For example, skull fractures are common and can be divided into fractures of the skull base and the vault of the skull.

Skull base fractures do not always directly damage the brain. Some of the symptoms and signs associated with skull base fractures include, for example, loss of hearing and dizziness, or paralysis on one side of the face. These occur because of the vulnerability of certain cranial nerves, for example VII (facial paralysis) and VIII (hearing loss), being bruised or even severed as a result of skull base fractures. Furthermore, a fracture of the vault of the skull can result in an open brain injury, increasing the risk of infection of the brain tissue. Sometimes the depression in the skull associated with a skull fracture or the bone fragments themselves push on to or into the brain. This is known as a depressed skull fracture, and it should be noted that when bone fragments enter the brain, it could substantially increase the risk of the person developing post-traumatic seizures. In other cases, a skull fracture constitutes a long crack in a straight line along the surface of the skull. These are known as linear skull fractures and are perhaps not as ominous as depressed skull fractures.

Returning to the acceleration and deceleration forces typically associated with traumatic brain injury, it is important for clinicians to understand how these are transmitted inside the skull. The effects of these forces, as well as the shape of the inner bony structures of the skull, are associated with a specific and typical regional pattern of injury to the brain. Bigler (2007) provided an excellent overview of how this regional injury to the brain is related to the interface of the brain with the inner bony surfaces of the skull. The anterior poles of the frontal and temporal lobes of the brain are more vulnerable to contusions. In fact, this regional pattern of contusions is probably one of the defining characteristics of severe traumatic brain injury and leads to the rather predictable impairment of executive control function and information processing, among other cognitive difficulties. Bigler (*ibid.*) further pointed out that the close proximity of the hippocampus to the sphenoid ridge makes this a specifically vulnerable area in traumatic brain injury. The hippocampus forms part of the limbic system; hence, the hippocampus is of special importance because it is not only involved in memory, but, very importantly, emotion also.

It should be noted that, in many instances also, contusions are not limited to the anterior poles of the temporal and frontal lobes. Often, the brain is bounced inside the skull when force is transferred. Under these conditions, while the site of initial impact may result in predictable focal contusions, the side opposite to the blow is often severely injured also. This type of injury is known as a *contre coup* injury. Nevertheless, whichever way the head is accelerated or decelerated, the anterior parts of the temporal and frontal lobes are likely to be more vulnerable to injury because of the way mechanical force is transmitted throughout the brain. As a result, anosmia (loss of sense of smell) is a good clinical marker of frontal involvement after traumatic brain injury, given the proximity of cranial nerve I to the ventral aspects of the frontal lobes. The transmission of force, however, does not only affect the specific regions such as the frontal and temporal lobes. Because of the transmission of force throughout the brain, diffuse shearing and tearing of white matter (the axons of the neurons) can often take place. This is known as a diffuse axonal injury. Sustaining a diffuse axonal injury mostly results in a person being deeply unconscious immediately following injury. Diffuse axonal injury can often follow injuries resulting from severe acceleration or deceleration. An example of this is the injuries typically sustained in high-speed motor vehicle accidents.

Finally, severe traumatic brain injuries can result in bleeding, either deep inside the brain or around the coverings of the brain. Unfortunately, bleeding that occurs in the brain has nowhere to drain, because of the skull providing complete encapsulation, and hence in some cases may result in an increase in pressure inside the brain. Bleeding inside the brain is known as an intracerebral haemorrhage. These are commonly seen in the temporal and frontal lobes, but can also occur in other areas of the brain. Sometimes blood enters the ventricles. The meninges covering the brain can also be torn during severe injuries. Generally, this leads to bleeding between the skull and the outer layer of the brain (an epidural haematoma) or between the brain and the inner coverings of the brain (a subdural haematoma). Both of these complications can exert pressure effects on the brain, thus resulting in a secondary injury to the brain. Some patients require emergency neurosurgery to relieve the pressure resulting from certain types of bleeds. Bleeding inside the brain is a common example of how the primary mechanical injury resulting from traumatic brain injury can evolve into a secondary injury of the brain. Next, some other aspects of the secondary injury are briefly discussed.

The secondary injury

Perhaps the most significant difference between primary and secondary injuries to the brain is that the effect of the latter potentially can be reduced or limited in some cases by medical or surgical intervention. This is in contrast to the actual mechanical injury, where prevention is perhaps the area where healthcare professionals and policymakers should focus their efforts. Undoubtedly other areas, such as ambulance response time, airlifting casualties to hospital, and resuscitation at the scene may be a focus for improvement or development also. At the present, however, for many patients, improvements in these areas may still not be enough ever to completely avoid the risk of secondary injury in traumatic brain injury; there are, of course, also limits to the scientific knowledge base for treating traumatic brain injury during the acute phase. Many of the processes contributing to the secondary injury of the brain are not yet well understood, and more research in this area is much needed. While neurosurgical procedures have developed substantially in this area, according to Park, Bell, and Baker (2008), at this point there appear to be substantial limits to what can be achieved with pharmacological treatment of the secondary injury after traumatic brain injury.

In most cases, almost immediately after the primary (mechanical) injury, there follows a range of complex biochemical changes in the brain. For example, the levels of acetylcholine, free radicals and excitatory amino acids may rise. These and other biochemical changes can result also in reduced blood supply to the brain. Ultimately, this results in less oxygen and glucose reaching the brain tissue. As we know, brain tissue is extremely sensitive to starvation of oxygen and glucose and cannot survive for very long periods without these essential nutrients. There are also other mechanisms involved in oxygen and blood supply to the brain. Park, Bell, and Baker (*ibid.*) provided a comprehensive review of the biological mechanisms involved in the secondary injury after head trauma. An important factor appears to be the central role of calcium homeostasis in the secondary injury of both grey and white matter after traumatic brain injury (*ibid.*). This has additional relevance, as it is becoming increasingly clear that white matter damage may have significant implications for the post-acute prognosis or outcome of patients with traumatic brain injury (*ibid.*).

The secondary injury is, however, not only associated with biochemical changes occurring in the brain. In addition, intracerebral swelling (hydrocephalus), as well as bleeding, often take place in more severe traumatic brain injuries. These can increase intracranial pressure, thus further contributing to poor blood supply and less oxygen and nutrients reaching brain tissue. Post-traumatic cerebral infarction is relatively common: for example, Tian and colleagues (2008) reported an incidence of twelve per cent within the first two weeks following injury. Tawil, Stein, Mirvis, and Scalea (2008), on the other hand, reported an incidence of eight per cent and a significantly increased risk of mortality associated with post traumatic cerebral infarction after severe traumatic brain injury. There are also, of course, the direct pressure effects on the brain to consider. Perhaps the most dramatic evidence of the concept of a secondary injury is provided by these changes in the brain. Park, Bell, and Baker (2008) pointed out that patients who initially are able to converse after arrival at hospital, but then deteriorate and die, illustrate the point about the secondary injury being clearly separate from the primary (mechanical) injury and that it is here that future developments of treatments would most probably be focused. Finally, some of the biochemical changes associated with the secondary injury may exert a more direct negative effect by irritating the brain tissue. All these complex and interacting processes can and often do further injure the brain and have an additional adverse effect on the final outcome of the patient.

Determining severity

"How severe was the injury?" is a question we are likely to be asked many times during our careers. There are several reasons for clinicians to try to accurately assess the severity of traumatic brain injury. One of the most obvious reasons is, of course, that injury severity, along with several other factors, has a bearing on long-term outcome. While superficially appearing to be a simple process, determining with complete accuracy the actual severity of a traumatic brain injury can, in many cases, prove frustratingly difficult and challenging to even the most experienced clinicians. Many clinicians will be all too familiar with, and aware of, the dilemmas associated with determining the severity of a traumatic brain injury. This is specifically relevant in a post-acute rehabilitation setting, where ratings often have to be performed retrospectively and crucial data may not be readily available to assist with the process of determining severity. Perhaps the first task is not actually to rate severity in the first instance, but merely to determine the presence or not of a traumatic brain injury in a given patient.

What is meant by determining the presence or not of a traumatic brain injury? Not all injuries to the head result in a brain injury. Indeed, head injuries are extremely common, and most patients with a head injury make a complete recovery. It is, however, not always easy to distinguish between when a person has suffered a head injury and when a head injury actually extends to include an injury to the brain. Usually, a combination of clinical signs and findings from special investigations can be a way to confirm that a person has possibly suffered a traumatic brain injury. Traumatic brain injury is usually (but not always) associated with a period of loss or disturbance of consciousness. Post trauma amnesia tends to be a good clinical marker of traumatic brain injury also. In addition, structural abnormalities on brain imaging are common following severe traumatic brain injury. Generally, these clinical markers tend to be considered together to determine the presence and, ultimately, the severity of a traumatic brain injury.

Traditionally, the severity of traumatic brain injury has been rated as mild, moderate or severe (Guilmette, 1997), based on the Glasgow Coma Scale (Teasdale & Jennet, 1974), period of loss of consciousness, and length of post trauma amnesia, or, indeed, a combination of these markers of severity. Injuries are classified as mild where the Glasgow Coma Scale is between thirteen and fifteen, loss of consciousness is less than thirty minutes, and post trauma amnesia does not extend beyond one hour. Moderate brain injuries equate to a Glasgow Coma Scale of 9–12, and loss of consciousness between one and twenty-four hours. Traumatic brain injuries are classified as severe where the Glasgow Coma Score equals eight or less, loss of consciousness extends over a period of more than twenty-four hours, and post trauma amnesia exceeds twenty-four hours. Other forms of evidence of a traumatic brain injury include positive findings on computed tomography (CT) or magnetic resonance imaging (MRI) scans of the brain. However, we do not always have ready access to these clinical data, which can make it difficult for clinicians to determine the severity of the injury suffered by a patient.

Fortunately, Malec and colleagues (2007) provided an excellent model for overcoming the, at times, unreliability of single indicators of severity, as well as providing a clinical tool for retrospectively determining the severity of traumatic brain injury. In the Mayo Traumatic Brain Injury Severity Classification System (Malec et al., 2007), data from different sources are used in an attempt to overcome some of the significant difficulties sometimes encountered when faced with missing clinical data, for example, the absence of a Glasgow Coma Scale score or findings from neuro-imaging. Combining Glasgow Coma Scale score, post trauma amnesia, loss of consciousness, and findings from neuro-imaging, traumatic brain injury in this model is classified as moderate–severe (definite), mild (probable) or symptomatic (possible). It appears that the Mayo system correctly classifies more cases of traumatic brain injury as opposed to when a single indicator of potential severity, for example, neuro-imaging, is used.

Neuro-imaging

Brain imaging is not only used to determine severity. The development and also wider availability of high quality anatomical imaging, for example, CT and MRI scans of the brain, has, without any doubt, more generally contributed immensely to the acute and post-acute care of patients with traumatic brain injury. In many cases, findings from scans reveal the tell-tale pattern of contusions and other abnormalities classically associated with traumatic brain injury, ensuring diagnostic accuracy. As an illustration, a person might make a complete physical recovery after a traumatic brain injury, but present with behavioural or emotional difficulties, which can be interpreted as "being difficult", until appropriate imaging may suggest a link to the injury, thus ensuring appropriate treatment or rehabilitation. Nevertheless, in many cases scans are normal. These findings, however, should be interpreted with caution, especially during the very early stages following injury. Scan results can change over time. In this regard, Bigler (2001) warned that the absence of positive findings on CT or MRI does not necessarily always rule out the presence of a traumatic brain injury. Hence, clinicians should, in some cases, perhaps be cautious when interpreting scan findings or when attempting to reconcile these data with clinical presentation.

Every clinician should be aware that there are limitations to the information that can be provided by brain imaging. Biglar (*ibid.*) pointed out some of the important caveats we should be aware of when presented with data from neuro-imaging. One of the main difficulties appears to be the problems related to the interpretation of findings from CT and MRI scans, as these can potentially reveal only structural or anatomical damage (*ibid.*). The functional (metabolic) problems resulting from focal anatomical lesions associated with traumatic brain injury are not revealed by CT or MRI scans. These can only be detected by functional images (for example, single photon emission computed tomography [SPECT] scans) (*ibid.*). Furthermore, these functional changes can often be distant from the focal, anatomical lesion(s) sustained as a result of a traumatic brain injury, and may explain the limited convergence between neuropsychological findings and data from anatomical scans (*ibid.*). Ideally, then, findings from different investigations (for example, brain scans, clinical signs, family reports, and neuropsychological test results) should be integrated before conclusions are drawn in individual cases. Ultimately, these should also be compared with the patient's actual psychosocial outcomes in the community.

Psychosocial factors

Traumatic brain injury is a leading cause of disability in virtually every part of the world. It is one of the major causes of death in most countries of the world, but, as a result of medical advances, more people now survive. Traumatic brain injury is known to have devastating psychological, social, and physical effects on individuals and their families. The cost to society, both sociologically and financially, is enormous. For the individual, having survived a life-altering event does not mean that the impact or effects will necessarily recede over time. Indeed, many studies have highlighted the problems experienced by survivors of traumatic brain injury. For example, Dikmen, Machamer, Powell, and Temkin (2003), in a recent study that investigated prospectively the longer-term outcome (between three and five years) of moderate to severely brain-injured individuals, found a high level of morbidity to exist in this population. While this finding has not been replicated consistently (see, for example, Wood, 2008; Wood & Rutterford, 2006), the vast majority of studies tend to report chronic disability, most notably related to psychosocial functioning, but also for cognitive difficulties (e.g., Draper & Ponsford, 2008).

The most common causes of traumatic brain injury include motor vehicle accidents, falls, assaults, and sports injuries (National Institutes of Health, 1998). Other less commonly encountered causes of traumatic brain injury include blast injuries and industrial accidents. Males are more than twice as likely to sustain a traumatic brain injury. Symptoms following traumatic brain injury tend to be chronic and typically include cognitive impairments, personality (or behavioural) changes, depression and anxiety, apathy, impulsivity, impaired self-awareness, and aggression, among many others. Traumatic brain injuries also have the potential to accentuate pre-injury difficulties in some people: for example, pre-existing mental health problems. The complex impairment and disability that usually follow severe traumatic brain injury generally has a profound impact on the capacity of health and social care systems to provide appropriate rehabilitation. While overall the number of survivors may seem low compared to other chronic disease entities, for example, cancer, the burden placed on these systems can be as enormous, especially so when, for example, considering the long-term economical consequences associated with traumatic brain injury.

The highest incidence of traumatic brain injury is among individuals aged between fifteen and twenty-four, and seventy-five years or older, with a smaller peak in children aged five years or younger (National Institutes of Health, 1998). Although Andelic, Sigurdardottir, Brunborg, and Roe (2008) reported that while the median age for a traumatic brain injury was twenty-nine years, the highest incidence of hospitalizations was for young children and elderly males. These data are important to consider, as the very young and the old can experience additional, unique difficulties as a result of traumatic brain injury. For example, younger children and adolescents can have their schooling adversely affected, limiting their financial and social independence in later life. Indeed, paediatric traumatic brain injury is a particularly serious public health problem (see, for example, Martin & Falcone, 2008). Older adults, as a result of improved health and corresponding life expectancy, now have increased physical mobility into old age, leading to increased involvement in, for example, motor vehicle accidents, including as pedestrians (older adults and other special populations are discussed in Chapter Twelve). Life expectance following survival of traumatic brain injury has traditionally been thought to be close to that of the general population, but this is not a universally accepted finding (e.g., Ratcliff, Colantonio, Escobar, Chase, & Vernich, 2005). Indeed, more recently, Cameron, Purdie, Kliewer, and McClure (2008) reported their research findings, which indicated that survivors of traumatic brain injury experienced increased mortality over a period of ten years post injury. Naturally, then, of equal importance to mortality figures are survival figures, to plan and facilitate the provision of rehabilitation and service development.

Incidence and prevalence

Many healthcare professionals who look at data surrounding the incidence and prevalence of traumatic brain injury report how they are soon struck by how difficult it can be to interpret the reported numbers and figures related to traumatic brain injury. It is clear that there is enormous variation. For example, Rose and Johnson (1996) came to the conclusion that for the UK an average incidence figure for all traumatic brain injuries of approximately 250 per 100,000 of the population has been considered by some to probably represent a relatively accurate figure. But this figure is relatively high compared to the National Institutes of Health Consensus Statement (1998) estimated incidence figure of 100 per 100,000 of the general population for the USA. More recently, the Royal College of Physicians and British Society for Rehabilitation Medicine (2003) reported an annual incidence of approximately 150 per 100,000, with eight per 100,000 of these representing a severe traumatic brain injury. This figure is somewhere between those of the National Institutes of Health (1998) and Rose and Johnson (1996). In a recent study by Maegele and colleagues (2007) on incidence, severity, and outcome after traumatic brain injury, 130,000 pre-hospital emergencies were screened for specifically severe traumatic brain injury, revealing an annual incidence of 7.3 per 100,000 in an urban population of Western Europe. In this study, then, the incidence of severe traumatic brain injury was slightly lower but strikingly similar to the eight per 100,000 figure suggested for the UK.

Bruns and Hauser (2003), in their review, concluded that the incidence of all traumatic brain injuries (excluding head injuries not affecting the brain) is as high as approximately 180 to 250 per 100,000 population per annum in the USA. Nevertheless, some of the data for the UK and the USA appear broadly similar. However, on the other hand, the data reported for some other countries in the world vary quite dramatically. The incidence in many other countries, including, for example, in Europe as well as South Africa, may be higher (Bruns & Hauser, 2003). Other studies, though, have reported a lower incidence, for example, Andelic, Sigurdardottir, Brunborg, and Roe (2008) reported an annual incidence of eighty-three per 100,000 for an urban (Oslo) population in Norway. In contrast, Hillier, Hiller, and Metzer (1997) found an incidence as high as 322 per 100,000 in South Australia. However, other researchers (Tate, McDonald, & Lulham, 1998) found a much lower incidence of approximately 100 per 100,000 of the general population in New South Wales in Australia. Of these persons, about twelve per 100,000 sustained a severe traumatic brain injury, higher than the figure of eight per 100,000 suggested for the UK. These data, though, are similar to those reported for a large Canadian study, where an annual incidence of 11.4 per 100,000 was revealed (Zygun et al., 2005). Clearly, then, data regarding incidence reveal great variability and can at times appear confusing. Perhaps some of these data in part represent some of the very different social and economic issues facing different countries of the world.

Why are annual incidence figures so difficult to interpret? There are probably many reasons for this: for example, the high early mortality associated with severe traumatic brain injury. Furthermore, the actual diagnostic coding of all injuries following trauma in many cases may not highlight the presence of a traumatic brain injury when the patient has several other life-threatening injuries. Also, there are often missing data, making it extremely difficult to accurately determine the severity of the traumatic brain injury, and it is possible that many mild injuries are incorrectly included among these data. Conversely, some patients with what was initially thought to have been a mild injury, but later transpired to be a severe traumatic brain injury, may be missed off databases. Nevertheless, annual incidence figures do, to some extent, inform the planning and provision of acute care services, for example. But other data may be more useful to those working with the longer-term consequences of traumatic brain injury: for example, post-injury mood and anxiety disorders. Here, estimates of the numbers of disabled survivors probably provide much more meaningful data.

The prevalence of disabled survivors of traumatic brain injury in the UK general population is thought to be about 100–150 per 100,000 of the general population (British Society of Rehabilitation Medicine, 1998). More recent data provided by Maegele and colleagues (2007) revealed that 39.2 per cent of survivors of traumatic brain injury continued to present with persisting difficulties. This means that it is likely that even in less densely populated areas there is a great probability of a significant number of survivors requiring essential, specialist, long-term health and social care. While actual numbers may be relatively low in some less densely populated areas, what cannot be ignored is that the rehabilitation input required is invariably intense and long term for this clinical population. Finally, the limited data for rural areas tend to reveal poorer outcome (Coetzer & Blackwell, 2003; Gabella, Hoffman, Marine, & Stallones, 1997). Indeed, Schootman and Fuortes (1999) found that persons living in a rural area and who suffered a traumatic brain injury were twice as likely to be dependent on other people and in poor health when compared to individuals living in more densely populated areas. Next, we turn our attention to what is done to rehabilitate the survivors of traumatic brain injury.

Provision of rehabilitation

Unfortunately, the picture with regard to rehabilitation, especially long-term rehabilitation after traumatic brain injury, tends to be bleak. In general, for persons surviving a traumatic brain injury, limited rehabilitation programmes have been developed in the UK (Hutchinson & Pickard, 2006). For example, Dombovy and Olec (1996) reported that the findings from their study revealed that only eight of sixty-seven discharged survivors of traumatic brain injury received rehabilitation services. Perhaps more importantly, with regard to long-term difficulties, few individuals appear to be followed up by community-based brain injury rehabilitation services. In a survey of thirty-five community neuro-rehabilitation teams in South East England, McMillan and Ledder (2001) found that less than three per cent of individuals disabled by a traumatic brain injury were seen by these services. This finding implies that there are possibly large numbers of post-acute patients who receive very little specialist support. The picture is unlikely to be substantially different in other countries of the world.

A substantial proportion of persons with traumatic brain injury are left with long-term disability. For example, Selassie and colleagues (2008) reported that an estimated forty-three per cent of a huge sample of persons with traumatic brain injury in the USA developed long-term disability. Potentially of even greater concern, while physical disabilities after traumatic brain injury over time may modestly reduce or stabilize, the mental health consequences associated with traumatic brain injury can result in very long-term disabilities that often do not receive the necessary treatment or attention required (Handel, Ovitt, Spiro, & Rao, 2007; Lewis, 2001). In addition, it is becoming increasingly evident that psychiatric difficulties are common after traumatic brain injury (Labbate & Warden, 2000; Van Reekum, Cohen, & Wong, 2000). A striking finding was that the continuation of disability, or its new onset after recovery, was more strongly associated with anxiety, depression, and low self-esteem, rather than the long-term cognitive impairments or actual severity of the injury (Whitnall, McMillan, Murray, & Teasdale, 2006). These difficulties are the ones likely to have a significant impact on patients' functioning in the community. We can only conclude that a large proportion of survivors are most probably being cared for or supported by family members or other carers in the community. Indeed, where possible, family therapy should ideally form part of neuro-rehabilitation (Bowen, 2007). Rao and Lyketsos (2002) point out that as more individuals survive severe traumatic brain injury and, as a consequence, present with psychiatric problems, increasingly psychiatrists will need to become involved in the care of these survivors.

Whitnall, McMillan, Murray, and Teasdale (2006) point out that, in view of the disability following traumatic brain injury being strongly associated with anxiety and depression, remediation may be possible even many years after a person sustained the injury. Perhaps because of this, fortunately, the picture is not universally one of loss of hope or a dearth of appropriate services for patients. In many parts of the world excellent services for traumatic brain injury survivors have been developed. Indeed, while generally there are excellent acute services for brain-injured persons, the gap in service provision is often present at the post-acute, long-term level of service provision. But, while it cannot be denied that there are gaps in service provision, there are many services that do provide longer-term follow up to deal with the cognitive, behavioural, and emotional difficulties associated with traumatic brain injury. Some of these services include, for example, the holistic rehabilitation programmes developed across the world, including Europe (Sarajuuri & Koskinen, 2006), the USA (Trexler, Eberle, & Zappala, 2000), and the UK (Wilson et al., 2000), among others. Community-based programmes incorporating principles of holistic rehabilitation have also been developed (Coetzer, Vaughan, Roberts, & Rafal, 2003). Holistic rehabilitation programmes are specifically designed to address longer-term emotional difficulties after brain injury and may be ideally placed to provide the support and rehabilitation that many survivors need, especially those that present with a combination of emotional and cognitive problems. Is there evidence that these programmes benefit patients?

There are many studies reporting the effectiveness of post-acute rehabilitation, and only a few are mentioned here to illustrate this point. Svendsen and Teasdale (2006) concluded that post-acute rehabilitation could have long-term beneficial effects, including reductions in anxiety and depression. In a landmark randomized controlled study of community-based rehabilitation, Powell, Heslin, and Greenwood (2002) reported that significant benefits could be derived from rehabilitation, even several years after injury. Finally, regarding specifically holistic rehabilitation programmes, there is increasing evidence that these are effective in connection with psychosocial outcome (e.g., Klonoff et al., 2006), and also for those patients who were previously unable to successfully function within the community (e.g., Cicerone, Mott, Azulay, & Friel, 2004). While there is a lack of specialist rehabilitation services, it should be acknowledged that other services often provide long-term input to patients. For example, clinicians based in many generic services, for example, community-based mental health teams or psychiatric units, often provide excellent long-term support for brain-injured persons. Van Reekum, Bolago, Finlayson, and Garner (1996) suggested the need for both treatment and prevention of psychiatric illness after traumatic brain injury. However, rehabilitation, certainly from a more strategic viewpoint, is not the only initiative to reduce the impact of traumatic brain injury on society.

Preventative strategies

It should be obvious to any observer that strategies to prevent or reduce traumatic brain injury are necessary (National Institutes of Health Consensus Statement, 1998). Unfortunately, up to fairly recently, their effectiveness remained unclear (Warnell, 1997). Even in very specific populations with traumatic brain injury, surveillance and preventative systems are difficult to establish. For example, Runyan, Berger, and Barr (2008) reported that an ideal system for the measurement of the incidence of inflicted traumatic brain injury in young children probably does not exist at this point. Furthermore, with such a specific and more unusual mechanism of injury, alternative strategies to overcome the problem of low sample sizes when investigating preventative interventions might include the utilization of case-control designs (Shapiro, 2008). Finally, Minns, Jones, and Mok (2008), in a study conducted in Scotland, identified that inflicted traumatic brain injury in young children did appear to be more prevalent in areas with the lowest or poorest levels of housing, employment, crime, income, education, and health. These data could potentially prove invaluable when devising interventions or policies intended to reduce the incidence of traumatic brain injury in this very vulnerable population.

While there are clear difficulties with surveillance and prevention, it is somewhat reassuring to know that at least some preventative strategies have been reported to be successful. For example, Salvarani, Colli, and Júnior (2009) reported how the American "Think First" programme was adapted for use in Brazil and specifically targeted the use of seatbelts and helmets among younger people. Implementation of this programme appeared to have resulted in a reduction of injury severity at the end of the programme (ibid.). Furthermore, it is now widely acknowledged that in the UK the campaigns for wearing seatbelts in cars and also against drink driving were definitely successful in reducing the number of serious injuries resulting from motor vehicle accidents. These initiatives need to be ongoing and are often encapsulated in law and social policies. Examples of laws and policies followed by many countries include speed limits, the prohibition on operating hand-held telephones while driving, and stricter requirements for obtaining a driving licence, including more intensive driver training.

It has also been thought that, to some extent, it may be more pragmatic in the first instance to specifically target the populations that have, based on the findings from epidemiological research, been considered to be more vulnerable to sustaining a traumatic brain injury. For example, Zygun and colleagues (2005) suggested that, because males and older adults appeared to be more at risk for sustaining a traumatic brain injury, these groups should perhaps be targeted more specifically by preventative initiatives, whereas Andelic, Sigurdardottir, Brunborg, and Roe (2008), and also Thomas, Stevens, Sarmiento, and Wald (2008), suggested a need for preventative programmes targeting specifically prevention of falls among older adults. As an example of the latter, Sarmiento, Langlois, and Mitchko (2008) provided a description of the "Help seniors live better, longer" initiative by the Centers for Disease Control and Prevention in the USA. This multi-organizational initiative was launched to raise awareness about strategies to prevent, recognize, and respond to traumatic brain injury in a particularly vulnerable group, older adults aged seventy-five or above (*ibid.*).

None the less, there are, of course, problems with preventive initiatives. It should be remembered that measuring the effectiveness of preventative strategies is never easy. Researchers need accurate baseline figures for the incidence of traumatic brain injury before they can attempt to determine the effectiveness of preventative strategies. Moreover, we need to understand the willingness of groups to engage in preventative programmes. In this regard, Stallones, Gibbs-Long, Gabella, and Kakefuda (2008) investigated the readiness of rural communities in the USA to take part in traumatic brain injury prevention programmes and formulated a "community readiness" model to identify those counties more likely to take part in such initiatives. Furthermore, it can often be near impossible to secure funding for such work without demonstrating, in the first instance, some evidence of ongoing effectiveness in injury prevention and reduction. It should be emphasized, however, that healthcare professionals can be very effective advocates for change regarding the introduction of proven road safety measures, and examples of this actually do exist (Breen, 2004). Notwithstanding this important task for healthcare professionals, the reality is that providing rehabilitation mostly dominates the health agenda and, as a result, many healthcare professionals simply do not have the time or financial resources to invest in preventative work. In fact, it would probably be fair to say that many clinical services struggle to provide anything beyond acute and sub-acute rehabilitation, and that long-term follow-up for the cognitive, behavioural, and emotional difficulties so common to traumatic brain injury is often lacking.

Case report

There is an abundance of case reports in the literature outlining the nature and typical consequences of traumatic brain injury. Some of these are written by patients, others by treating clinicians, and yet others by academics or researchers. The following case report is from my clinical practice and is intended to provide an overview of the patient's journey commonly observed after traumatic brain injury.

Mr L was a twenty-year-old male who sustained a severe traumatic brain injury following a road traffic collision. He was thrown out of the vehicle during the collision, sustaining a severe traumatic brain injury, but only very minor other injuries. His Glasgow Coma Scale (Teasdale & Jennett, 1974) was 6/15 and he remained unconscious for approximately two weeks. Furthermore, Mr L's period of post trauma amnesia extended over a period of approximately two months. All of these indexes of severity confirmed that he had most probably sustained a severe traumatic brain injury. Retrospectively applying the Mayo Traumatic Brain Injury Severity Classification System criteria (Malec et al., 2007) classified the injury as moderate–severe (definite). The initial CT scan of the brain (performed during his stay in an acute care hospital) revealed generalized cerebral swelling. No focal lesions were reported as being present on CT. Mr L spent a couple of months in the acute hospital before he was transferred to a rehabilitation unit for approximately ten weeks.

Following his stay in the rehabilitation unit, Mr L was discharged home. Ultimately, Mr L made an almost complete physical recovery. However, his personality was judged, by persons who knew him well and for an extended period of time prior to his injury, to have changed significantly following the accident. More than ten years after Mr L sustained his injury, he was referred for an assessment to determine his potential suitability for community-based brain injury rehabilitation. During the initial clinical assessment, the patient reported struggling with depression and anxiety. Initial neuropsychological testing revealed subtle impairments of verbal memory as well as executive control functions. These were thought to be clearly compatible with the expected effects of a traumatic brain injury. The patient's history revealed an unusually high number of failures to resume his studies or to return to gainful employment. He had poor self-awareness of how his impairments affected his outcome and had no clear ideas as to why he could not hold down a job. He had become depressed over time, but could not lay his finger on exactly why this had happened or what possibly caused it.

This case illustrates a few points about the epidemiology, outcome, and also some patients' journey after traumatic brain injury. The patient was a young male, representing the part of the general population thought most likely to sustain a traumatic brain injury. He did not return to employment, again a very common outcome. The patient made a full physical recovery, but was left with behavioural changes, cognitive impairment, and emotional difficulties, all very common complications of traumatic brain injury. He presented with depression and anxiety, the most common mental health problems associated with traumatic brain injury. While Mr L had very good acute and sub-acute care, he did not access any post-acute, community-based brain injury rehabilitation services for a decade. Hence, he remained dependent on the government for financial support and accommodation, among other things. Finally, it was not his cognitive impairment or any physical problems that exerted the greatest effect on his poor outcome, but, rather, his emotional difficulties and poor self-awareness. Perhaps the non-physical difficulties, including depression and anxiety, represent one of the nettles commissioners, service providers and clinicians will inevitably have to grasp to more effectively rehabilitate persons who continue to present with chronic disability many years after traumatic brain injury.

Summary points for this chapter

1. Traumatic brain injury is a major public health problem across the world.
2. In addition to rehabilitation programmes, there is a need for preventative strategies, to try to minimize the effects traumatic brain injury have on society.

3. Traumatic brain injury has a tri-modal distribution, involving the very young, young males, and the elderly.

4. The annual incidence of severe traumatic brain injury varies between seven and twelve per 100,000 of the general population, whereas the prevalence of disabled survivors appears to be somewhere between 100 and 150 per 100,000.

5. The anterior poles of the temporal and frontal lobes are particularly vulnerable, and diffuse axonal injury is common also, resulting in a predictable pattern of impairment.

6. Many patients make a relatively good physical recovery, but are unlikely to return to pre-injury levels of employment.

7. The greatest challenge appears to be that many patients are left with disabling cognitive impairment, behavioural changes, and emotional difficulties, but have limited access to specialist post-acute rehabilitation services.

8. Disability is strongly associated with anxiety and depression, and these may respond to appropriate treatment long after injury.

CHAPTER TWO

Clinical presentation

Introduction

W hat represents the "signature" symptomatology of trau-matic brain injury? Severe traumatic brain injury tends to result in a somewhat predictable combination of symptoms, including cognitive impairment, emotional difficulties, personality changes, physical problems, and altered behaviour in general being the more common areas involved. Lezak, Howieson, and Loring (2004) and, more recently, Roebuck-Spencer and Sherer (2008) provided excellent overviews of the clinical presentation, including cognitive impairment, resulting from traumatic brain injury. Lishman (1998) comprehensively reviewed the clinical symptomatology associated with traumatic brain injury, with perhaps a more specific focus on psychiatric syndromes. Lishman (*ibid.*) posited that there were four main categories of psychiatric problems following traumatic brain injury. These constituted neurosis, psychosis, cognitive impairment, and personality changes (*ibid.*). The clinical symptoms associated with traumatic brain injury can have a profound effect on many different areas of a patient's life and may manifest in several areas, including the person's physical abilities, role in the family, employment, education, quality of life, or leisure and social functioning, among others.

In general, the full range of cognitive impairment may be present after severe traumatic brain injury (Lezak, Howieson, & Loring, 2004). Nevertheless, certain domains of cognitive functioning are more commonly impaired than others after severe traumatic brain injury. Most notably, these include problems with attention, memory, and executive control function (*ibid.*). The fact that these cognitive domains are more frequently impaired is understandable in view of the brain regions most likely to be damaged as a result of a severe traumatic brain injury (see also Chapter One). Nevertheless, in many cases, other cognitive areas can be and are impaired also. For example, some patients exhibit problems related to language, including word finding difficulties, poor comprehension, reduced ability to read or write, and difficulties related to naming objects. Others may have specific problems with calculation or constructional abilities. It is important to remember that there are huge differences in presentation, even when two persons of similar demographic backgrounds appear to have sustained remarkably similar injuries. Each patient tends to present slightly differently, for complex reasons that are not yet, and perhaps never will be, well understood.

Essential features

Impairment of executive control function is probably one of the symptoms, if not *the* hallmark symptom, of traumatic brain injury. It can often pose numerous difficulties for patients trying to live their lives out there in the real world. Impairment of executive control function has been associated with poor outcome with regard to social integration and employment (Struchen et al., 2008). Executive control function can, in essence, be defined as usually constituting those cognitive functions involved in the planning, initiation, sequencing, and monitoring of complex behaviours that are goal directed (Royall et al., 2002). It is easy to see how impairment of executive control function can influence other areas also. Indeed, executive control function appears to be implicated in several areas crucial to everyday functioning, such as the ability to solve problems, insight and understanding, starting or completing tasks, and planning of activities. Furthermore, it is likely that impairments of executive control function may manifest itself to relatives as alterations in character or personality changes, rather than an impairment of cognitive function *per se*. Examples of how impaired executive control function might, on the surface, appear to be personality changes, may include the person dealing differently (compared to the past) with complex social situations, not becoming involved in any tasks without excessive prompting, not understanding their limitations after traumatic brain injury, or never completing tasks before starting new ones. These changes in behaviour can, at times, prove somewhat perplexing to relatives and others.

Changes in behaviour perhaps, at least on a clinical level, largely overlap with personality changes, and thus will be considered together. Common behavioural changes, for example, may include apathy, changes in sexual desire (both increased or decreased libido), and hyperactivity. Although personality changes tend to overlap with behavioural changes, personality changes after traumatic brain injury perhaps essentially refers more to the more complex and enduring patterns of behaviour or aspects of character usually associated with a person, as opposed to levels of arousal or activity. Lishman (1998) defined personality change as representing an alteration in habitual patterns of behaviour and attitudes, manifesting itself in changed reactions to people and events. McAllister (2008), on the other hand, described impulsivity, irritability, affective instability, apathy, and lack of awareness as constituting the common clusters of symptoms representing personality changes after traumatic brain injury. Examples of personality changes include the person being less tactful, speaking their mind without first thinking, not picking up on social cues, over-familiarity, excessive jocularity, and being unconcerned by important events, among many others. Personality changes are mostly reported by relatives or friends, rather than by the patient. Problems of executive control function, which may underpin some of the personality changes described above, can significantly colour the presentation of emotional difficulties also.

Personality change after traumatic brain injury is probably common. A recent study by Rao, Spiro, Handel, and Onyike (2008) used *DSM-IV* (American Psychiatric Association, 1994) criteria to investigate personality changes after traumatic brain injury among fifty-four patients. About one third ($N = 17$) of this sample was diagnosed as meeting the diagnostic criteria for personality change due to a general medical condition (*DSM-IV*), mostly representing patients with more severe traumatic brain injury (Rao, Spiro, Handel, & Onyike, 2008). This group was also less likely to be employed post-injury (*ibid.*). Personality change after traumatic brain injury can sometimes be difficult to identify, but a few pragmatic definitions do exist. For example, McAllister (2008) pointed out that, generally speaking, personality change can present in a couple of ways: an accentuation of pre-morbid personality traits, or a more fundamental change in behaviour patterns. However, we also need to understand that personality changes after traumatic brain injury should probably not be viewed as a unitary concept or in isolation, as there can be a substantial interaction with many other symptoms. Indeed, it would be a rather narrow interpretation to see personality change after traumatic brain injury as resulting purely from neurological damage (see also Chapter Eleven).

Fleminger (2008) reminded us that personality changes overlap with both changes in cognitive ability as well as mood. An example of how impaired executive control function might exert an effect on the presentation of emotional difficulties might be as follows. The lack of initiation that occurs with some frequency after traumatic brain injury can sometimes appear to be somewhat similar to, or be confused with, the loss of drive that, in some instances, could actually constitute aspects of a depressed mood. Indeed, Glenn (2002) pointed out that because of this, problems of executive control function need to be disentangled from other systems or symptoms it may influence. Often, both impaired executive control function and emotional difficulties are present following traumatic brain injury. Indeed, emotional problems after traumatic brain injury are common: for example, Horner, Selassie, Lineberry, Ferguson, and Labbate (2008), in their study, identified that forty per cent of their sample of 1560 adults self-reported clinically significant levels of anxiety or mood problems. Generally, emotional difficulties may include anxiety, loss of confidence, anger, irritability, mania, frustration, and depression, among others. Some of these, and the research regarding the frequencies with which they can occur, are discussed a bit later in this chapter.

We do not always understand how these emotional difficulties evolve, though. Several factors are likely to contribute to the onset and maintenance of emotional difficulties following traumatic brain injury. Horner, Selassie, Lineberry, Ferguson, and Labbate (2008) identified that the main risk factors for depression or anxiety in their sample were physical problems, younger age, being female, and, finally, not having enough social support. Broadly speaking, some of the factors involved in emotional difficulties after brain injury are likely to be biological, environmental, or psychological, or a combination of these. Pre-injury factors, most notably personality factors, can, of course, also affect the clinical presentation, and the typical cognitive impairments described above may also interact with, or even have a causative effect on, emotional problems after traumatic brain injury. For example, forgetting important appointments as a result of memory impairment may make a patient anxious; likewise, being unable to perform cognitive tasks as smoothly and effortlessly as before may make the person very irritable, depressed, or, indeed, lead to anger outbursts. Clearly, psychological factors can have a potent effect on clinical presentation. In addition, physical problems may have a potent effect on a person's mood, for example. Some of the issues pertaining to the aetiology of emotional problems after traumatic brain injury are discussed a bit later in this chapter.

Physical impairment, although perhaps slightly less common, include motor difficulties (for example, loss of strength or co-ordination), post trauma seizures, loss of sense of smell or taste, visual field defects, hearing problems, loss of sensation, and post trauma headaches, among others. Besides these symptoms, relatively commonly associated with the more severe cases of traumatic brain injury, patients can also have many other physical difficulties if they suffered multiple injuries in addition to the brain injury. Indeed, this scenario is rather common (see, for example, the case report later in this chapter) following serious road traffic accidents, for instance. Safaz, Alaca, Yasar, Tok, and Yilmaz (2008) described some of the common physical complications, including swallowing difficulties, pressure ulcers, incontinence, heterotopic ossification, seizures, and deep venous thrombosis, associated with traumatic brain injury. The physical symptoms described above can profoundly limit participation in some everyday activities, including work, study, travelling, and driving, among many others. For example, Rapport, Bryer, and Hanks (2008) reported that survivors of traumatic brain injury who were not able to return to driving showed poorer community integration. Limited participation, in turn, can in itself have a dramatic effect on emotional wellbeing. Clearly, then, it is very important for most clinicians to attempt to identify as accurately as possible, or diagnose in a systematic way, the complex emotional problems that can be present in some patients following traumatic brain injury. Accurate diagnosis and formulation is often the starting point for appropriate intervention. A brief overview of one of the most widely used diagnostic classification systems for mental disorders is provided next.

Diagnostic classification systems

How can the clinician working in a brain injury rehabilitation setting identify and communicate the presence of emotional problems following traumatic brain injury? The perhaps overly simplistic answer to this question is to use a diagnostic system. It would be fair to say that there are probably two main diagnostic systems in use throughout the world today to describe and diagnose mental disorders. First, the International Classification of Diseases (ICD): for example, the *ICD-10 Classification of Mental and Behavioural Disorders* (World Health Organization, 1992), used more outside of North America and second, the *Diagnostic and Statistical Manual of Mental Disorders*, fourth edition (*DSM-IV*) (American Psychiatric Association, 1994), used more extensively in North America. This book follows the *DSM-IV* (American Psychiatric Association, 1994) classification system. However, it should be remembered that there was much mutual influence between those preparing *DSM-IV* and *ICD-10*, and that, for example, the codes and terms in *DSM-IV* are compatible with *ICD-10*. The *DSM-IV* classification system provides an invaluable framework into which to organize and identify some of the emotional problems following traumatic brain injury. It has also been used fairly extensively in research, specifically in the area of mental disorders after traumatic brain injury.

DSM-IV uses a five-axial diagnostic system. At the heart of this system is an intention to list the diagnostic criteria of mental disorders as guidelines for commonly encountered disorders seen by clinicians. Axis I is used for the core mental disorders, except mental retardation and the personality disorders, which are reported on Axis II; Axis III is used for medical conditions; Axis IV for psychosocial problems; while Axis V is used for reporting the patient's overall level of functioning. While the term "mental disorder" is used in *DSM-IV*, and to some may appear rather reductionistic, a dualism between the physical and mental is actually not intended. Each of the mental disorders are seen as representing a clinically significant level or presence of behavioural or psychological pattern associated with distress, disability, increased risk of suffering, or loss of individual freedom. In accordance with the *DSM-IV* diagnostic system, in this book the term "mental disorder" is used also, but only mood and anxiety disorders are covered. While *DSM-IV* uses the specifier term, "due to a General Medical Condition", for those disorders that were thought to have resulted from, for example, a clear biological factor such as a brain injury, very importantly there is no intention to mean that there is a basic difference between the same mental disorders when biological factors are identified, as opposed to where no biological factor can be found (American Psychiatric Association, 1994).

Obviously, there are both benefits and limitations to the use of a diagnostic system such as *DSM-IV*, and, at times, there has been fierce debate as to its usefulness, with equally strong arguments made on both sides. Indeed, it has probably proved to be one of the topics that can instantaneously divide colleagues! Nevertheless, undeniably, one of the main benefits is that these types of diagnostic systems do facilitate communication between clinicians. It can also facilitate research, again by providing a common clinical language. Furthermore, in accordance with a biopsychosocial model, mental disorders in *DSM-IV* are seen as resulting from psychological, behavioural, or biological dysfunction. Its main strength, though, is probably that it helps prevent us from missing treatable clinical conditions in our patients. Some of the limitations of *DSM-IV* include the following: there are not always clear distinctions between diagnostic categories, or, indeed, between the presence or absence of a mental disorder (American Psychiatric Association, 1994); the *DSM-IV*, published during 1994, may now be seen as somewhat dated and a new edition is perhaps overdue.

With regard to limitations more generally, it would be entirely fair to conclude that diagnostic systems such as *DSM-IV* cannot possibly encapsulate all the vast complexities of humans. Moreover, some of the disorders listed perhaps have less than ideal diagnostic certainty. Accordingly, from this perspective, there has been fierce criticism against diagnostic systems such as the *DSM-IV* (see, for example, Boyle, 2007; Moncrieff, 2007). Some of the problems with psychiatric diagnosis are thought to be related to a lack of scientific foundations and, hence, the potential to contaminate research finding (Boyle, 2007), or poor evidence for persons with specific psychiatric diagnoses having a distinct underlying biological pathology which, in turn, may, in some cases, question the (pharmacological) treatment of these mental disorders also (Moncrieff, 2007). Finally, it should be kept in mind that any reasonable, or perhaps even basic, skills in the use of such diagnostic systems generally requires a truly considerable investment in training, formal assessment of knowledge, and supervised practice in clinical settings over extended periods of time.

Nevertheless, having a diagnostic system such as *DSM-IV*, or unitary clinical language, most probably does help to ensure that clinicians are more aware of, and can plan for the treatment of, some of the emotional difficulties that can follow traumatic brain injury. Without such a system, and relying exclusively on formulation, we might run the risk of failing to identify in the first instance what the patient clinically presents with. Ultimately, formulation of the factors contributing uniquely in the individual case is likely to almost always follow the initial diagnostic phase. In addition, perhaps each part of this process, while essential in isolation, takes on much more meaning with regard to the patient's rehabilitation when combined and seen as one process. For example, the clinician, first and foremost, has to identify that a person with traumatic brain injury is presenting with a major depressive disorder (otherwise this will be missed, to the serious detriment of the patient) before proceeding to identify the most likely biological, psychological and social factors contributing to the clinical presentation at that point in time. It should also be remembered that it is considered good practice to regularly review and, if necessary, update diagnoses and formulations. While it is, of course, acknowledged that many different mental disorders have been described in *DSM-IV*, this book addresses the anxiety and mood disorders only. What follows next is a general overview of these disorders after traumatic brain injury.

Mental disorders after traumatic brain injury

Why is it important to have a general understanding and working knowledge of mental disorders after traumatic brain injury? Primarily, to overcome the perennial problem of patients with traumatic brain injury who present with co-existing mental disorders not being offered an appropriate clinical service. In some areas, there seems to prevail a rather dualistic view that a patient can only present with one diagnosis, that is, either a mental illness or a traumatic brain injury, but not both. A referral may be refused, because "the patient does not have a mental illness because he (or she) has had a brain injury". Conversely, clinicians in brain injury rehabilitation services may conclude that the person is mentally ill, and hence the traumatic brain injury does not require any specialist neuro-rehabilitation. These views are, of course, entirely unhelpful, and in some cases harmful, for patient care. As we know very well, diagnostic systems such as *DSM-IV* do not address aetiology *per se*, or even assume a biological aetiology; rather, the focus is on describing and organizing symptoms into clusters that represent a defined mental disorder. Clearly, there is a huge potential for patients with traumatic brain injury to present with a co-morbid mental disorder and there is more than enough evidence to support this assertion.

While some specific mental disorders, for example, schizophrenia, are probably less common after traumatic brain injury (Fleminger, 2008), generally speaking, many of the common mental disorders, including emotional difficulties such as anxiety and depression, are frequently seen after traumatic brain injury (Deb, Lyons, Koutzoukis, Ali, & McCarthy, 1999; Koponen et al., 2002). For example, Silver, Kramer, Greenwald, and Weissman (2001), in a study of a large sample of people in the general population, found an association of a history of brain injury and an increased lifetime risk for developing various types of psychiatric illnesses. They interviewed more than 5000 people, and found that 361 persons who reported a history of a brain injury (defined as head injury resulting in loss of consciousness or confusion) were identified. Within this group, the risk for psychiatric illness was reported to be significantly increased. However, the nature of this relation, including a potential temporal relation between sustaining an injury and the subsequent development of a psychiatric disorder, remains unclear (*ibid.*). In addition, a further problem with this study also appeared to be the self-report of both the history and severity of head injury, without objective verification from, for example, medical records.

Koponen and colleagues (2002) reviewed sixty patients to determine the presence of psychiatric problems over an average of thirty years (range 27–48 years) after sustaining a traumatic brain injury and found an increase of psychiatric illness, with forty-eight per cent of patients meeting the *DSM-IV* diagnostic criteria for an Axis I disorder. Of these, the highest proportion (almost twenty-seven per cent) met the *DSM-IV* criteria for major depression, with panic disorder and phobia, respectively, at about eight per cent (*ibid.*). The mean age at which the patients sustained their traumatic brain injury was approximately twenty-nine (range 10–55 years) and the average time since injury was approximately thirty-one years (range 27–48 years) (*ibid.*). This study highlighted the potentially very long-term nature of the mental health difficulties persons with traumatic brain injury can experience. However, on the other hand, it should be noted that Ashman and colleagues (2004) did not find an increased risk over time for developing Axis I disorders after traumatic brain injury. Some of these data can be confusing and cast some uncertainty on the aetiology, nosology, and epidemiology of mental health problems after traumatic brain injury.

Aetiology of mental disorders after traumatic brain injury

Rogers and Read (2007) provided a systematic review of the literature related to the onset of psychiatric illness after traumatic brain injury. Based on the data from their review, Rogers and Read concluded that various non-organic factors, for example, pre-injury personality and post-injury psychological reactions and adjustment to disability are involved in both the onset and maintenance of mental health problems after traumatic brain injury. Other authors (e.g., Lishman, 1998; Van Reekum, Cohen, & Wong, 2000), on the other hand, have emphasized the importance of biological factors contributing to psychiatric illness after traumatic brain injury. For example, Jorge (2005) outlined how the latest anatomical and functional neuroimaging technologies help us to understand the biological factors implicated in psychiatric illness after traumatic brain injury. However, it should be remembered that many mental disorders supposedly associated with traumatic brain injury do not actually show a clear relation to the presence of general or specific lesions as revealed by post-acute MRI brain scans (Koponen et al., 2006). Clearly, there remain significant gaps in our knowledge regarding brain lesions associated with trauma and the onset of psychiatric difficulties. To further complicate the picture, there appears to be evidence that not all psychiatric disorders seem to be increased after traumatic brain injury. According to Van Reekum, Cohen, and Wong (2000) there are credible data and thus robust evidence for a causative effect for major depression, bipolar disorder, and some of the anxiety disorders, but very little evidence for an increase in, for example, psychosis or new-onset substance abuse after traumatic brain injury.

McAllister (2008) described what he termed the neurobiopsychosocial paradigm to help us understand how neuro-behavioural changes can be associated with traumatic brain injury. Neuro-behavioural change may represent a direct effect of the injury, a development of a new illness process, psychological reaction, including the meaning or loss associated with the injury, or environmental changes, including changes in care-givers or routines. Dealing more specifically with personality changes, and drawing on the work of Cummings (1993), McAllister (2008) pointed out that the five major frontal–subcortical circuits were vulnerable to traumatic brain injury and three of these were particularly relevant to personality changes. Damage to the orbitofrontal cortex appears to result in impairment of social behaviours and self-monitoring, while damage to the dorsolateral prefrontal cortex results in poor executive control function and damage to the medial temporal regions can result in memory impairment, particularly the integration of current experience and emotional memory. Finally, there is also emerging evidence that, following traumatic brain injury, there can be a change in the regulation of the neurotransmitters involved in behaviour and cognition (*ibid.*). However, biological changes do not represent the only contributory factor involved in emotional difficulties after traumatic brain injury.

Other factors are also highly likely to contribute to the individual patient's clinical presentation. For example, Bay and Donders (2008) reported that perceived stress after traumatic brain injury is associated with depressive symptoms. It should be noted, though, that Bay and Donders' sample consisted of persons with mild to moderate traumatic brain injury. This finding may, therefore, not necessarily apply to all persons who have suffered a moderate to severe or very severe traumatic brain injury. Nevertheless, other factors, such as age, can also be important to consider. For example, Marquez de la Plata and colleagues (2008) reported that older adults generally had a poorer outcome with regard to disability over the first five-year period after traumatic brain injury. And, with specific regard to mental health problems, Deb and Burns (2007) assessed 165 adults with traumatic brain injury for psychiatric illness one year after injury and reported that patients between eighteen and sixty-five years of age were more at risk of developing psychiatric problems. But, in contrast, Ashman and colleagues (2004) found no evidence for such a relation between age and psychiatric problems. Post-injury and demographic factors are, however, not the only areas we need to consider when trying to understand mood and anxiety disorders after traumatic brain injury.

Another important, but sometimes contentious, area to consider is the possible contribution of pre-morbid factors to the onset or maintenance of mental health problems after traumatic brain injury. Indeed, McAllister (2008) pointed out that not only do psychiatric problems appear to follow traumatic brain injury, they may also predispose the individual to traumatic brain injury. Of further interest here is the specific roles possibly played by pre-injury personality factors. Lishman (1998), for example, pointed out that sometimes pre-morbid personality traits may be accentuated by traumatic brain injury, while at the same time or in others, there may be behaviours or symptoms more generally present or, indeed, expected in patients who have suffered a traumatic brain injury. Glenn (2002) posited that while personality traits were commonly accentuated after traumatic brain injury, clinicians also needed to consider alternative factors or contributors to the patient's presentation, such as pre-morbid intellectual ability, social relationships, and vocational, economic, or academic roles predating the injury. It is also likely that at least some of these factors might show strong interaction effects: for example, vocation and economic status may be related. Clearly, there are still significant gaps in our knowledge about the epidemiology, nosology, and risk factors regarding the development of mental health problems after traumatic brain injury (Kim et al., 2007). Two case reports are now used to highlight some of the points discussed thus far in this chapter.

Case reports

The literature is awash with case reports intended to illustrate the "typical" clinical presentation associated with traumatic brain injury. For example, as early as the start of the twentieth century, Meyer (1904) proposed that neuropsychiatric symptoms could result from brain trauma (Neylan, 2000). Indeed, it was proposed that Meyer's contributions to medical science to this day form the foundations of the biopsychosocial approach currently embedded in the multi-axial nosology of mental illness (Neylan, 2000). One of the most well known early reported cases of behavioural change after traumatic brain injury was that of Phineas Gage. Hence, Phineas Gage has taken on almost iconic status in the scientific literature pertaining to traumatic brain injury, with his case being analysed and re-analysed and discussed to this day by many researchers in the field. While new case reports, some containing data regarding brain imaging also, are published each year, we can still learn much from this classic case report.

Phineas Gage was one of the earliest survivors of a severe traumatic brain injury, and Damasio (1994) provided an extremely detailed case description which contains many clinically relevant observations and insights about brain–behaviour relations. In short, Phineas Gage was severely injured in Vermont following a blasting accident involving a tamping iron during the mid-nineteenth century. The accident, involving explosives, resulted in a tamping iron being blasted through the frontal region of his brain. Astonishingly, Phineas Gage did not lose consciousness and was taken by horse and cart to be seen by Dr Harlow shortly after the accident. Perhaps the most striking aspect regarding his subsequent (post-acute) clinical presentation was how Phineas Gage, after making what was thought to be an amazing physical recovery, started to present with personality changes and emotional problems. Or perhaps, as time passed, people became more aware of his problems; or we may never actually know with certainty what he was like before and after his injury, or, indeed, exactly which parts of his brain were destroyed by the accident (Macmillan, 2008). However, we do now know the reported difficulties experienced by Phineas Gage to be very common after traumatic brain injury, but these insights did not exist at the time and many found Gage's presentation rather puzzling. Indeed, there are many modern-day cases similar to Phineas Gage. Below follows a case report from my caseload, again outlining some of the common impairments that, in many persons, constitute the core clinical presentation after traumatic brain injury.

Miss I, a university graduate, was in her early twenties when she suffered multiple injuries, including a severe traumatic brain injury, following a motor vehicle accident. Her Glasgow Coma Scale was 5/15. She was initially admitted to the nearest hospital, but then, as a matter of urgency, transferred to a specialist neurosurgical unit at a nearby university teaching hospital. With regard to her traumatic brain injury, it was documented in her medical notes that she sustained bilateral frontal cerebral contusions, extradural haemorrhage, subarachnoid haemorrhage, and cerebral oedema. She had a tracheostomy while she was in the intensive care unit and later a percutaneous endoscopic gastrostomy (PEG) feed was inserted. Her period of post trauma amnesia was approximately four weeks. The period of loss of consciousness was near impossible to determine with any reasonable degree of accuracy in view of the sedation she required because of her very extensive injuries. Miss I was eventually transferred to a nearby regional specialist inpatient neurological rehabilitation unit. She spent a total of six months in hospital and was then discharged into the care of her parents.

Following discharge, she was seen in the community for further assessment and follow-up. Initial clinical assessment revealed severe physical difficulties (resulting in part from her orthopaedic injuries), significant problems related to pain, subtle cognitive impairment, and obvious emotional difficulties. Baseline neuropsychological testing performed about ten months after the accident revealed impairments in the areas on information processing, memory, and executive control function. Over time, and with substantial physiotherapy input, she gradually improved with regard to the physical difficulties and, after a couple of years, was able to walk independently again, albeit at a slower pace and with poor confidence. Pain remained a huge problem and interfered, for example, with her sleep pattern. Particularly enduring were her emotional difficulties. Miss I presented with significant and persistent anxiety and depression. With regard to anxiety, she tended to become anxious about the future, started to worry about anything and everything, and gradually lost her confidence. She also experienced profound feelings of anger, as the accident was known not to have been her fault and resulted from careless driving on the part of another motorist. She became increasingly despondent, could not see a future, and hardly socialized any more. Miss I experienced loss of appetite, a disturbed sleep pattern, extreme fatigue, and poor concentration, the latter resulting in memory lapses also.

Miss I presented with a rather predictable combination of physical, cognitive, and emotional impairments following her severe traumatic brain injury. These impairments in turn resulted in significant disability. She lost her independence and initially had to return to living with her parents. She was not able to return to her pre-accident employment. She could not return to driving. Undoubtedly, these disabilities also affected her clinical presentation. It is important that we understand the symptomatology, especially in the emotional area, and for this purpose it may be useful to more closely scrutinize some of Miss I's symptoms. Starting with her sleep disturbance, upon closer examination it was clear that she was randomly woken during the night by pain, but that she consistently experienced terminal insomnia also. The latter is likely to be more compatible with some of the diagnostic features of a major depressive disorder. Furthermore, qualitatively, her mood represented obvious signs of depression, including a loss of sense of future and feelings of guilt. But the former (sense of future) could, of course, also represent a realistic view because of the significant disability she now faced, while the latter (guilt) would be more in keeping with a depressed mood. Her poor concentration and fatigue could be equally well accounted for by either the traumatic brain injury or a mood disorder, or, indeed, a combination of both. Finally, the anxiety she experienced was clearly about future events, and as such was compatible with some of the features of a generalized anxiety disorder, but again, given her impairments and resulting disability, these were, at some level, probably realistic fears.

Miss I was followed up for several years and provided with multi-disciplinary rehabilitation input. This included neuropychology, physiotherapy, speech and language therapy, and periodic medical review. The psychological intervention constituted psychotherapy, including during a later phase of her rehabilitation, cognitive–behaviour therapy. Eventually, she returned to part-time studies, part-time employment, and living more independently. However, it would be fair to say that she continued to experience anxiety and depression and, because of this, remained vulnerable to relapse. This case perhaps illustrates several points about severe traumatic brain injury, including the complex interplay between the physical, cognitive, and emotional symptoms experienced by patients. It also illustrates the problem of long-term disability in young adults and the profound effect this can have on their lives. Finally, this case shows us the importance of diagnosing anxiety and mood disorders after traumatic brain injury and the fact that quite often both can be present. For rehabilitation efforts to be optimally effective, members of the multi-professional team need to understand the role of anxiety and depression and how this relates to other symptoms and impairments commonly associated with traumatic brain injury.

In essence, then, diagnostic systems such as *DSM-IV* (American Psychiatric Association, 1994) can possibly provide the framework within which potentially treatable mental disorders can be identified and diagnosed. This is important for obvious reasons, but the process of diagnosis is only the start of a more comprehensive process that should also, of course, include a formulation of the factors (psychological, biological, social, and environmental) that actually trigger and maintain the disorder. Anxiety and depression are probably the most common difficulties after traumatic brain injury and there are many factors, especially psychological, that can either maintain or ameliorate the person's clinical presentation. It is these factors that, ideally, should be incorporated into a post-diagnosis formulation. We cannot know only what the patient clinically presents with, because we also need to understand why they present with this specific constellation of symptoms or problems on this occasion and under these circumstances. Only then can a realistic treatment plan that augments the patient's overall rehabilitation programme be devised and, ultimately, its effectiveness eventually be reviewed.

Diagnostic issues

It has already been mentioned that *DSM-IV* (American Psychiatric Association, 1994) uses a five-axial diagnostic system. To recap, Axis I is used for the core mental disorders (excluding mental retardation and the personality disorders); personality disorders are reported on Axis II; Axis III is used to record medical conditions; Axis IV for psychosocial problems; finally, Axis V is to assess and record the patient's overall or global (psychological, social, and occupational) level of functioning (*ibid.*). An important concept to be aware of is that while clinically a patient may present with enough diagnostic criteria to satisfy the requirements for making a diagnosis of one of the specific anxiety or mood disorders (for example, major depressive disorder) to be recorded on Axis I, the *DSM-IV* in most cases specifies that when one of these disorders follow a biological event, it should be recorded differently to reflect this fact. The biological event is determined by the patient's history, the physical examination, or laboratory tests (*ibid.*). For example, in the aforementioned case, the diagnosis would still be recorded on Axis I and would, of course, reflect the usual symptoms of a major depressive disorder, but it would be specified as a mood disorder due to a general medical condition and the medical condition noted: for example, traumatic brain injury.

There are further deviations from the usual multi-axial recording procedures. The most important for us to be aware of is the diagnosis of personality changes after traumatic brain injury. As we know, personality or behavioural change is common after traumatic brain injury and can overlap with at least some of the symptoms common to anxiety and mood disorders. What we do not know with certainty, in most cases perhaps, is which biological, psycho-logical, and environmental factors contribute to these changes. However, if it becomes clear over time that the patient's presenta-tion actually more accurately reflects a personality change which only had its onset after the traumatic brain injury, the correct diag-nosis according to *DSM-IV* (American Psychiatric Association, 1994) would be personality change due to a general medical condi-tion, with the biological event judged to be the causative factor (traumatic brain injury, in this case) specified as part of the diagno-sis and additionally recorded on Axis III also. Furthermore, it is important to be aware that, although the diagnosis contains the term "personality", unlike the personality disorders, this diagnosis is recorded on Axis I (*ibid.*) and bears no resemblance to the Axis II personality disorders. The particular personality change should be specified, where possible, as, for example, disinhibited type or labile type, among others (*ibid.*).

Finally, it can sometimes be near impossible to determine the technically correct diagnosis of, say, an individual who, for exam-ple, suffered from a major depressive disorder in the past and who now presents with symptoms of depression following a severe trau-matic brain injury. How do we code this person's diagnosis? Does he or she suffer from major depressive disorder, or a mood disor-der due to a medical condition? Or would a more accurate view be that the person's pre-injury vulnerability to depression has been accentuated by the traumatic brain injury? Or is it possible that the person presents with understandable despair, having increasingly become aware of the devastating impairment and disability result-ing from his or her traumatic brain injury? Can history, physical examination, or laboratory tests always provide all the answers under these conditions? Of course not. And is it not perhaps anyway, in many cases, also possibly equally important to under-stand the psychological and other factors that may account for the person's presentation at this time?

McAllister (2008), having considered the symptoms commonly associated with traumatic brain injury, concluded that psychiatric illness may under these circumstances not always meet *DSM-IV* criteria, and proposed a "relaxed fit" when making a diagnosis. Williams, Evans, and Fleminger (2003) reminded us that diagnoses are perhaps best seen as being multi-factorial and that they can evolve or change over time. In fact, Williams, Evans, and Fleminger (2003) posited that diagnoses perhaps represent clinical formulations that hold or encapsulate clinical information with the purpose of informing treatment, but also to be modified as things change during treatment and, as such, probably equals working hypotheses. This viewpoint does not, however, necessarily explicitly address the issue of what "causes" the diagnosis and that this should be combined with the actual process of making the diagnosis. In this book, a singular aetiology, and specifically a biological aetiology in each and every case, is not automatically assumed. Instead, it is acknowledged that anxiety and mood disorders are common after traumatic brain injury, but for many possible reasons. Because of this, in this text, making the correct diagnosis is emphasized, while psychological factors contributing to the disorder and psychological approaches to the management of these mental disorders are highlighted while acknowledging that other factors, for example, biological, contribute also.

Anxiety and mood disorders in DSM-IV

Several anxiety and mood disorders are described in *DSM-IV* (American Psychiatric Association, 1994). A summary of these is now provided below, to aid the reader in putting these into a broader diagnostic context during later chapters when the specific disorders are reviewed. With regard to anxiety disorders, essentially the following are included in *DSM-IV*:

1. Panic disorder without agoraphobia.
2. Panic disorder with agoraphobia.
3. Agoraphobia without a history of panic disorder.
4. Specific phobia.
5. Obsessive–compulsive disorder.
6. Post traumatic-stress disorder.
7. Acute stress disorder.
8. Generalized anxiety disorder.
9. Anxiety disorder due to a general medical condition.
10. Substance-induced anxiety disorder.
11. Anxiety disorder not otherwise specified.

Chapters Five to Nine address the more common anxiety disorders following traumatic brain injury. With regard to mood disorders, depressive disorders and bipolar disorders are included in *DSM-IV* (American Psychiatric Association, 1994):

1. Major depressive disorder.
2. Dysthymic disorder,
3. Depressive disorder not otherwise specified.
4. Bipolar I disorder.
5. Bipolar II disorder.
6. Cyclothymic disorder.
7. Bipolar disorder not otherwise specified.
8. Mood disorder due to a general medical condition.
9. Substance-induced mood disorder.
10. Mood disorder not otherwise specified.

Chapters Ten and Eleven deal with the more frequently reported mood disorders following traumatic brain injury. For example, most papers reporting bipolar disorder after traumatic brain injury appear to not specify type (I or II), hence the lack of specification in this book also. Having emphasized the importance of diagnosis in this chapter, the next chapter (Chapter Three), provides an overview of the clinical (or bedside) assessment of persons with traumatic brain injury, with specific emphasis on disentangling symptoms and identifying mood and anxiety disorders in this population.

Summary points for this chapter

1. Traumatic brain injury commonly results in a hallmark combination of symptoms including cognitive impairment, emotional difficulties, personality changes, physical problems, and altered behaviour patterns.
2. Impairment of executive control function can possibly influence the presentation of symptoms in other areas also, and clinicians should specifically assess for this.
3. Mental disorders are relatively common after traumatic brain injury, with anxiety and depression the most frequently reported.

4. While certainly not perfect, diagnostic systems can be helpful in identifying the often overlooked or misunderstood emotional difficulties associated with traumatic brain injury.

5. Some uncertainty remains as regards the exact aetiology of mental disorders following traumatic brain injury, but there is preliminary evidence for biological factors being important.

6. Nevertheless, other factors, including psychological and environmental, also, and perhaps more significantly, contribute to the onset and maintenance of emotional problems after traumatic brain injury.

7. While there are predictable and expected symptoms after traumatic brain injury, there is also great individual variation after similar injuries in different persons.

CHAPTER THREE

Assessment

Introduction

Whereas an understanding of the pathophysiology (Chapter One) and awareness of clinical presentation (Chapter Two) of traumatic brain injury are both essential, ultimately, in everyday clinical practice, it is the process of evaluating patients that constitutes the first step in rehabilitation. A thorough initial assessment of patients with traumatic brain injury is essential on all occasions. But this is not always a straightforward process. Patients tend to present with symptoms in different domains, which can make it difficult for the clinician to make sense of their symptoms and associated difficulties. Furthermore, some symptoms may be rather subtle in nature. And some of the symptoms, for example, poor attention, memory, and fatigue, may make it difficult for patients to persevere with the assessment process or, indeed, other interactions with healthcare professionals (Ashman, Gordon, Cantor, & Hibbard, 2006). Making an accurate assessment of patients' neuro-behavioural symptoms is important for a few reasons, perhaps the main reason being that assessment has obvious implications for the management of the patient (McAllister,

2008). To ensure optimal management of patients, assessment of the brain-injured person should cover several important areas. For example, as Lishman (1998) pointed out, clinical assessment can be time-consuming and, ideally, needs to cover a physical examination, history taking, mental status examination, and psychological assessment.

This chapter focuses on history taking and mental status examination. It provides an overview of the process of clinical assessment that most clinicians, irrespective of professional background, should be able to use as a starting point for developing their generic assessment skills within this clinical population. Hence, it does not cover in any detail the specifics of any of the more profession-specific assessment methodologies used, for example, within neurology, neuropsychiatry, occupational therapy, or neuropsychology. The reader needing more information specifically on neuropsychological testing (for some patients constituting a specialist component of the overall assessment process) should consult a text such as, for example, Lezak, Howieson, and Loring (2004). Likewise, for more information regarding the physical examination of patients with neuropsychiatric difficulties, the interested reader may wish to consult, for example, Sadock and Sadock (2007). Finally, Taylor and Price (1994) provide an excellent chapter on the neuropsychiatric assessment of patients with traumatic brain injury, including the use of special investigations such as brain imaging and electrophysiological testing.

Two of the most widely used models of bedside clinical assessment developed specifically for application in brain-injured populations have been described by Strub and Black (1993) and Hodges (1994). These remain classic texts, and the reader who requires much more detailed information would be well advised to consult these. In this chapter, the models of assessment described by these authors are broadly followed, most notably that described by Strub and Black (1993). Hodges (1994) divided cognitive functions into distributed (throughout the brain) and localized cognitive functions, and how to assess these by the bedside within the context of the referral, the patient's history, the physical examination, and the information provided by family members. Similarly, Strub and Black (1993) recommended that broadly three areas were covered during the mental status examination, including pre-injury history, behavioural observations, and, finally, an assessment of cognitive functions. We will first discuss history taking, before proceeding to the assessment of the patient's mental status, including (bedside) cognitive assessment, although it should be remembered that this book is about mood and anxiety disorders after brain injury and the reader will not be provided with the detailed information needed to actually reliably perform a cognitive assessment. Rather, the focus is on cognitive functions' relation to mood and anxiety disorders, interpretation, and the overall process of performing an assessment. Later in the chapter the use of questionnaires is discussed, before concluding with a brief discussion about integrating and making sense of different findings. Finally, a case report is presented to illustrate some of the points discussed earlier on in the chapter.

Clinical assessment in practice

In short, clinical assessment can be divided into three main components, history taking, mental status examination, and diagnostic formulation, comprising the following and commonly performed in the sequence outlined below.

1. Consideration of information contained in referral letter.
2. Inspection of medical records.
3. Exploring the patient's presenting complaints.
4. Patient history.
5. Mental status evaluation (behaviour and emotions).
6. Mental status evaluation (cognitive).
7. Interviewing of family member.
8. Additional information gained by administering questionnaires.
9. Provisional diagnosis.
10. Formulation and treatment plan.

Below follows an overview of this process and some of the pitfalls that may be encountered when performing a clinical assessment aimed at identifying mood and anxiety disorders in persons with traumatic brain injury.

Obtaining a history and reason for referral

Any clinical assessment should always include obtaining a thorough history from the patient (or with the assistance of a family member of the patient), including the presence of pre-injury mental health problems or psychiatric illness. Involving a family member in the assessment process is doubly important. Many patients' clinical symptoms, most notably memory impairment and poor self-awareness can complicate the process of history taking and consequently yield muddled results. It is worth remembering that family members are usually the only people who have known their injured relative before the injury well enough to reliably confirm the presence of any suspected personality changes. Regarding the possible effect of pre-injury variables on post-injury presentation, for example, Ashman and colleagues (2004) report that a pre-injury history of mental health problems is predictive of post-injury mental health difficulties. Many other pre-injury factors can also contribute to post-injury presentation. For example, pre-injury unemployment has been linked to post-injury depressed mood (Bowen, Neumann, Conner, Tennant, & Chamberlain, 1998). Strub and Black (1993) suggest that there were four main areas to cover during history taking, including both pre-injury history and history related to the patient's presentation, and that ideally one should involve a family member in this process. The four main areas are behaviour changes, functional psychiatric disorders, pre-morbid functioning, and the patient's general medical status (Strub & Black, 1993). Below follows an outline of the history taking process, incorporating the model described by Strub and Black (1993) with that used by myself and many other colleagues working in brain injury rehabilitation settings.

After considering and reviewing all available information from the referral letter and accompanying medical notes (including brain scans), the first area to cover during assessment is obtaining a description of the patient's presentation by asking them to provide an outline of how it came about that they are attending hospital today. It is important to make initial behavioural observations from this early stage, for example, taking note of impaired self-awareness, memory problems, disinhibition, emotional lability, and other behaviours. If the patient can deal with this, he or she may be asked about how the injury was sustained and what, if any, consequences there have been for them. This should include date of onset, symptoms, and changes in behaviour since the injury. It can be useful to obtain information as to how the person sustained his or her traumatic brain injury, as this may, in some cases, shed some light on possible mechanisms of injury. This can be useful as, for example, a high-speed motor vehicle accident may raise the suspicion of diffuse axonal injury, whereas a missile wound may imply a more focal injury. Furthermore, it is important to take note of any clues as to the length of amnesia immediately pre and post injury, as this can help with an early judgement of the severity of the injury the patient sustained.

The next step, on many occasions, is to try to more accurately determine the severity of the injury (see also Chapter One). Sometimes this is straightforward: for example, where a person was rendered unconscious for a month, there can be little doubt in the clinician's mind that this equates to a severe traumatic brain injury. At other times, the information needed to determine severity is available in the medical notes or covered in the referral letter. In yet other cases, it can be fraught with difficulty: for example, where there are no data pertaining to severity, no witnesses, and the patient reporting not being sure either, as might be the case where a person was assaulted while on holiday abroad and no hospital records are available. Here, it is almost impossible to judge with complete accuracy the severity of the injury sustained. Nevertheless, ideally and where possible, the following information should be obtained to inform the process of judging severity: period of loss of consciousness, period of post trauma amnesia, Glasgow Coma Scale (Teasdale & Jennet, 1974) score, if the patient needed neurosurgery, and, finally, if the period of coma actually is representative of the patient having been sedated and paralysed due to multiple injuries, rather than having been in a coma (unconscious). If, as is always the case in post-acute brain injury rehabilitation, the judgement of severity is performed retrospectively, Malec and colleagues (2007) provide a useful model for guiding this complex process and systematically organizing the data pertaining to injury severity (see Chapter One for a more detailed description of this process).

After concluding the patient presentation and clinical judgement of severity, generally I find it more productive to do the pre-morbid history before proceeding to the mental status. Patients tend to need time to adjust to what is inevitably a new and potentially anxiety-provoking situation for them, which can result in under-performance if the bedside cognitive assessment is performed too soon in the consultation. Taking into consideration this possible caveat, the process of history taking is initiated by obtaining a developmental history. Many people find it less anxiety provoking to tell you about "who they are" rather than being "tested and put on the spot", perhaps suspecting that they may under-perform and consequently feeling anxious about this. Hence, obtaining the developmental history may provide further time for the patient to warm to the situation first. What is covered, broadly, includes the following: birth, the mother's health during pregnancy, milestones, academic and social functioning at school, qualifications obtained, employment history, and social relationships. Next, the family history could be reviewed, covering neurological and psychiatric illness, the presence of potentially early cognitive decline, and premature death.

The history is usually concluded with covering the patient's past medical history, including previous head injuries, neurological illness, psychiatric illness, use of substances (both prescription medicines and illicit drugs), major surgery, and any medical problems that may have a bearing on the patient's current presentation. To some, it might seem that this is an overly detailed covering of the history where it should, in most cases, be clear that the patient's problems stem from having sustained a traumatic brain injury. Alas, we should remember that persons with traumatic brain injury are definitely not immune to, or protected from, other significant health related events or factors. Indeed, it is not uncommon to uncover a history of another traumatic brain injury predating the one that triggered the current referral. Or, for example, the presence of significant learning difficulties at school. Moreover, the clinical presentation of traumatic brain injury should always be viewed within the context of person's biopsychosocial pre-injury history. Hence, it should be emphasized that, in reality, the above areas probably represent the minimum that should be covered during an initial assessment of the patient with traumatic brain injury, before proceeding to the assessment of mental status.

Assessment of mental status

After obtaining the presentation and history from the patient, we can generally proceed to perform the mental status examination (including, of course, bedside cognitive assessment). The presentation and history naturally provide the essential background against which the assessment of mental status should subsequently be interpreted. The bedside clinical assessment of mental status described here, while drawing on the work of Hodges (1994) and Strub and Black (1993), as well as my and my colleagues' experience, is broadly divided into three areas. These three areas are the objective behavioural observations, assessment of mental function (including subjective patient report), and the assessment of cognitive function. Objective behavioural observations include, but are not limited to, the patient's handedness, gait, speech, self-care, level of co-operation, distractibility, eye contact, expression of affect, and initiation or volition. But, while there is not necessarily a prescribed structure for making behavioural observations or reviewing mental symptoms, the cognitive assessment is a different matter altogether, and here a strategy can avoid many of the common pitfalls associated with interpreting the findings from bedside cognitive assessments.

One of the strengths of Strub and Black's (1993) proposed model for bedside cognitive assessment relates to the hierarchical manner in which they recommend it to be performed. What this essentially means is that there is a bottom-up influence to consider with regard to the assessment of cognitive functions. Hence, one would start the cognitive assessment with the most fundamental or basic cognitive functions before proceeding to the more complex cognitive functions. This is sensible, because the higher-level cognitive functions, for example, executive control function, relies heavily on more fundamental functions, such as attention. Hence, an impairment of a basic cognitive function will, in many cases, have a bearing on the person's performance with regard to higher-level functions. And this can potentially confuse the unsuspecting clinician who starts the assessment by testing, say, executive control function because it is implicated in most cases of severe traumatic brain injury. If the patient struggles with tests of executive control function because of poor attention, it would, of course, be incorrect then to conclude that the patient's primary cognitive impairment is that of impaired executive control. For this reason, it is recommended that the cognitive assessment starts off with a review of the more fundamental cognitive functions, such as attention or concentration.

However, before starting to assess attention, clinicians should be aware that if there are any even more basic functions, usually, but not always, perceptual in nature, that may dramatically affect the findings of the bedside assessment also. Examples of these types of difficulties include hearing loss, loss of motor function, and visual problems. To return to attention and concentration, there is another important factor to keep in mind. Attention or concentration is one the cognitive areas notoriously sensitive to the presence and influence of anxiety and depression. Indeed, in *DSM-IV* (American Psychiatric Association, 1994), poor concentration is listed as one of the diagnostic criteria for a few mood and anxiety disorders, for example generalised anxiety disorder, post traumatic stress disorder and major depressive disorder. As already pointed out, impaired attention is likely to colour the other cognitive functions we assess also. But attention can, in itself, also be affected by other, non-cognitive symptoms of traumatic brain injury. For example, Battistone, Woltz, and Clark (2008) investigated twenty persons with traumatic brain injury to look at speed–accuracy trade-offs regarding processing speed deficits and compared the findings to a control group. The data from this research revealed that deficits in processing speed after traumatic brain injury can be accounted for by at least two factors: that there is a fixed limit to the patient's ability, or that there may be a problem related to volition or cautiousness, accounting for reduced performance (*ibid.*). Hence, problems of attention, including processing speed, may, in some cases, relate to other, perhaps hidden, symptoms also.

Clearly, we need to be sure about the patient's level of attention, fluctuations in this, the possible contribution of non-cognitive factors, and distractibility before proceeding to assess the next cognitive function in the hierarchy, language. Generally, comprehension, naming, word generation, reading, writing, and repetition are covered during this part of the assessment. Assessing language functions is extremely important, as impairments in this area can have profound negative effects on people's everyday functioning. For example, a person with word-finding difficulties may make a poor initial impression during first encounters in social situations with other people. Or persons with problems related to compre-hension, even if subtle, may find it really difficult to deal with more formal or official written or spoken communications to which they have to respond: for example, those from Social Services. To get by in modern society, it is very important to be able to communicate effectively. An inability to do this may have significant effects on a person's mood or levels of anxiety. Finally, with regard to the assessment of language, note again how this level of cognitive func-tion can affect the next level: poor comprehension of language-based instructions will almost always contaminate the findings from, for example, bedside tests of memory, or, indeed, further up the hierarchy, including executive control function also.

Memory should always be carefully assessed, not least because of the significant effect impaired memory can have on both mood and anxiety. Again, having one's memory tested can be an anxiety-provoking task. But this is a complex relation, as persons who are aware that they may have some memory difficulties may present with increased anxiety. Regarding the clinical bedside assessment, it is useful to test immediate and delayed recall for both visually and auditorily (language) presented material. Furthermore, if possi-ble (for example, if there is a relative present who may confirm the accuracy of the patient's answers), it is often useful to test autobio-graphical and perhaps also other, more ecologically valid recall of everyday events. Finally, the testing of executive control function is something of an art. This should never be under-invested in during the assessment, due to the potentially wide-ranging effects of impaired executive control function on behavioural and emotional presentation. Generally, the following areas of executive control function are covered during the bedside cognitive assessment. Initiation, problem solving, planning, and set-shifting. The assess-ment of executive control function after traumatic brain injury is complex and, ideally, a formal neuropsychological testing is more effective at eliciting problems in this area, especially where the presentation tends to be more subtle. Finally, it should be remem-bered that executive control function also influences other cognitive functions (top-down influence).

In some situations, clinicians elect to abandon the less structured bedside cognitive assessment altogether in favour of a standard-ized, comprehensive neuropsychological testing. Where cognitive difficulties are very subtle, this is probably a sensible approach. But there are significant caveats to consider. While this book does not specifically address neuropsychological testing, it is worth mentioning at this point that there are issues specifically related to cognitive testing after traumatic brain injury in the presence of mood and anxiety disorders. It is well known that anxiety and depression can influence test results in normal populations. This is, of course, also the case in brain-injured populations. For example, in a study looking at recall of a word list, depressed mood was associated with reduced delayed recall as well as recognition (Keiski, Shore, & Hamilton, 2007). Perhaps it is also worth considering, then, that depression and anxiety after traumatic brain injury possibly can artificially decrease scores on neuropsychological tests, in effect hiding the real magnitude of the cognitive impairment, or drawing attention away from emotional difficulties by producing results suggesting cognitive impairment to be the person's main problem.

Depression after traumatic brain injury has been associated with impairment of executive control function also (Jorge et al., 2004). But, while there is evidence that a depressed mood can influence a person's performance on neuropsychological tests, this has definitely not been a universal finding. For example, Chaytor, Temkin, Machamer, and Dikmen (2007) looked at the neuropsychological test performance, mood symptoms, and everyday functioning of 216 adults with traumatic brain injury and found that depression was actually not strongly associated with neuropsychological test performance. Nevertheless, it is worth again bearing in mind the potential effect of impaired executive control function on many other areas also, including a person's mood (see also Chapter Two). While not a universal finding, in view of the potential negative effect of emotional disturbances on cognitive functioning, clinicians should perhaps always interpret neuropsychological test results with some caution in this population when there is suspected or confirmed co-morbidity with anxiety or mood disorders.

There are alternatives to both standardized neuropsychological testing and bedside cognitive assessment. Indeed, in some clinical situations, the bedside cognitive assessment is replaced or augmented by a shorter screening of cognitive functions. Many of these instruments exist, and it is beyond the primary focus of this book to provide an overview of this aspect of assessment. The most common instrument used here is probably the mini mental state examination (Folstein, Folstein, & McHugh, 1975). More recently, screening instruments that can provide more detailed assessments have been developed, for example, the repeatable battery for the assessment of neuropsychological status (Randolph, 1998). It should be noted, though, that findings from these types of assessments can be notoriously difficult to interpret, especially if the clinician blindly uses the summed score that is usually yielded by such instruments. It is probably more important for the purposes of bedside assessments to try to make as much use as possible of qualitative observations and to combine this with the patient's actual performance on some of these tasks in an effort to try and determine which factors were responsible for the patient's overall performance. This often entails trying to identify the main factor that could possibly account for the patient's performance. For example, was it primarily anxiety that resulted in a reduction in performance of the patient's suspected modestly impaired cognitive function, or, indeed, was anxiety and other emotional factors possibly the core problem on this occasion? These can be trying questions, and a rule of thumb is to use data from as many different sources as possible before making an initial judgement.

At this point in the consultation, the clinician should attempt to put together or integrate the less precise (and definitely preliminary) but qualitatively rich data from the bedside cognitive assessment. Ideally, this process should result in at least two things. First, with the bedside cognitive assessment completed, can a judgement be made that these initial findings are likely to be compatible with the expected effects of traumatic brain injury? Or are there factors from the history that may provide a better account for the patient's presentation? Second, which other hypotheses does the clinician now, during the remainder of the mental status assessment, need to explore in greater depth, including the presence of anxiety and mood disorders that may become a focus of treatment? And how could these be assessed? Initially completing the mental status assessment and focusing on these and other areas can help to explore the possible presence of anxiety or depression. As part of this process, the clinician should, of course, also screen the patient for the presence of symptomatology of mental health difficulties other than anxiety or depression, such as schizophrenia and other psychotic disorders or substance-related disorders. As pointed out earlier, these diagnostic entities are not covered in this book, as the primary focus is on anxiety and mood disorders. The reader interested in a comprehensive discussion of clinical assessment of psychiatric disorders could consult, for example, Sadock and Sadock (2007), or a similar textbook.

Let us return to the assessment of mood in persons with traumatic brain injury. The patient should be asked directly about their mood and allowed ample time to explore this in an unhindered fashion, to enable the clinician to obtain enough data to try to judge this complex area of clinical presentation. The clinician should try to observe expression of affect, while, of course, also noting the content of what is reported by the patient. From the patient's report, it can be helpful for us to try to determine the presence or absence of, for example, feelings of guilt, excessive rumination, if the person has a foreshortened sense of the future, thoughts or plans of suicide, and other possible markers of a depressed mood. Some persons with traumatic brain injury describe their experience of having suffered a traumatic brain injury as constituting a loss, including their independence or sense of identity. Others may display irritability, anger, or sorrow. Emotional lability may also feature, making it difficult to judge if a significantly depressed mood has been a consistent feature of the person's everyday experience. To fill in the picture further, other areas with a potential bearing on a depressed mood should be reviewed also, including the patient's sleep pattern, appetite, changes in weight, loss of energy, to mention but a few. As a further example of how difficult it can be to disentangle symptoms in this population, sleep disturbances and fatigue are, of course, common to traumatic brain injury, hence findings should be interpreted with care once again.

While depression is likely to be the most common mental health complication of traumatic brain injury (see Chapter Ten), signs potentially indicative of an elevated, expansive, or irritable mood should, of course, also be assessed for. This may indicate the more unusual presence of mania or hypomania after a traumatic brain injury. Tell-tale symptoms of hypomania or mania may include, for example, increased goal-orientated behaviour, increased talkativeness, grandiosity, and distractibility, among others. These symptoms are, of course, potentially indicative of hypomania or mania, and would be recognized as such by most clinicians working in mental health settings and who are familiar with *DSM-IV* (American Psychiatric Association, 1994). But, yet again, the diagnosis of mania or hypomania after traumatic brain injury is not at all straightforward. For example, there are significant difficulties here related to judging whether these symptoms can be more accurately ascribed to personality changes associated with traumatic brain injury and what genuinely represents a hypomanic or manic episode. Another example of overlapping symptomatology in this regard is distractibility: a common cognitive symptom after traumatic brain injury; a common symptom of a hypomanic and manic episode also. This latter example again reinforces the importance of performing a bedside cognitive assessment as part of the mental status assessment in this clinical population; often, this is a very useful aid to narrowing down the differential diagnosis.

Anxiety can be explored by asking about the possible presence of panic attacks, physical symptoms of anxiety, avoidance behaviour, and other clinical markers of anxiety. Note that loss of confidence, which is common after traumatic brain injury, may contribute to symptoms of anxiety and that anxiety may be related to other symptoms. For example, anxiety following traumatic brain injury has been associated with sleep disturbances (Rao et al., 2008). Symptoms of obsessions and/or compulsions need to be questioned. Again, findings related to this area can be difficult to interpret or disentangle. What is obsessional slowness and what is more likely to be apathy resulting from traumatic brain injury? And what is a true compulsion and what more accurately constitutes an impairment of memory? This part of the assessment of course requires objective observations to be made and contrasted with the patient's subjective, or phenomenological, reports. For example, a person may answer that he or she has not been affected by their injury, while displaying obvious signs of anxiety, such as avoidance behaviour or symptoms of panic attacks, mistaken for physical illness. Conversely, the Achilles' heel of assessing anxiety symptoms after traumatic brain injury is probably the fact that many of the primarily physical symptoms of traumatic brain injury can easily be mistaken for anxiety symptoms. For example, headaches, dizziness, and tremor are symptoms of traumatic brain injury that can be really confusing when trying to assess for the presence of anxiety. For this and other reasons, once the mental status assessment has been completed, some clinicians turn to other strategies in an attempt to obtain slightly more objective or repeatable data about depression and anxiety by administering questionnaires that explore these areas.

The use of questionnaires

Can questionnaires really contribute anything useful to the process of assessment? Perhaps unsurprisingly, the use of questionnaires with brain-injured persons is considered to be controversial. As with the bedside assessment of mental status, one of the main problems related to using questionnaires as an additional assessment tool after traumatic brain injury is the possible overlap in symptomatology between anxiety and mood disorders and the common difficulties and symptoms associated with traumatic brain injury. These might include the fact that some items used in questionnaires cannot distinguish between some of the very similar physical symptoms of traumatic brain injury and anxiety, respectively, for example. In addition, Hiott and Labbate (2002) remind us of the difficulties encountered when attempting to untangle the symptoms of post traumatic stress disorder from other psychiatric problems that often follow traumatic brain injury. The problem is amplified when attempting to blindly (without a clinical assessment or in-depth knowledge of diagnostic systems) use questionnaires to elucidate anxiety and mood disorders in the presence of traumatic brain injury, as can, unfortunately, be the case in some research.

A further problem with questionnaires is that many of these have not been at all standardized for use in brain-injured populations. Potentially, one of the most striking examples to highlight problems associated with the use of questionnaires again pertains to post traumatic stress disorder. Sumpter and McMillan (2005) found that when using questionnaires to identify post traumatic stress disorder after traumatic brain injury, the rate was around fifty-five per cent. However, when using clinician-applied *DSM* diagnostic criteria, the rate of post traumatic stress disorder after traumatic brain injury rather dramatically dropped to about three per cent (*ibid.*). The authors conclude that this finding illustrates confusion between the clinical presentation of post traumatic stress disorder and traumatic brain injury and recommended that questionnaires be used for screening purposes only in this population (*ibid.*). Another factor to consider when using questionnaires with brain-injured persons concerns the adaptation of the questionnaire specifically for use in this population. Some of these issues relate to font size (to compensate for potential visual problems), length of the questionnaire (to address possible problems of fatigue), and complexity of language (to compensate for possible problems of attention or comprehension).

There are a limited number of questionnaires claiming to identify emotional difficulties, including anxiety and depression, which have specifically been developed for use with brain-injured persons. In the first instance, some general outcome measures, for example, the European Brain Injury Questionnaire (Teasdale et al., 1997), do attempt to identify emotional factors also (depression, for instance). The European Brain Injury Questionnaire (*ibid.*) is a questionnaire that is fairly easy and quick to administer. It has a large standardization sample of brain-injured persons and relatives from which the normative data were derived. Because of the relative or family member normative data, it also has a parallel version that is completed by a family member or carer. The difference score between the family rating and the person's self-rating can provide an approximate indication of the patient's level of self-awareness: for example, when the person significantly underestimates her difficulties when compared to the family member's views. This aspect of the European Brain Injury Questionnaire (*ibid.*) can be very useful. Self-report, patient-completed questionnaires may miss many of the subtle difficulties common to traumatic brain injury. This is often due to contamination effects resulting from poor self-awareness that can influence the patient's report on many items. Furthermore, having some indication of both emotional factors and self-awareness is of considerable importance. These generally routinely administered outcome measures can sometimes provide useful quantitative data when trying to detect the presence of anxiety and depression in persons with traumatic brain injury. An obvious limitation to consider is that routinely administered outcome measures like these at best provide only very general information about the possible presence of depression and anxiety.

Clearly, there are significant limitations to using general outcome measures to try to detect emotional problems after traumatic brain injury. Fortunately, some widely used questionnaires, for example, the Beck Depression Inventory (Beck, Steer, & Brown, 1996), that have been standardized for other clinical populations have shown some promise as a screening tool for use with brain-injured persons also (Green, Felmingham, Baguley, Slewa-Younan, & Simpson, 2001). However, questionnaires standardized for other populations cannot be blindly used for persons who have suffered traumatic brain injury. In contrast to the Beck Depression Inventory (Beck, Steer, & Brown, 1996), commenting on the use of the Zung Depression Scale (Zung, 1965) in a traumatic brain injury population, Huang, Spiga, and Koo (2005) warned that patients' increased endorsement of somatic items on this scale may actually be the result of the somatic or physical problems associated with traumatic brain injury. For some scales, too, conflicting results are reported. Dawkins, Cloherty, Gracey, and Evans (2006) reported that the Hospital Anxiety and Depression Scale (Zigmond & Snaith, 1983), while requiring a cautious approach to the interpretation of some items, was a useful questionnaire for identifying anxiety and depression after brain injury. But, conversely, Al-Adawi and colleagues (2007) reported that, for an Omani population with traumatic brain injury, it was not a reliable questionnaire to identify or screen for anxiety and depression. More recently, Whelan-Goodinson, Ponsford, and Schonberger (2009) provided evidence that the Hospital Anxiety and Depression Scale (Zigmond & Snaith, 1983) was effective in identifying emotional distress after traumatic brain injury, but that clinicians should be careful when using cutoff scores in this population. Nevertheless, some questionnaires, for example, the Brief Symptom Inventory (Derogatis, 1975), have shown very good reliability and validity for detecting anxiety and depression in persons with traumatic brain injury (Meachen, Hanks, Millis, & Rapport, 2008).

What about the use of questionnaires aimed at detecting more specific mental disorders, for example, obsessive–compulsive disorder, as opposed to screening more generally for the presence of anxiety or depression in persons with traumatic brain injury? Instruments such as the structured clinical interview for *DSM* (Spitzer, Williams, Gibbon, & First, 1992) and the Yale–Brown obsessive–compulsive scale (Goodman et al., 1989) can possibly assist the clinician by enhancing diagnostic accuracy and determining the symptom severity of obsessive–compulsive disorder. Of some interest to clinicians working in brain injury rehabilitation settings is the fact that both these instruments have been used in populations with acquired brain injury also. The structured clinical interview (Spitzer, Williams, Gibbon, & First, 1992) has, for example, been used to determine the incidence of depression, anxiety, and substance use disorders after traumatic brain injury (Hibbard, Uysal, Kepler, Bogdany, & Silver, 1998) and personality disorders in patients with a history of traumatic brain injury (Hibbard et al., 2000), as well as obsessive–compulsive disorder following various other types of acquired brain injury (Berthier, Kulisevsky, Gironell, & Heras, 1996). Regarding the Yale–Brown obsessive–compulsive scale, it is noteworthy that it has been used to determine symptom severity of obsessive–compulsive disorder following traumatic brain injury (Berthier, Kulisevsky, Gironell, & Lopez, 2001) and other types of acquired brain injury also (Berthier, Kulisevsky, Gironell, & Heras, 1996). Again, as with some of the instruments discussed earlier on, it should be kept in mind that self-report questionnaires might have to be interpreted with great caution when used in persons with brain injury who present with symptoms of obsessive–compulsive disorder.

Because of some of the problems outlined above, there have been some interesting and innovative developments intended to overcome some of the unique difficulties related to the use of questionnaires in this population. For example, Turner-Stokes, Kalmus, Hirani, and Clegg (2005) acknowledged the problems related to cognitive, language, and somatic symptoms when using questionnaires to identify depression in brain-injured patients and developed a six-point visual scale, the depression intensity scale circles. This was designed as a simple tool for the graded assessment of depressed mood in persons with brain injury and consists of six circles organized with increasing proportions of dark grey to depict depressed mood (*ibid.*). Turner-Stokes, Kalmus, Hirani, and Clegg reported that the depression intensity scale circles identified depression as per *DSM-IV* (American Psychiatric Association, 1994) criteria and provided preliminary evidence that the tool was indeed valid and reliable for use in this population. It also appears to be very quick and easy to administer. A particular difficulty pertains to the assessment, specifically with questionnaires, of behavioural or personality changes resulting from impaired executive control function. An example of an innovative development in this area is the executive interview (Royall, Mahurin, & Gray, 1992), with some evidence that performance on this screening test is associated with other tests of executive control function as well as actual disability in persons with traumatic brain injury (Larson, Leahy, Duff, & Wilde, 2008). Further innovative developments such as these are needed to assist busy clinicians to more reliably identify anxiety and mood disorders after traumatic brain injury.

In summary, then, while questionnaires may have some role in augmenting the clinical diagnosis of mental health problems resulting from traumatic brain injury, there are also considerable limitations we need to be aware of. While questionnaires may be quick to administer and can attach some numerical value to symptoms, there can also be many false positives related to incorrect endorsement of items overlapping with the physical problems associated with traumatic brain injury. Clearly, there is a need for much more information to supplement the clinical assessment. In an ideal world, clinicians would have access to neuro-imaging, results from questionnaires, and neuropsychological testing, to mention but a few, after completing the initial clinical examination of the patient. It is to be hoped that access to these data would make the diagnostic process somewhat simpler in what can, in many cases, represent a very complex clinical population. In reality, though, many clinicians often have limited access to at least some of these data. Almost by default, this makes the clinical assessment of patients perhaps the most important aspect of the diagnostic and, ultimately, management or rehabilitation process. On the bright side, many of the newer, multi-disciplinary brain injury rehabilitation services often do have different professionals ensuring that at least some of the data crucial to the diagnostic process are available to colleagues.

Putting it all together

There is a great need for more detailed assessment of patients with traumatic brain injury in an attempt to identify the potential presence of mental health disorders (Handel, Ovitt, Spiro, & Rao, 2007). But how do we do that, in the presence of what is often a rather complex constellation of symptoms, including cognitive impairment and pre-injury histories that are not always easy to make sense of? One of the main aims of clinical assessment is to conclude with a diagnosis and treatment plan. How can we be sure of the symptoms that constitute the diagnosis in a particular patient? In practice, when in doubt and, of course, also where possible, clinicians are perhaps most likely to use data from as many sources as possible before concluding that a specific symptom has been accurately identified: for example, that what was observed was actually a perseveration and not a memory impairment the person presented with. While this approach represents a clinician perspective, there is probably at least some empirical support for this approach also. For example, in a study that looked at the assessment of impulsive behaviour in persons with traumatic brain injury attending inpatient rehabilitation, Votruba and colleagues (2008) conclude that impulsive behaviour is multi-dimensional and, as a result, suggested that rating scales, neuropsychological tests, and clinical assessment data should be combined.

McAllister (2008) points out that there were two main contributing factors to the neuro-behavioural consequences of traumatic brain injury. These two factors are the personality changes associated with traumatic brain injury and the increased rate of mental health problems, respectively (*ibid.*). Perhaps we need to consider, in the first instance, what can be directly (physically or biologically) attributed to the traumatic brain injury, while being aware that there is an increase in mental health difficulties or psychiatric illness after such injury. Next, there needs to be an organization of data obtained from different sources, for example, questionnaires, family reports, and so forth, before identifying the primary symptom(s). With regard to hierarchically organizing symptoms, it may be useful to be aware of which are the potentially most confusing traumatic brain injury related symptoms and which are potentially the primary symptoms of the suspected mental disorder. Perhaps even more important is the point made by McAllister (*ibid.*) that we do need to be clear about what is causing the symptoms, as this will have significant implications for the treatment plan. Often, a multi-professional case conference of clinicians familiar with the patient can prove to be a helpful mechanism for presenting, organizing, and making sense of clinical data, resulting in a detailed formulation being made. Finally, and more generally, when it comes to the process of diagnosis, perhaps the most practical and time-honoured approach favoured by many clinicians who actually see patients on a daily basis is to combine the making of a diagnosis and case formulation into a seamless, integrated process. A case report is now presented to illustrate some of the main points covered in this chapter.

Case report

Mr R was in his fifties and in full-time employment as an engineer when he fell down a flight of stairs. He was rendered unconscious and taken to hospital by ambulance. Here, it soon transpired that he had suffered a severe traumatic brain injury. It was recorded in the medical notes that he sustained a serious depressed skull fracture and contusions of the brain. He remained in hospital for several weeks. Post-discharge clinical assessment revealed the presence of cognitive impairment, including poor executive control function, as well as a depressed mood. In addition, Mr R also presented with anxiety, usually when confronted by failures as a result of memory problems or failure to perform complex tasks he could do before. His partner reported significant changes in his personality, including impulsivity and lack of insight into his difficulties. Baseline neuropsychological testing revealed impairment of memory and executive control functions, among others. A psychiatrist later diagnosed features of obsessive–compulsive disorder being present, and accordingly prescribed medication for this. Subsequent administration of questionnaires confirmed this, but poor memory also played a role in some of his ritualized behaviours. Three subsequent sets of neuropsychological test results were thought to be indicative of the presence of a possible cognitive decline, spanning a period of six years since he sustained the injury.

This case illustrates, among other things, how diagnoses of anxiety and mood disorders can, after traumatic brain injury, evolve over time. It also reminds us of the limitations of questionnaires and that clinical diagnosis is paramount. Furthermore, the problem of overlapping symptomatology was illustrated by the patient's memory difficulties at least being a contributory factor to some of his repetitive behaviours. Another interesting point concerned the evidence from neuropsychological testing results about the possible presence of cognitive decline. This is important to consider because, while there is perhaps not conclusive evidence of later cognitive decline after traumatic brain injury, some authors have indeed reported that this can occur. For example, Fleminger, Oliver, Lovestone, Rabe-Hesketh, and Giora (2003) found some evidence that traumatic brain injury may increase the risk for Alzheimer's disease later in life, particularly among men. Finally, this case highlighted the important contribution different professionals can make to the ongoing process of diagnosis and treatment of individuals with traumatic brain injury. The next chapter provides a brief overview of some of the basic principles underpinning psychological approaches to managing anxiety and mood disorders more generally.

Summary points for this chapter

1. The identification of anxiety and mood disorders after traumatic brain injury requires comprehensive clinical assessment to try to detect the presence of these disorders.
2. Clinicians need to understand the interaction between symptoms commonly associated with traumatic brain injury and those more indicative of anxiety or mood disorders.
3. Questionnaires appear to play a limited role, perhaps at most adjunctive to the process of clinical diagnosis.
4. Personality changes common to traumatic brain injury can significantly confuse the clinical picture in some cases.
5. The process of making a diagnosis should, ideally, include a formulation of all the biological, psychological, and environmental factors uniquely contributing to the individual patient's presentation.
6. Different professionals familiar with a given patient can uniquely contribute to the process of diagnosis and formulation.

CHAPTER FOUR

Psychological approaches to the management of anxiety and mood disorders

Introduction

The previous chapter provided an overview of the process of clinical assessment in traumatic brain injury, with some emphasis on identifying anxiety and mood disorders in this population. Chapters 5–11 address the identification of the specific anxiety and mood disorders that can follow traumatic brain injury, as well as provide a brief overview of psychotherapeutic approaches to their management as part of an overall rehabilitation programme. A general understanding of psychological therapy is necessary before attempting to apply any strategies to this aspect of brain injury rehabilitation. This chapter briefly discusses a general framework for understanding psychotherapeutic approaches, before proceeding to provide an overview of evidence-based psychological therapies for anxiety and mood disorders, in clinical populations without traumatic brain injury. The reason for this approach is that almost all of the psychotherapeutic approaches to managing emotional difficulties after traumatic brain injury were developed from techniques or models applied first to persons with anxiety and mood disorders where there was no history of neurological disorders such as stroke, traumatic brain injury, or encephalitis, for example. In view of this, we need to have a good understanding of psychological approaches to managing anxiety and depression in other clinical populations, before considering their use with persons who have suffered traumatic brain injury. The application of general models of psychotherapy to brain injury rehabilitation has been discussed elsewhere also (Coetzer, 2006, 2007). This chapter concludes with a brief discussion of the potential application and adaptation of individual psychotherapy in brain-injured clinical populations. This book does not address group psychotherapy as an approach.

The most fundamental question is perhaps if there is really a need for a more general theoretical framework to inform psychotherapeutic work with brain-injured persons. Should we not just simply apply whatever specific techniques have been proved to be effective in other clinical populations? To some extent, this is exactly what has happened, but there may also be a role for a more fundamental or integrated understanding of psychological therapies in neuro-rehabilitation. For example, Prigatano (2005) posited that a broad psychotherapeutic model was indeed necessary in brain injury rehabilitation. Nowadays, there are many different schools (or techniques/methods) of psychotherapy, including the many different variants of the cognitive–behaviour therapies, psychodynamic therapies, humanistic therapies, existential approaches, brief psychotherapies, psychoanalytical approaches, to name but a few. Each of these has its own underlying theory and techniques or guidelines for application to clinical practice. Almost all have been applied to, and researched in, populations presenting with anxiety or mood disorders. The fact that in practice many different psychotherapeutic approaches have been applied to persons suffering from the same mental disorder (for example, anxiety or depression) with generally similar treatment outcomes have made some researchers question if there are not more basic underlying or generic factors that can account for similar therapeutic outcomes, rather than the specific theoretical underpinnings of these specific model(s). Also, perhaps somewhat provocatively, it could be stated that very complex or overly detailed psychotherapeutic models or systems have a high potential for ultimately proving to have limited clinical utility; comprehension by both therapist and patient of how a specific therapeutic endeavour works is perhaps a more important general factor for success than thought?

Psychotherapy: communalities or specifics?

Among academics and clinicians alike, a debate that has raged for many years centres around the question of what it is that accounts for change during psychotherapy. Or, put differently, what exactly works? Is it the specific techniques, or is it the more general factors (for example, the therapeutic relationship) that might account for observed therapeutic change? Several authors (e.g., Beutler, Moleiro, & Talebi, 2002; Sprenkle & Blow, 2004) have argued that psychotherapy is effective because of the common factors they share, rather than the specific techniques related to their underpinning theories or models (or schools) of psychotherapy. While there is certainly at least some credibility contained in this argument, it should also be acknowledged that in many situations specific interventions might be more effective than others and clearly generic factors may have more of a background function here. Nevertheless, a more generic or basic understanding of how psychotherapy works is probably fundamental to working psychotherapeutically with most clinical populations, including persons presenting with anxiety or depression after traumatic brain injury. It would be fair to say that before considering specific therapeutic interventions, the practitioner needs to have a firm understanding of the more basic or overall processes of psychotherapy.

An understanding of the more fundamental or basic processes involved in psychotherapy practice perhaps allows us to stand back and consider what might be contributing to effectiveness (or, conversely, poor outcome) in individual cases. Considering more general processes, of course, does not preclude the selection and application of specific interventions. With regard to more general models, Orlinsky and Howard (1995), over several years, developed their generic model of psychotherapy, outlining and describing the six characteristics they thought were shared by most of the individual psychotherapies. Theirs is a research theory and, as such, transcends specific schools of psychotherapy, intending rather to identify and describe the more generic facets of psychotherapy.

These characteristics or facets of the psychotherapeutic process individually represent several variables, and mostly operate at the same time (*ibid.*). These six facets include the therapeutic contract, therapeutic operations, the therapeutic bond, self-relatedness, in-session impacts, and the phases of treatment made up by sequential events within and also between psychotherapy consultations (*ibid.*). Below follows a more detailed description of the six facets contained in this model.

The generic model of psychotherapy

In essence, Orlinsky and Howard's (1995) generic model of psychotherapy is a simple model that defines and describes six general characteristics shared by most psychotherapy systems. These six characteristics (listed above) were defined as follows. The therapeutic contract refers to the respective roles of the patient and therapist, as well as practicalities such as the length of sessions and duration of treatment and, finally, the practitioner's treatment model. This treatment model in some way encapsulates elements of specific schools of psychotherapy. Therapeutic operations in psychotherapy constitute the person presenting information that, in turn, is evaluated by the clinician with a view to determining which technical intervention might be indicated or deemed most suitable under the specific circumstances. The patient, of course, actively co-operates in this process. In many ways, this essentially mirrors diagnostic processes (see Chapter Three for more information about assessment and diagnosis).

The therapeutic bond is the relationship that develops over time during therapy and is manifested by each person's investment in their respective roles as well as the personal rapport that develops. Clearly, this is a two-way process. On the other hand, the self-relatedness of persons refers to how people respond to themselves during interactions with others and the environment, including their self-awareness. Perhaps somewhat related or connected to the previous characteristic is the in-session impacts in psychotherapy, which include emotional relief and insight, among others. Indeed, much earlier, Orlinsky and Howard (1986) had already highlighted the importance of emotional expression taking place during psychotherapy. Finally, the sequential events that form the phases of treatment in psychotherapy (Orlinsky & Howard, 1995) can be thought of as events during sessions that combine over time and psychotherapy sessions to form the phases of the overall interventions. Orlinsky and Howard's (1995) model can potentially provide an overall perspective needed to understand more generally what happens in psychotherapy and, accordingly, steer the overall process, including when working with persons who present with anxiety or depression. Nevertheless, it should be acknowledged that, while an overall understanding can be helpful, practitioners increasingly in this day and age of evidence-based healthcare need to know which specific interventions or techniques are useful for which conditions, and also try to understand when these specific interventions appear to work better.

What works for anxiety and depression?

Before applying specific psychological interventions to an individual case, clinicians need to make a judgement regarding the said intervention's known effectiveness in similar clinical populations. This probably lies at the heart of providing evidence-based healthcare. Hence, before one can even start to consider the potential usefulness of certain psychological techniques with brain-injured persons specifically, one needs to be aware of their effectiveness in patients without traumatic brain injury who present similarly. Woody and Ollendick (2006) reviewed the techniques that have been identified as being effective in the management of anxiety disorders, before listing several general principles that appear to be common across all these techniques. After reviewing previous work conducted in this area by Chambless and Ollendick (2001), Woody and Ollendick (2006) identified the following representative techniques as most likely to be effective for the respective anxiety disorders:

● generalized anxiety disorder: cognitive–behaviour therapy; relaxation therapy;
● obsessive–compulsive disorder: exposure and response prevention;

- post traumatic stress disorder: stress inoculation and exposure therapy;
- panic disorder: cognitive–behaviour therapy; relaxation therapy;
- the phobias: cognitive–behaviour therapy; exposure therapy; systematic desensitization.

Furthermore, according to Woody and Ollendick (2006), the general principles common to the above techniques are as follows:

- misconceptions (beliefs) need to be challenged through discussion and specifically questioning the person's evidence for these beliefs;
- incorrect beliefs need to be tested by using behavioural experiments;
- the intensity of fear responses needs to be reduced by using repeated exposure;
- avoidance of feared situations needs to be prevented;
- skills for coping with feared situations need to be improved.

These general principles operate at behavioural, cognitive, and affective levels (Woody & Ollendick, 2006). A recent meta-analytic review by Norton and Price (2008) provided further evidence for the effectiveness and general effects of certain psychological therapies. Norton and Price (2007) looked at the effectiveness of cognitive–behaviour therapy for anxiety disorders across the different individual diagnoses by reviewing the outcome data from 108 studies and found that cognitive–behaviour therapy and exposure therapy individually or in combination, or coupled with relaxation therapy, were uniformly effective across the spectrum of anxiety disorders.

With regard to treatments for depression, similarly to Woody and Ollendick (2006), Follette and Greenberg (2006) reviewed the techniques that have been identified in the literature as being effective in the management of mood disorders, before listing several general principles that appear to be common to all these techniques. Follette and Greenberg (2006) identified the following individual psychological therapies as most likely to be effective for the psychotherapeutic treatment of depression:

- behaviour therapy;
- cognitive therapy;
- interpersonal therapy;
- emotion-focused and brief dynamic therapy;
- problem solving therapy;
- self-control therapy.

Some of these findings have also been supported by similar results from a recent meta-analysis by Ekers, Richards, and Gilbody (2007). These authors compared behaviour therapy for depression with other accepted psychological treatments for depression by including 1109 participants from seventeen studies into a meta-analysis and found that behaviour therapy was superior to supportive psychotherapy and brief psychotherapy, but equal to cognitive–behaviour therapy (Ekers, Richards, & Gilbody, 2008). However, when assessing the effectiveness of techniques for depression, other more general factors should, of course, also be considered. For example, Biegler (2008) pointed out the importance of considering also the potential for self-knowledge to promote autonomy after successful psychological therapy for depression. Furthermore, according to Follette and Greenberg (2006), the general principles common to the above techniques for managing depression are as follows:

- beliefs and behaviours need to be challenged by new experiences;
- ensure access to contingent reinforcement and decrease reinforcement for avoidant and depressive behaviours;
- the patient's social functioning needs to be improved;
- the patient's awareness, acceptance, and emotional regulation need to be improved and change in ineffective emotional responses strengthened;
- the family and social environments need to be improved to avoid depressive behaviours becoming established and rooted;
- the intervention should be structured and focused.

One of the strengths of the very important work of Follette and Greenberg (2006) and Woody and Ollendick (2006) is the fact that they have attempted to move beyond the identification of evidence-based techniques by focusing their efforts on identifying the principles common to these techniques also. In this respect, their and others' work perhaps at some level can link into or even mirror many aspects of Orlinsky and Howard's (1995) generic model of psychotherapy. The generic model of psychotherapy and its application to persons with traumatic brain injury has been discussed in greater depth elsewhere (Coetzer, 2006, 2007). Some support for the suggestion that the generic model of psychotherapy (Orlinsky & Howard, 1995) could also have application to psychotherapeutic practice with brain-injured persons was indirectly proposed by Pollack (2005). He suggests that the main issue is perhaps not that persons with traumatic brain injury do not respond to psychotherapy, but, rather, that because, in effect, almost every aspect of their existence, including sense of self, have been changed in such a manner that these difficulties cannot possibly be addressed by a single psychotherapeutic approach or technique. In effect, while selecting and using techniques, perhaps more importantly, we also need to have an overall feel for, or understanding of, why different techniques work (or not) and under what circumstances. However, before proceeding, it is important to consider the usefulness of individual psychotherapy as an approach to brain injury rehabilitation.

Is psychological therapy indicated after traumatic brain injury?

While, as outlined above, there appears to be growing evidence for the effectiveness of certain psychological interventions for anxiety and depression, a question that continues to crop up is whether psychotherapy might be useful to persons with traumatic brain injury also. And, more specifically in this book, whether it can be useful to those who present with emotional difficulties such as anxiety and mood disorders. In the past, it was thought that psychotherapy as an intervention had little to offer persons who have suffered brain injury. Reduced self-awareness (or insight), memory impairment, and executive control impairment have been considered to pose some of the more serious obstacles to effective psychotherapeutic work. However, increasingly over the past couple of decades, specific psychotherapeutic approaches have been used in brain injury rehabilitation. For example, approaches drawing on principles of behaviour therapy and more recently cognitive–behaviour therapy (e.g., Kinney, 2002) have for some time been considered to be appropriate for treating specific difficulties associated with brain injury. Examples of these more commonly encountered difficulties include aggression, anxiety, and depression, among others. Nevertheless, we do need to have an understanding of the more fundamental factors considered to underpin the process of working psychotherapeutically with persons who have suffered traumatic brain injury. Interestingly, more recently, biological factors underpinning psychotherapy have also been considered and, for example, Linden (2006) reported on the functional brain changes associated with receiving psychotherapy.

Let us now return to the point that certain general principles or factors may well be implicated in psychotherapeutic approaches to rehabilitating some of the difficulties resulting from traumatic brain injury. Prigatano, Borgaro, and Caples (2003) posited that there are four generic components to the psychological management of the common difficulties stemming from traumatic brain injury. These components were thought to be reinforcement of desirable behaviours, ensuring that the patient is provided with adequate information, helping the person to develop self-awareness, and, finally, nurturing and using the therapeutic relationship to help the patient make more effective or functional choices. Clearly, Prigatano, Borgaro, and Caples' (2003) proposed general factors have considerable overlap with the facets of the generic model of psychotherapy of Orlinsky and Howard (1995). For example, the therapeutic relationship, self-awareness, and in-session impacts, as well as therapeutic operations and reinforcement or helping a patient to make choices, can be seen as, respectively, meaning virtually the same thing. Hence, while there may not yet be an extensive evidence base for the effectiveness of specific psychotherapeutic techniques after traumatic brain injury, there are now theoretical models that can inform more generally the psychotherapeutic interventions with this population. However, any psychological therapy approach derived from work in other groups of patients is likely to need some adaptation and modification before it can be applied to persons with traumatic brain injury.

Adaptations to psychotherapy practice

Psychotherapy with brain-injured persons undoubtedly presents the clinician with unique challenges. Judd and Wilson (2005) in their qualitative study reported some of the more commonly encountered obstacles during psychotherapy interventions in this population. According to these authors, some of the more frequently reported difficulties experienced by clinicians working with persons who had suffered a traumatic brain injury included, for example, memory problems and negative reactions (Judd & Wilson, 2005). These and other difficulties common to traumatic brain injury, including poor attention, distractibility, impairment of executive control function manifesting itself as lack of implementation of strategies and poor insight, apathy, and language difficulties require the clinician to adapt the process and strategies for delivering psychological therapy. Rather than considering the adaptations specific psychotherapeutic interventions (for example cognitive–behaviour therapy) might require, it is perhaps more useful to consider the more generic adaptations to psychological therapy for this population.

Several authors have suggested adaptations to psychological therapy that can be useful when treating patients with traumatic brain injury. For example, Prigatano (1999) advised therapists to go slowly, be honest and empathic, focus on the present while knowing the contribution of history, help persons to gain perspective on reality, and try to assist them to derive a sense of meaning. It is interesting to see the importance of pre-injury history (see Chapter Three) emerge yet again. Moreover, one of Prigatano's suggestions does appear to resonate with cognitive–behaviour therapy: to look at the ways persons might think, as this could have a considerable influence on making them feel better. Coetzer (2006), considering the cognitive, physical, behavioural, and emotional difficulties some patients face, described some of the more generic adaptations to individual psychotherapy. These included shortening sessions, making use of memory aids such as session summaries or audio recordings, reviewing notes at the start of sessions, limiting the number of (therapist) responses during the consultation, and constantly being aware of potential problems of self-awareness that might limit the patient's capacity to develop insight. Below are listed some of the more common and potentially useful practical adaptations to the provision of psychological therapy for persons with traumatic brain injury.

1. Providing shorter sessions to minimize the potential negative effects of fatigue or poor attention.
2. Sessions may be spread out over time to facilitate the long-term processes of adjustment, coming to terms with identity change, and developing more accurate self-awareness.
3. Using a noise-free clinic or treatment environment to limit distractions during psychotherapy consultations.
4. Making use of strategies to compensate for memory problems: for example, recording sessions in one form or another, or the very powerful technique of using metaphors.
5. Starting sessions with a summary from the previous session to compensate for memory difficulties and ensure integration or continuity of the themes that make up the overall psychotherapeutic process.
6. Limiting both the number and length of the therapist's verbal responses to maximize the potential for accurate understanding and prevent distraction or memory lapses.
7. Using questioning or role reversal to check for patient understanding: for example, at the end of sessions or when discussing results from neuropsychological testing.
8. Providing written information: for example, with regard to homework assignments or general information about traumatic brain injury and its likely consequences.
9. Where indicated and mutually agreed, asking a friend or relative to help with the implementation of, for example, homework assignments.
10. Being constantly aware of potential countertransference issues unique to working with this population: for example, feelings of frustration, anxiety, or, indeed, that change is impossible and accordingly to have access to appropriate supervision to discuss these dilemmas.

While these and other adaptations can be useful, it should, of course, be kept in mind by all therapists that sometimes, despite our best efforts, adjustments to process, and personal commitment, patients may not benefit from psychotherapy as an approach to, or component of, their rehabilitation. There follows a case report to illustrate some of the above points.

Case report

In Chapter Two, Miss I was presented to further illustrate what was termed a "typical" clinical presentation after traumatic brain injury. Here, aspects pertaining to her psychological therapy are presented to provide an overview of the processes and factors that made up and influenced her psychotherapy. To briefly recap, Miss I was in her early twenties when she suffered a severe traumatic brain injury, following a motor vehicle accident. Her Glasgow Coma Scale was 5/15. She sustained bilateral frontal cerebral contusions, extradural haemorrhage, subarachnoid haemorrhage, and cerebral oedema. In addition, Miss I also suffered multiple other injuries. After her stay in the acute hospital, Miss I was eventually transferred to a nearby regional specialist inpatient neurological rehabilitation unit, where she spent several months before she was discharged into the care of her parents. After Miss I was discharged, she was seen in the community for further assessment and follow-up, mainly for physiotherapy and psychotherapy. Miss I's main rehabilitation input, though, was in the area of psychotherapy, which spanned several years.

Miss I was first seen by me while she was still an inpatient. At this point, a clinical assessment was performed to inform her rehabilitation post discharge, constituting the factor of therapeutic operations described by Orlinsky and Howard (1995). Once she was discharged, she was seen on an outpatient basis. The first consultation essentially covered a discussion of her neuropsychological test results performed earlier, as well as providing general information about traumatic brain injury. It was emphasized that it was impossible to predict her outcome with complete accuracy at that point in time. Based on the clinical assessment and neuropsychological test findings, she was offered psychotherapy, occupational therapy, speech and language therapy, and physiotherapy as part of a holistic, multi-disciplinary rehabilitation plan. It was also clarified where (community hospital nearest her home), for how long (open ended, but for regular review), time of each session (approximately one hour), and how frequently (once every fortnight to start with) she would be seen for psychological therapy. While acknowledging that separating the discussion of the different rehabilitation profession-als' input is perhaps an artificial divide, we shall focus here on the psychotherapy aspect of her rehabilitation only. It would be fair to conclude, then, that the initial contact, as outlined above, repre-sented the therapeutic contract as described by Orlinsky and Howard (1995).

During the early phases of psychotherapy, the following themes were presented by Miss I. She explored the impossible question of why this had happened to her and her feelings of intense anger towards the driver of the vehicle that crashed into her. Miss I felt very acutely the losses she had suffered as a result of her consider-able disability. She found it very difficult to emotionally process the changes to her normal routines stemming from the accident. Clini-cally, she presented with a depressed mood. Providing to Miss I the time and space to explore her emotions was one of the major ther-apeutic strategies during this phase. It also served to robustly develop the therapeutic relationship, as outlined by Orlinsky and Howard (1995). At about this time, some of the baseline outcome measures were repeated, and from these data it appeared that Miss I's self-awareness had increased, perhaps accounting in part for her mood becoming more depressed. In Orlinisky and Howard's (1995) generic model, this would be seen as the factor pertaining to self-relatedness. Up to this point, Miss I was clearly defensive about expressing her emotions during consultations, for example, report-ing anger towards the driver, but not displaying any non-verbal behaviours congruent with this emotion. Increasingly, over time, and perhaps as a function of increased self-awareness, Miss I expressed more openly and congruently her emotions during ses-sions and reported feeling relief when doing so. With regard to Orlinsky and Howard's (1995) model, this probably was compati-ble with their description of in-session impacts.

As time progressed and Miss I became less focused on, and more comfortable with, her feelings related specifically to the accident and its effects on her life, the intensity of her depressed mood appeared to reduce. However, it now also became much more apparent that she was experiencing significant general anxiety.

Interestingly, her pre-accident history revealed some vulnerability to depression and anxiety. Returning to post-accident functioning, she would, for example, worry about the future to the point where it would influence her activities of daily living. In response, two more psychotherapeutic strategies were added at this point: mutual goal setting and cognitive–behaviour therapy. These, of course, again constitute aspects of therapeutic operations in Orlinsky and Howard's (1995) model. With the help of goal setting, Miss I eventually returned to part-time education, voluntary work, and then paid employment. Cognitive–behaviour therapy was valuable in helping with rumination and anxiety, though she struggled to implement many of the techniques "in the moment". Strategies from mindfulness were useful in this regard. Nevertheless, while Miss I made some significant gains during her rehabilitation, the fact is that she remained vulnerable with regard to anxiety and depression. Finally, some of the most useful general adaptations to psychotherapy in this case were the use of metaphors, slightly shorter session times when fatigue was a problem, and starting every consultation by reading over the previous session's notes to compensate for memory problems and maintain a focus on the main themes in psychotherapy. Moreover, providing very long-term follow-up increasingly spread out (later on sessions were between four and five weeks apart) was probably also invaluable in helping with longer-term issues, for example, changes in identity and roles. All the aforementioned, of course, reflect the different stages or phases (with some overlap) that constitute the overall, longitudinal phases of treatment in psychotherapy (Orlinsky & Howard, 1995).

Conclusions

It would be fair to conclude that psychotherapy is increasingly emerging and being accepted as a more common component of many modern post-acute rehabilitation programmes, most notably in the USA and the UK, but in other countries also. While it is acknowledged that there are unique challenges associated with psychotherapy for persons with brain injury, current opinion is that the cognitive, behavioural, and emotional difficulties associated with traumatic brain injury do not necessarily always have to prevent the provision of verbally mediated therapies for brain-injured persons and, indeed, can be compensated for during consultations (Paterson & Scott-Findlay, 2002). There is, however, a glaringly obvious and possibly more important point to consider. Perhaps the bottom line for those working in brain injury rehabilitation settings is that besides psychotherapeutic approaches or environmental intervention (for example, help with returning to work, access to support groups, or having a more supportive family) and, in some cases, pharmacological treatment, there appears to be precious little that can be offered to patients to help them with intense or chronic mood and anxiety disorders after traumatic brain injury.

Several authors have advocated the need for psychotherapy to address emotional issues, including anxiety and depression, in people with brain injury (for example, Block, 1987; Bracy, 1994; Miller, 1993; Prigatano, 2005). The approaches proposed for psychotherapeutic work with brain-injured persons cover a broad spectrum of schools of psychotherapy, ranging from a person-centred approach (for example, Bracy, 1994) to a psychoanalytical approach (for example, Kaplan-Solms & Solms, 2000). A word of caution is necessary, though. Individual psychotherapy is not the treatment of choice for all persons with traumatic brain injury and does not necessarily result in long-term benefits for everyone, even when constituting only part of a comprehensive rehabilitation programme. Indeed, Prigatano (1999) reminds us that while psychotherapy can be incredibly useful to some patients, for others it could turn out to be an enormous waste of their time. Future research in the area is likely to focus on identifying prospectively and more precisely who might be more likely to benefit from psychotherapy after traumatic brain injury.

Summary points for this chapter

1. The generic model of psychotherapy (Orlinsky & Howard, 1995) provides a potentially useful model for understanding the overall process of psychotherapy.

2. There are several evidence-based psychological approaches to the management of mood and anxiety disorders in populations without a history of traumatic brain injury.

3. These approaches may also be useful for persons presenting with anxiety and depression after traumatic brain injury.

4. Psychotherapy may be one of only a few pragmatic approaches available to manage depression and anxiety after traumatic brain injury.

5. Psychological therapy with brain-injured persons may require some general adaptations to maximize the potential for success.

6. Psychotherapy is not indicated for all survivors of traumatic brain injury, and some may not benefit from this approach.

CHAPTER FIVE

Panic disorder

Introduction

The previous chapters covered the nature of traumatic brain injury, including clinical presentation, clinical assessment, and general principles of psychotherapy. The remainder of the core chapters in this book address the specific anxiety and mood disorders in the context of traumatic brain injury, before concluding with a chapter which provides a brief overview of special populations and traumatic brain injury. The first of these chapters deals with panic disorder. The *DSM-IV* (American Psychiatric Association, 1994) essentially defines panic disorder as the occurrence of unexpected and recurrent panic attacks. A panic attack, in turn, is described as encompassing a distinct period of significant anxiety, represented by symptoms such as trembling, dizziness, fear of dying, increased heart rate, sweating, and others. Other examples of symptoms of panic disorder may include the person fearing that he or she is losing their mind, or sometimes becoming convinced that they are dying from a heart attack or other dreaded physical illness. Key here is the intensity of anxiety experienced.

The diagnosis of panic disorder can be specified as with or without agoraphobia. Agoraphobia is not a diagnosis in its own right, hence does not have a diagnostic code. Agoraphobia can be defined as anxiety and avoidance related to being in a place or circumstances (for example, away from the person's home) from which escape might be difficult or where assistance might not be readily available should the person experience a panic attack. Returning to panic disorder, *DSM-IV* also specifies that the panic attacks accompanying panic disorder are not the result of specific physiological phenomena, the effects of drugs or other substances, or another biologically mediated condition. If this is the case, an anxiety disorder due to a general medical condition should be diagnosed. Also, panic disorder should not be confused with medical conditions such as seizures, or with substance induced anxiety, such as, for example, a person presenting with severe anxiety resulting from taking illicit drugs or withdrawing from alcohol or other, including prescription, drugs. For example, in the latter situation, a substance-induced anxiety disorder should be diagnosed in the *DSM-IV* diagnostic system (American Psychiatric Association, 1994).

Patients usually report finding the unexpected onset of panic attacks particularly anxiety provoking and distressing, as well as experiencing the somatic symptoms as really intensely uncomfortable. Some persons develop more general anxiety between panic attacks, often related to anticipating (and therefore fearing) suffering a panic attack in the future. Panic attacks clearly can be very distressing and, not surprisingly, many patients report finding them very disabling. Hence, it is not uncommon for patients with panic disorder to present with avoidance behaviour and, as a result, experience significant negative effects on their normal activities of daily living. Examples of this may include the person being unable to travel or to do the shopping because of anticipatory anxiety, but the effect is not necessarily limited to chores or routine tasks. Pleasurable or recreational activities such as going to the cinema may also be avoided through a fear of possibly suffering a panic attack. While there are exceptions, panic attacks are usually relatively short-lived and self-limiting. However, this does not appear to provide any degree of reassurance to many people who suffer panic attacks.

Diagnostic issues

From a psychological perspective, panic disorder has been formulated more generally as constituting an over-interpretation of normal or expected physical symptoms, of which there can, of course, be several after traumatic brain injury. With the significant somatic colour of many of the symptoms of panic disorder, diagnostic confusion when this disorder presents after traumatic brain injury is perhaps to be expected. For example, Williams, Evans, and Fleminger (2003) advised that panic disorder, because of the depersonalization and derealization that can be present in some cases, should be distinguished from temporal lobe epilepsy. As outlined above, according to *DSM-IV* guidelines, new onset panic disorder that is clearly associated with a traumatic brain injury should be diagnosed and coded as an anxiety disorder due to a general medical condition. Not only biological factors should be considered, though.

Many persons can present with a loss of confidence after traumatic brain injury. This can result in, for example, reduced activities outside of the home or appearing anxious about doing tasks that were probably almost second nature to them prior to the injury. While this presentation, especially where the person seems to be almost housebound, may appear similar to panic disorder with agoraphobia, it should not be confused with this diagnosis. It is important to carefully assess for the presence of panic attacks before making the diagnosis of a panic disorder. Hence, psychological factors can sometimes account more accurately for the clinical presentation and, under these circumstances, a diagnostic label of panic disorder would be entirely meaningless. Finally, because there is very limited specification in the traumatic brain injury literature of panic disorder as regards the presence or not of agoraphobia, panic disorder will be considered here more generally, without this diagnostic specification. Below follows some general suggestions on how to disentangle panic disorder from other symptoms in the presence of traumatic brain injury.

Symptom differentiation

Considering diagnostic criteria as well as actual observed clinical presentation of patients, in the specific context of traumatic brain injury, the following general differentiation between symptoms that may either lend weight to or, alternatively, reduce the index of suspicion of panic disorder, may assist us in the process of making a differential diagnosis.

The most confusing symptoms potentially related to traumatic brain injury, and not necessarily always panic disorder, are likely to include:

- dizziness;
- trembling;
- derealization.

Conversely, the most telling symptoms indicative of the potential presence of a panic disorder in some persons are likely to include:

- symptoms indicative of severe anxiety, for example, fear of dying or going mad;
- the unpredictability associated with panic attacks;
- persistent worrying about having more panic attacks.

The above are merely clinical guidelines to assist the clinician in making a differential diagnosis and should definitely not be seen as hard and fast rules. The initial working diagnosis and formulation for each individual person would be based on much more, including, for example, clinical assessment and an understanding of how common panic disorder actually is after traumatic brain injury.

Panic disorder after traumatic brain injury

Almost predictably, panic disorder appears to be relatively common after traumatic brain injury. For example, Deb, Lyons, Koutzoukis, Ali, and McCarthy (1999) defined a sub-sample of 120 persons aged between eighteen and sixty-four with a history of traumatic brain injury and found that about nine per cent met the diagnostic criteria for panic disorder during the first year after suffering their injury. Perhaps this finding is to be expected given the large numbers of patients with traumatic brain injury who present with unpleasant physical symptoms during the early stages post-injury.

These symptoms can, of course, provide fertile grounds for the development of anxiety disorders in general and, more specifically, panic attacks. For example, some of the perceptual symptoms that can accompany traumatic brain injury must be very frightening for patients, and it is not only symptoms that can be a source of intense anxiety. Surely, hospital environments can also be hugely anxiety provoking for some patients, especially if one cannot even remember how it came about that one now finds oneself in an unfamiliar hospital environment.

In an interesting speculation about the nature of the disorder, Deb, Lyons, Koutzoukis, Ali, and McCarthy (1999) hypothesized that panic disorder may actually represent a novel expression of post traumatic stress disorder, because of the amnesia for the event resulting from traumatic brain injury. But what about the later stages after traumatic brain injury? Is panic disorder common during these stages also? Indeed, Van Reekum, Cohen, and Wong (2000), in their comprehensive review, pooled the data from three separate studies and found that just over nine per cent (26/282) of patients presented with panic disorder. This figure appears to be strikingly similar to the figure reported for a more recently injured population. Moreover, in a study that looked at mental health difficulties more long-term after traumatic brain injury, Koponnen and colleages (2002) found that just over eight per cent of their group, followed up, on average, thirty years after injury, presented with a panic disorder. It should be kept in mind, though, that after such a long period of time since injury, it is probably impossible to confidently attribute panic disorder directly to the biological effects of the injury and surely psychological or environmental factors should be considered also under these circumstances. Finally, some case studies of panic disorder after traumatic brain injury have also been reported.

What is also emerging from some studies is the fact that many patients' emotional difficulties cannot be neatly fitted into a single diagnostic category. Hibbard, Uysal, Kepler, Bogdany, and Silver (1998) evaluated 100 patients on average eight years after traumatic brain injury and found that major depressive disorder was the most common disturbance, but that specific anxiety disorders, including panic disorder, was one of the most common mental disorders in this population also. However, rather interestingly, it should be noted that there was very high co-morbidity in this sample and many of the patients had two diagnoses of mental disorders (Hibbard, Uysal, Kepler, Bogdany, & Silver, 1998). Evidence for the presence of panic disorder after traumatic brain injury is also not limited to group studies. For example, Scheutzow and Wiercisiewski (1999) described a case of a patient who was diagnosed with panic disorder during his rehabilitation process. In this case, the patient presented with symptoms, including avoidance of activities, of panic disorder related to a fear of having a cardiac arrest. Clearly, a contributory factor in panic disorder can be a misinterpretation or lack of understanding of physical symptoms common to traumatic brain injury. But what potential role does patients' understanding, or insight more generally, after having sustained a traumatic brain injury, have on anxiety disorders?

The role of self-awareness

Self-awareness, or insight, is possibly one of the hallmark phenomena of traumatic brain injury. In essence, it represents an individual's understanding of their impairments, their significance, and associated impact on everyday living. Impaired self-awareness can pose one of the most significant obstacles to patients' participation in rehabilitation and should probably always be considered as a potentially contributory factor to the patient's presentation by clinicians who work in rehabilitation settings. While not exactly the same thing, self-awareness can, on many levels, be equated to insight or understanding and, not surprisingly, relatives sometimes use these terms to describe the changes they observe in a family member after a traumatic brain injury. Much has been written about self-awareness and its relation to depression after traumatic brain injury, and for this reason self-awareness is covered more comprehensively later in the chapter that deals with depression (Chapter Ten). Nevertheless, while less work has been done in the context of anxiety disorders, it is important to cover here more generally the potentially important role of self-awareness in the onset, evolution, and maintenance of anxiety symptomatology after traumatic brain injury.

While self-awareness can be either protective against, or contributory to, depression in the context of traumatic brain injury, increased self-awareness is more likely to lead to increased anxiety and, as such, even motivate the person to try to change or take part in rehabilitation. For example, Fleming, Strong, and Ashton (1998) investigated fifty-five patients with severe traumatic brain injury and reported that, among other findings, self-awareness was associated with greater anxiety and stronger motivation to change. More recently, O'Callaghan, Powell, and Oyebode (2006), in a qualitative study with ten persons who had suffered moderate to severe traumatic brain injury, reported that patients, through personal discovery and the reactions of other people, learnt about their deficits and responded with emotions of fear and loss. Obviously, self-awareness is only one of many factors associated with, or implicated in, anxiety disorders after traumatic brain injury. For example, discrepancies between pre-injury and post-injury selves have been strongly associated with anxiety also (Cantor et al., 2005). We shall now turn to a case report of a patient who presented with panic disorder after traumatic brain injury, and how there was, as in the Hibbard, Uysal, Kepler, Bogdany, and Silver (1998) study, co-morbidity with other mental disorders also.

Case report

Mr R, who was briefly discussed earlier in this book (Chapter Three), was in his mid-fifties and in full-time employment when he fell down a flight of stairs, hitting his head in the process. According to witnesses, following the fall, he regained consciousness within minutes, but by the time he arrived at the hospital, his Glasgow Coma Scale (Teasdale & Jennet, 1974) was 7 out of 15. At that time his computed tomography (CT) scan of the brain revealed multiple fractures to the occipital bone, including a depressed skull fracture. Initially, while in the intensive care unit of the hospital, Mr R's neurological condition unfortunately dramatically deteriorated, most probably due to suspected swelling of the brain. Fortunately, some days later he started to improve. Mr R was awake and responding to commands after about ten days. About three months after his injury, a magnetic resonance image (MRI) of the brain was obtained, which revealed contusions of the left lateral occipital lobe, right temporal pole, and right medial-orbito frontal area. Mr R eventually made a good physical recovery and was discharged home.

Clinically, when seen for post-acute rehabilitation, Mr R initially presented with poor concentration, emotional lability, increased frustration, difficulties in reading, dizziness, and impaired balance. Baseline neuropsychological testing revealed the presence of numerous cognitive difficulties, including poor concentration, impaired visual memory, visio-spatial problems, and impaired executive control function. Despite intensive rehabilitation input, including occupational therapy, Mr R failed to return to his previous employment. Mr R reported that he could only attend to one thing at a time. Relatives reported subtle changes in social skills: for example, having become less tactful or at times talking incessantly without a gap for others to speak. Over time, he became increasingly depressed and eventually met the diagnostic criteria for both major depressive disorder as well as some of the diagnostic criteria for obsessive–compulsive disorder. He also consistently described feeling as if he was dreaming, that things were unreal, and while realizing, on an intellectual level at least, that he had suffered a traumatic brain injury, he wished that at some point he would "wake up". This desire to return to his former self he would endlessly and repetitively discuss during rehabilitation sessions, expressing strong emotions of frustration in the process.

Later during his presentation, Mr R started to experience panic attacks. He described these as representing overwhelming anxiety, to the point where he would fear that he might "pass out". Some of these panic attacks were in response to his cognitive impairment (in his case most probably memory problems and difficulties with complex problem solving) resulting in failure in everyday tasks. For example, Mr R once forgot to pay for his parking and when he tried to exit, he was unable to do so. He could not figure out why (because he had not paid) and became overwhelmed with anxiety, making it even less possible for him to solve the problem. On other occasions, the panic attack would come out of the blue. For example, one evening he and his family were going to order a take-away meal and he suddenly became overwhelmed with severe anxiety, physical sensations that he was seriously unwell, and thought that he would collapse. He also feared that he might have suffered a seizure. Mr R eventually, in addition to psychological therapy, saw a psychiatrist, who prescribed medication. About six years post-injury Mr R reported that while he continued to present with anxiety, the intensity of his emotions were reduced, but that he feared suffering a full-blown attack. As a result he became very intolerant of any potential changes to his deeply ingrained daily routines, fearing that he would experience a panic attack if his routines were disturbed.

Returning to the psychological component of Mr R's rehabilitation, the following strategies were followed. Mr R's psychotherapy intervention initially constituted forging a therapeutic bond and providing robust information about traumatic brain injury. The latter was an attempt to increase his understanding and self-awareness. Much of the subsequent psychotherapeutic work focused on themes of loss, not only the more tangible aspects of loss, such as employment, but much more about having lost the person he used to be, or, put differently, having lost his identity. The second main theme was about his inability to accept these losses and changes and a constant desire to be like he was in the past. Finally, with regard to his panic attacks, the following psychotherapeutic strategies were used. First, provision of information about what panic attacks actually were and, conversely, what they were not. Second, using this information with more general cognitive–behavioural strategies to help him manage some of the emotions he continued to experience and to set behavioural goals. There was also some psychotherapeutic work pertaining to acceptance, including living life as it was now to the full. It was, however, unclear how successful the latter was, at least until much later in the psychotherapeutic process.

Below follows a brief overview of the literature regarding psychotherapeutic approaches to managing panic disorder after traumatic brain injury.

Psychological approaches to management

Relaxation therapy, cognitive–behaviour therapy, and behaviour therapy have all been reported to be effective as psychological therapies for the management of panic disorder in persons without a history of traumatic brain injury (e.g., Landon & Barlow, 2004;

Norton & Price, 2007). Also, cognitive–behaviour therapy has been proposed to be a useful treatment in general for persons with traumatic brain injury, but it must be delivered in such a way that patients are engaged through the therapeutic relationship, and lasting behaviour change is ensured through repeated verbal mediation as well as behavioural practice (Manchester & Wood, 2001). With specific regard to panic disorder after traumatic brain injury, cognitive–behaviour therapy has been suggested to be useful (Williams, Evans, & Fleminger, 2003), but can and should be modified and developed in a creative way to better suit the unique emotional difficulties that persons who have suffered a traumatic brain injury generally tend to present with. Indeed, Williams, Evans, and Fleminger (2003) asserted that cognitive–behaviour therapy should be developed beyond the treatment of narrow diagnostic categories when applied to the rehabilitation of persons with acquired brain injury to help them with acceptance and adjustment.

Gracey, Brentnall, and Megoran (2009) provide a detailed account of how cognitive–behaviour therapy can be modified to better suit the needs of a patient who presented with significant anxiety-related difficulties after having suffered a severe traumatic brain injury. They described the case of a thirty-one-year old female who suffered a severe traumatic brain injury in a car crash, as evidenced by the presence of a left frontal subdural haematoma and post trauma amnesia extending to three weeks. The patient attended a six-month holistic rehabilitation programme where first cognitive–behaviour therapy was modified to include behavioural experiments as part of the rehabilitation process and second, "positive formulations" to facilitate adjustment and work on issues related to identity change were used. The patient presented with a combination of emotional difficulties, perhaps not meeting formal diagnostic criteria, but including depression, obsessional checking behaviour, and elements of post traumatic stress disorder, but most pressing, actually, were the panic attacks she presented with. To facilitate acceptance, adjustment, and understanding, as part of the cognitive–behaviour therapy approach, collaborative behavioural experiments to test out her assumptions about "threats to the self", as well as "safety behaviours", were devised and carried out with good effect. Finally, a "positive formulation" that she was "a someone after all" resulted from the behavioural experiments and the strategy of developing her identity through activity (Gracey, Brentnall, & Megoran, 2009).

Clearly, cognitive–behaviour therapy can be modified to address some of the specific difficulties related to anxiety after traumatic brain injury. Regarding pointers from clinical practice towards other psychological therapies that may show some potential for being helpful, clinicians could consider relaxation techniques, exposure, provision of information (psychoeducation), or strategies from mindfulness approaches. Relaxation techniques have the potential to provide patients with the necessary skills to gain some control over the symptoms of a panic attack, whereas exposure may ultimately be helpful in boosting patients' confidence. Patients do report some relief from anxiety after being provided with information about the nature of panic attacks. Indeed, O'Callaghan, Powell, and Oyebode (2006) report that rehabilitation provided explanations and normalizing in a supportive environment, which may reduce fear and feelings of loss. Mindfulness, as an approach, has the potential benefit of assisting persons with traumatic brain injury to experience a general reduction in anxiety, but also can facilitate an increased awareness of physical symptoms and, in this way, provide a psychological mechanism for reducing the impact of the panic attacks the individual may experience. Mindfulness approaches may also help individuals with traumatic brain injury to live life more in the moment, potentially avoiding some of the common anxiety symptoms that can possibly be implicated in triggering full-blown panic attacks.

Riley, Brennan, and Powell (2004), in a qualitative study, looked at the role of threat appraisal in anxiety after traumatic brain injury and found that men and, perhaps unsurprisingly, persons who were assaulted, reported more avoidance behaviour. These authors suggested that rehabilitation should help facilitate patients' participation in valued roles and activities to counteract anxiety and avoidance. Clearly, this would have to be done in a supportive and gradual fashion to prevent the person from experiencing failure and then experiencing increased emotional distress as a consequence. Finally, while psychological approaches are possibly the treatment of choice in panic disorder after traumatic brain injury, drug treatments have an important role also, and the reader with a specific interest in the pharmacological management of panic disorder after traumatic brain injury could look at a paper by Scheutzow and Wiercisiewski (1999), who provide an overview of the topic. For more general guidance on the use of drugs in managing anxiety or mood disorders after traumatic brain injury, the reader could consult, for example, Fleminger (2008) or, for relatively recent reviews, Tenovuo (2006); Lee, Lyketsos, and Rao (2003), or Glenn and Wroblewski (2005).

In summary, considering both the above overview of research findings and pointers from clinical practice, the main psychological therapies to consider in panic disorder after traumatic brain injury include:

- cognitive–behaviour therapy;
- behaviour therapy, including exposure;
- relaxation techniques;
- provision of information (psychoeducation);
- mindfulness approaches.

Drawing upon some of the generic aspects of psychotherapy (see Chapter Four), most notably the therapeutic relationship and self-awareness, as well as experience from clinical practice, the next section explores the qualitative nature of patients' thoughts, behaviours, and emotions, as these may present during the process of providing psychological interventions. Moreover, some potentially useful strategies or techniques the clinician could consider employing are briefly mentioned.

Strategies and themes in psychotherapy

The very nature of panic disorder, to some extent perhaps, determines some of the themes patients may bring to the psychotherapeutic encounter. For example, fearing that the person has lost his or her mind as a result of the injury, or a fear that a physical illness has developed in response to having suffered a traumatic brain injury, or, indeed, as a result of the many other physical injuries that sometimes accompanies traumatic brain injury sustained in, say, a car crash. For many, simply just not understanding their symptoms is the main source of fear or panic. Another theme is the specific fear that the injury has resulted in post trauma epilepsy. This is, of course, a common dilemma of differential diagnosis. Hence, in some cases, post trauma epilepsy has to be excluded before it can be said with certainty that the patient is presenting with panic disorder. Sometimes, the panic attacks are related more to simply not understanding what is wrong or what has happened to them, especially while being an inpatient shortly after sustaining the injury. For example, one patient described coming around in hospital, unable to recognize where she was, and becoming intensely fearful as she thought she had been abducted.

Another common theme I have encountered in patients with panic disorder after traumatic brain injury is their reporting that they would in the past have been much more able to deal with anxiety and that part of the problem, in their view, was their reduced capacity to manage their panic attacks. This, in itself, can, of course, create something akin to a vicious circle and increase their anxiety. Some patients describe a combination of loss of confidence, embarrassment, and fear of "disintegrating" when in social company or out and about, and in response become quite housebound, but then, almost perversely, become more panicky about leaving the house as time goes on. Prognosis, or rather the lack of clarity with regard to prognosis, can be a major source of panic for some, especially once a person starts ruminating about what their outcome will be. If the patient, during the acute phase after injury, believes that their symptoms are static and that there will be no further progress, significant anxiety or panic attacks can be a very uncomfortable consequence, particularly for those patients who are more likely to mull over things, but who may now, as a result of the traumatic brain injury, be less able cognitively to figure things out.

With regard to strategies to attempt to address some of these themes in psychological therapy, in my experience it is crucial to prioritize a couple of tasks (or generic factors) initially: assessment and diagnosis, as well as the rapid forging of a therapeutic alliance. Regarding the therapeutic relationship, honesty and empathy is paramount here. Should the therapist succeed with these generic aspects of the process, it can often be very helpful to provide information about panic disorder, including the specific symptoms, and emphasizing that the unexpected onset of panic attacks are particularly troublesome for most people. It can be helpful to inform patients that this latter aspect of the disorder (attacks coming out of the blue) can make one vulnerable to misinterpretation of the symptoms. Furthermore, it can be useful to also emphasize that, mercifully, the symptoms of an individual panic attack in most cases are self-limiting and relatively short-lived. This may even provide the necessary comfort for a patient to be more willing to engage in behavioural strategies, such as exposure, to try to reduce the frequency and intensity of their panic attacks. Nevertheless, behavioural goals should always be set jointly with the patient. While we should, of course, guard against working at too fast a pace, or even coming across as impatient, an early therapeutic success, however small, when working with this disorder is invaluable and can really have profound effects on the likelihood of a good outcome over time.

Patients' views or interpretation of their panic attacks can be addressed by utilizing generic cognitive therapy strategies. For example, probing the patient about what they think their symptoms represent, or what it might mean to them, can be helpful in identifying possible cognitions contributing to the onset and maintenance of panic attacks. Once the core thoughts have been identified (for example, that they are suffering a heart attack or seizure, where this, of course, has been ruled out), the therapist may wish to provide the patient with more objective evidence of what a panic attack constitutes, sometimes even sharing with the patient the actual diagnostic criteria. Sometimes, for some persons (for example, where there are significant difficulties related to concentration or memory), it is not practically feasible to go through a detailed explanation of the general rationale for cognitive therapy, especially where severe anxiety dominates their experience and potentially makes them less receptive. Under these circumstances, the use of metaphors to illustrate the relation between thoughts and feelings and behaviours can be tried. For example, a simple exercise of two persons looking at exactly the same object or event, but describing it differently, can be a powerful metaphor for illuminating the basic rationale of many of the cognitive therapies. Finally, always try to use real examples (from the patient's actual experience) where possible, to try to move the therapeutic process from an intellectual understanding to a more robust personal internalization of the principles used in therapy.

More generally, within a well-established therapeutic relationship, reassurance can also go some way towards providing relief from the symptoms of panic disorder. The therapist, however, should never follow strategies that may adversely affect trust. It is crucial not to minimize patients' symptoms as "merely signs of anxiety", as this may result in a breakdown in the therapeutic relationship and unwillingness to work on, for example, a more behavioural level with the therapist to reduce the impact of the disorder. People do experience panic attacks as seriously unpleasant, and trying to suggest the opposite by "putting things into perspective" can be counterproductive. On the other hand, patients do report considerable relief when some empathy with their symptoms is expressed, and perhaps become more receptive to psychoeducational strategies. Again, this may open the door to more gently exploring complex issues such as self-awareness or other issues surrounding their anxiety, for example, a fear that their partner may leave them or that they will go to ruin financially. Issues or questions such as these can play on patients' minds and result in panic attacks and avoidance of, for example, discharge from hospital, social events, or attempts to return to work, where this is still feasible. Finally, it is important to help patients to minimize avoiding participation in other therapies, for example, physiotherapy or occupational therapy, as a result of the symptoms of panic disorder. Panic disorder can seriously adversely affect a person's participation in rehabilitation or activities related to reintegration into everyday life and, ideally, should be identified as early as possible to prevent behavioural patterns from becoming entrenched.

Summary points for this chapter

1. Panic disorder in the context of resulting from a traumatic brain injury should be diagnosed as an anxiety disorder due to a general medical condition.
2. Panic disorder following traumatic brain injury often presents with other emotional difficulties, for example, depression.
3. The somatic symptoms resulting from traumatic brain injury can confuse the clinical presentation of panic disorder.

4. Psychological approaches to the management of panic disorder include cognitive–behaviour therapy, relaxation, behaviour therapy, and psychoeducation.
5. Early diagnosis and establishment of the therapeutic relationship are perhaps prerequisites for successful cognitive and behavioural interventions.

CHAPTER SIX

Phobias

Introduction

I t would be fair to assert that most people are afraid of at least
some things. However, it is also true that these fears are not so
severe that they cannot manage to get by without having to
totally avoid these objects associated with their fears, or at least that
it does not significantly interfere with their daily routines. In many
ways, this difference lies at the heart of what constitutes a phobia. A
phobia (simple phobia) is defined in *DSM-IV* (American Psychiatric
Association, 1994) as a significant, excessive fear in response to the
presence or anticipation of a specific stimulus (situation or object).
Furthermore, the stimulus almost always results in immediate anxiety and the person is aware that his or her anxiety is excessive. The
person would, therefore, attempt to avoid the stimulus and this
mostly tends to interfere with social or occupational activities. An
example of a particular phobia is social phobia, where there is a
significant and enduring fear of social situations with a potential for
embarrassment. Other specific phobias may relate to animals,
heights, or driving, for example. Phobias may evolve in response to
identifiable, discrete events: for example, a phobia of dogs being

triggered after a dog has bitten the person. In other cases, there may appear to be no clear causative factor or precipitant.

The qualitative nature of phobias can be influenced or coloured by culture. Phobias should not be confused with more general or pervasive anxiety disorders such as, for example, panic disorder (with agoraphobia) because phobias are limited to, and triggered by, specific events, objects, or situations. Likewise, shyness and stage fright do not constitute social phobia. Moreover, the phobias are broadly divided into specific phobia and social phobia, which should be differentiated based on the fears of negative evaluation by other people (in the latter) as opposed to fears about, for example, objects or situations without being concerned about the evaluation of others (the former) (American Psychiatric Association, 1994). Some individuals with social phobia may also meet some of the criteria for avoidant personality disorder. In the context of traumatic brain injury, social phobia should, where possible, be disentangled from avoidance resulting from loss of confidence or significantly reduced ability to socialize as a consequence of cognitive (most notably speech and language or memory) impairment.

Diagnostic issues

Social anxiety can form part of many of the other mental disorders in *DSM-IV* (American Psychiatric Association, 1994), but social phobia should only be diagnosed where avoidance is not better accounted for within the context of another disorder. In contrast to some of the other anxiety disorders, *DSM-IV* guidelines do not explicitly state that new onset simple phobia associated with traumatic brain injury should be diagnosed as an anxiety disorder due to a general medical condition. Similarly, in social phobia, *DSM-IV* specifies that if a medical condition is present, the fear regarding social performance is not related to the said medical condition. Specific phobias can be specified as animal type, natural environment type, blood-injection type, situational type, or other type (*ibid.*). This sub-classification, however, is perhaps unlikely to be of any real clinical use in the context of traumatic brain injury. Social phobia can be specified as generalized if the person's anxiety pertains to almost all social situations (*ibid.*). This may have some utility in brain injury rehabilitation, as specific social fears may require a different psychotherapeutic strategy compared to more generalized social anxiety.

With regard to social anxiety within the context of traumatic brain injury, clinicians should be sensitive to factors such as loss of confidence, reduced cognitive ability to effectively take part in social situations, or apathy potentially confusing the diagnosis. These difficulties can all present as, or result in, avoidance of social situations, but may not represent social phobia. The astute clinician should always check for the presence of significant anxiety related to, or in anticipation of, social situations, before considering a diagnosis of social phobia. It should also be noted that, with regard to simple phobia, some patients do show (quite understandably) avoidance and fear of situations associated with the circumstances under which they sustained the injury in the first place, for example, driving, or hospital environments. Finally, some patients become socially isolated as a result of personality changes, lack of financial resources, inability to drive or use public transport, or other factors associated with their injury, and these should again not be confused with social phobia. There follows some general suggestions on how to identify phobias in the presence of traumatic brain injury.

Symptom differentiation

Based on observed clinical presentation as well as diagnostic criteria, in the specific context of traumatic brain injury, the following general differentiation between symptoms that may either lend weight to or, alternatively, reduce the index of suspicion for the presence of a phobia (including simple or social phobia) may assist in the process of making a differential diagnosis.

The most confusing symptoms that are potentially primarily related to traumatic brain injury and not necessarily always to a phobia are likely to include:

● dizziness mistaken for anxiety;
● general loss of confidence associated with changed abilities (as opposed to social fear);
● avoidance or change in previous routines.

The most telling symptoms indicative of the potential presence of a phobia are likely to include:

●   symptoms of severe anxiety, in response to a specific object or situation;
●   a recognition that the fear is unreasonable;
●   worries about having a phobia.

The above are, of course, merely clinical guidelines or suggestions to assist the clinician in making a differential diagnosis. The actual working diagnosis and formulation would almost always be based on more extensive clinical information or findings based on a comprehensive clinical assessment of the patient. Furthermore, an understanding of how common phobic disorders actually are after traumatic brain injury can, of course, also prove to be helpful.

Phobias after traumatic brain injury

From a psychological perspective, we would perhaps expect phobias to be fairly common after traumatic brain injury. In many cases, the circumstances under which the person sustained the injury would lend themselves to the development of anxiety and avoidance. For example, one could almost expect someone to exhibit fear and avoidance of driving and hospital visits after being involved in a serious car crash. Likewise, it would not be surprising if a person were to be anxious about, and accordingly avoided, being on the street late at night after being assaulted under similar conditions. It is possible, though, that a person may well, as a result of loss of consciousness (and consequently not remembering events), to some extent be protected from developing a phobia (see also Chapter Eight). It is, of course, also possible that persons may, after traumatic brain injury, be more prone to anxiety resulting from reduced cognitive abilities to perform everyday tasks, resulting in avoidance of certain situations. What do research findings and case reports tell us about phobias after traumatic brain injury, though?

Unfortunately, there are very few studies that specifically report the incidence and prevalence of social phobia or specific phobia after traumatic brain injury (Hiottt & Labbate, 2002). Nevertheless, Koponen and colleagues (2002) found that just over eight per cent of their sample of persons with traumatic brain injury met the *DSM-IV* criteria for a phobia. Interestingly, Labbate, Warden, and Murray (1997) reported a case where social phobia resolved after the patient sustained a traumatic brain injury, perhaps as a result of the injury replacing pre-morbid inhibition with disinhibition. Indeed, it is not uncommon for some persons to present with a personality trait or behaviour opposite to what was perhaps more usual for them prior to the injury. With regard to individual case reports, Kneebone and Al-Daftary (2006) reported a case of a thirty-two-year-old female who had a history of Down's syndrome and who, after having suffered a traumatic brain injury, presented with a specific phobia related to attending physiotherapy. In view of the lack of research regarding the incidence and prevalence of phobias after traumatic brain injury, further research in this area is much needed.

Case report

Ms C was seventeen years old at the time she was injured in a road traffic collision. She was a passenger in a vehicle that overturned when the driver was blinded by the lights of an oncoming car. She sustained a severe traumatic brain injury, while her other injuries were of a minor nature. Her Glasgow Coma Scale (Teasdale & Jennet, 1974) score was 6/15 on admission to hospital. Ms C remained unconscious for two days. Following treatment for her physical injuries at a local acute hospital, she was discharged home after a week for further convalescence. She then attempted unsuc-cessfully to complete her schooling. Fatigue was a major problem, and she could only manage to work one morning per week. She was referred for neuropsychological assessment three years after sustaining her injury. The initial bedside clinical assessment did not reveal any obvious cognitive impairment, but significant emotional and behavioural difficulties were noted. Ms C presented with anxi-ety, depression, and lack of motivation. Furthermore, over time, it became increasingly clear that she was suffering from social phobia and a phobia about driving, also. The latter became apparent when she started taking driving lessons and pertained specifically to driving on motorways. With specific regard to her phobia about driving on motorways, this responded very well in a short period of time to exposure (by the driving instructor) while at the same time receiving sessions of cognitive–behaviour therapy. Other aspects of this case have also been described elsewhere (e.g., Coetzer, 2006).

Psychological approaches to management

Psychological therapy is probably the treatment of choice for managing phobias after traumatic brain injury. In populations without traumatic brain injury, cognitive–behaviour therapy appears to be the treatment of choice for social phobia. Ponniah and Hollon (2008) reviewed thirty treatment studies utilizing therapeutic strategies such as social skills training, exposure therapy, and cognitive therapy (the latter two combined or individually) for social phobia and concluded that cognitive–behaviour therapy, involving cognitive restructuring, exposure and behavioural experiments, to be the psychological treatment of choice for this disorder. Can these therapeutic strategies be used in populations with traumatic brain injury also? Hodgson, McDonald, Tate, and Gertler (2005) report that cognitive–behaviour therapy indeed has a potentially beneficial effect on social anxiety after acquired brain injury. These authors randomized patients to a cognitive–behaviour therapy group or a waiting list group, with the treatment group receiving between nine and fourteen hourly individual therapy sessions (ibid.). The treatment group, when compared to the control group, showed significantly reduced anxiety (including social anxiety) and depression, with these gains maintained at one-month follow-up (ibid.).

With regard to other psychological approaches to the treatment of phobias after traumatic brain injury, Kneebone and Al-Daftary (2006) reported on a patient who presented with a specific phobia for physiotherapy treatment of her feet, which had the potential to significantly interfere with everyday activities: for example, getting into a car, as well as her rehabilitation more generally. As a result, a treatment strategy comprising a single session of flooding was used, resulting in a significant reduction in the phobia, to the extent that the physiotherapists could complete the patient's treatment (Kneebone & Al-Daftary, 2006). Impressively, this reduction in phobic behaviour was maintained at follow-up (*ibid.*). Given the nature of flooding as an intervention, though, perhaps it should be considered with caution, and, when identified as a potential treatment of choice, first be weighed against factors such as the likely interference with essential daily activities that the phobic behaviour might cause if left untreated. Finally, the finding that self esteem improved also in the Hodgson, McDonald, Tate, and Gertler (2005) study might be indicative that there could possibly be a role more generally for psychological interventions aimed at addressing loss of confidence or changes in identity and role in persons who present with social phobia after traumatic brain injury. These may include supportive and interpersonal psychotherapy, among other psychological interventions.

From a more psychoanalytic perspective, it has been suggested that a defensive personality style coupled with persistent denial after traumatic brain injury can prevent adjustment (Ownsworth, 2005). Accordingly, Ownsworth described the case of a forty-five-year-old female (JK) who presented with social phobia and depression after she had sustained a traumatic brain injury. JK was described as having a highly defensive personality style, and that following individual psychotherapy there was a reduction in defensiveness and subsequently also her social phobia and depressed mood (*ibid.*). It should be noted, though, that while there was some emphasis on the patient's denial and, indeed, that this was a focus of treatment, some of the therapeutic techniques described in Ownsworth's paper showed some obvious resemblances to mainstream cognitive therapy strategies and approaches. Nevertheless, this case report was an important illustration that, where needed, different psychotherapeutic strategies should be employed to address not only the patient's phobic behaviour, but also personality and other factors that may contribute to the presentation. In view of this it provides valuable pointers relevant to clinical practice.

In summary, considering the above overview and experience from clinical practice, the main psychological therapies to consider in phobias after traumatic brain injury are likely to include:

● cognitive–behaviour therapy;
● behaviour therapy, including exposure and, in some situations, flooding;

- relaxation techniques;
- supportive psychotherapy;
- interpersonal psychotherapy.

The next section explores pointers from clinical practice with regard to the qualitative nature of patients' thoughts, behaviours, and emotions as they may present during the process of providing psychological interventions. Moreover, some potentially useful generic factors (see Chapter Four) pertaining to strategies, the therapeutic relationship, and self-awareness that therapists may wish to consider are mentioned also.

Strategies and themes in psychotherapy

Epstein and Ursano (1994) proposed that social phobia after traumatic brain injury was related to patients' fear of how others would view them, especially in social situations, where they may be seen as unattractive or intellectually less able, including poor ability to follow conversation when several people are speaking. Patients may sometimes fear the embarrassment that could stem from their cognitive impairments being revealed in social situations (Epstein & Ursano, 1994). Clearly, for some, this could have significant potential to result in avoidance of social situations. Sometimes, it can be profound or even subtle speech difficulties that may make patients feel less competent to take part in social situations; at other times, it can be more obvious cognitive problems such as an inability to remember names, or what was said during the conversation, for example. Where speech proves to be an obstacle to social interaction, the patient should be referred for speech and language therapy. At other times, it may be the physical impairment associated with traumatic brain injury, for example, tinnitus, hearing loss, or being in a wheelchair that may result in significant social anxiety and consequent avoidance. Finally, some persons suffer other injuries also, resulting in scarring or loss of mobility, which can, of course, also adversely influence their ability to partake in activities, including social events. Where mobility is a major barrier to participation, the patient should be referred to a physiotherapist for assistance in this area. Many persons express a profound sense of loss resulting from their phobias and associated social isolation.

Another relatively common phobia reported by patients after traumatic brain injury concerns driving, experienced most commonly by those who were injured in motor vehicle accidents. This may occur even if the patient cannot actually remember the circumstances surrounding the accident. Phobias about leaving the house can also occur, and may perhaps relate to loss of confidence. Some patients, in my experience, after spending many months in hospitals, sometimes undergoing painful or unpleasant medical procedures, may, after discharge, become anxious about attending hospital appointments and start to avoid anything to do with healthcare. This is perhaps an important source of potential transference also, resulting in a patient experiencing negative emotions when seeing healthcare professionals, including, for example, those who were not at all involved in their acute care. Some persons explain a fear of exposure to any activity that has the potential to highlight their deficits or how they have changed since the accident. For example, Mr M (see Chapter Twelve for a full case report) indicated that he became very apprehensive merely when thinking about seeing anybody from work, as the interaction was very likely to highlight for him how, in contrast to his own, their lives had moved on while his remained static as a disabled person. He found these thoughts very painful and reported that it highlighted the huge losses he suffered as a result of his traumatic brain injury.

With regard to more generic therapeutic factors or strategies, the therapeutic relationship itself can contribute to providing a safe environment for patients, not only to explore their fears, but also to test and try out new behaviours before attempting real-life tasks. Any exposure, though, should be gradual. Exposure may also be more successful if the person has been provided with relaxation skills to apply before or during the feared situation. However, it should be remembered that, generally speaking, most relaxation skills require substantial practice (ideally to the point where it becomes almost automatic to apply) before it is really effective as part of an overall exposure strategy. Also, it is important to explain to patients what a phobia is and, crucially, why exposure can, for some, have a beneficial effect. In other words, explaining in simple terms how exposure works, before actually attempting it. Facilitating and encouraging patients to explore and define their fears in a safe environment can be the first step to helping them to try out more practical behavioural strategies (or homework assignments) to work towards overcoming the phobia they may be struggling with. If the phobia pertains to social situations, the actual therapeutic relationship can provide the environment for role-plays and other strategies that may be helpful prior to attempting socializing outside the consultation room situation. Another practical strategy is to help persons develop the skills to, where appropriate, tell others that they have had a traumatic brain injury and how their difficulties may under some circumstances affect communication. For example, forewarning a person that his or her name may be forgotten several times, or that noise or other distractions can be a real problem.

A strategy from cognitive–behaviour therapy that can sometimes be helpful is to try to help the patient to identify which aspects of the situation or object triggers the most anxiety and then to more objectively review these together. Furthermore, it can also be beneficial to encourage the patient to think more clearly about what the potential benefits of confronting the specific fear might be and, accordingly, to set specific goals that are genuinely relevant to them. Where possible, when assisting the patient in setting goals, try to ensure a high potential for reward (for example, social praise) when meeting the minimum steps for achieving the goal (for example, merely attending the social function, without necessarily contributing actively). As is often the case, it is important to ensure that any cognitive difficulties are compensated for as far as is possible, by, for example, providing printed homework sheets, reading material, and goal sheets. Repetition is also important, of course, to ensure that core ideas or insights are retained. All of these should be done against the background of a supportive therapeutic relationship characterized by openness, where the therapist must constantly try to understand the true nature and intensity of the patient's fears. Without this, unrealistic or even counterproductive goals may be set and patients alienated from the process of rehabilitation.

A robust therapeutic relationship can also form the basis for exploring perhaps more psychodynamic issues underlying the person's presentation with a phobia. For example, a person might have experienced a problematic relationship with his father during childhood around issues of achievement. Having then, during most of his life (perhaps not consciously), over-compensated by working excessive hours and becoming hugely successful as a professional, only to suffer a traumatic brain injury and consequently being less able to work at the same level as before the injury, may well trigger anxiety and avoidance when having to deal with male authority figures. It is extremely important to be fully aware of a person's pre-injury history, including factors pertaining to potentially relevant psychodynamic factors. These can significantly colour the person's post-injury presentation and therapists ignore these at their own peril. Once again, we should remember that while the diagnosis tells us what the constellation of clinical symptoms are likely to mean in "shorthand", it is the formulation, including psychodynamic factors, that tells us more about the "why, how, and when" for this person.

Summary points for this chapter

1. Phobias are perhaps less common after traumatic brain injury, but research in this area is also lacking.
2. New onset phobia after traumatic brain injury should usually not be diagnosed as anxiety disorder due to a general medical condition.
3. Social phobia is possibly the most commonly encountered phobia after traumatic brain injury; others may include a fear of driving or hospitals.
4. Behaviour therapy may be useful for some persons, especially exposure or flooding, but this should only be attempted within a supportive therapeutic relationship.
5. Cognitive–behaviour therapy and goal setting may be helpful to some persons who present with a phobia after traumatic brain injury.

CHAPTER SEVEN

Obsessive–compulsive disorder

Introduction

Obsessive–compulsive disorder has fascinated people for many years. As a result, obsessional behaviours have been immortalized in books, plays, and films, among many others. And it has been speculated that some famous individuals have suffered from obsessive–compulsive disorder. In fact, because of this exposure in the arts and media, an inaccurate stereotype has probably evolved in the public mind as to what obsessive–compulsive disorder might be. Many would see obsessive–compulsive disorder as merely an annoying tendency of an individual to be overly concerned with detail and cleanliness. This could not be further from the truth. Obsessive–compulsive disorder is very disabling and people have probably suffered from it long before the disorder was formally diagnosed. While many have been portrayed in films or literature as suffering from obsessive–compulsive disorder, interestingly a direct link with traumatic brain injury has not been portrayed in these media. However, more recently, it was suggested that Howard Hughes, the pioneer of aviation, may actually have experienced obsessive–compulsive disorder as a result of the numerous serious head injuries he suffered following several aeroplane crashes he was involved in during his lifetime (Gibson, 2005).

What, then, are the formal diagnostic criteria for this disabling disorder? According to the *DSM-IV* (American Psychiatric Association, 1994), obsessive–compulsive disorder constitutes repeated obsessions or compulsions severe enough to result in significant distress or be particularly time consuming for the individual. In most cases, the person is aware that these obsessions or compulsions are unreasonable or excessive. However, it is also possible for the patient to present with reduced insight into the nature of their problems associated with obsessive–compulsive disorder and, under these circumstances, the appropriate specifier would be added to the diagnosis. Compulsions are defined as repetitive behaviours that are engaged in with its main purpose being to reduce anxiety. Obsessions are recurrent and intrusive thoughts or images that cause significant anxiety to the person. Furthermore, *DSM-IV* specifies that obsessive-compulsive disorder is not directly due to a biological or general medical condition. Under these circumstances, *DSM-IV* specifies that an anxiety disorder due to a general medical condition should be diagnosed. It should also be noted that obsessive–compulsive disorder does not represent an enduring personality pattern that is present in an individual.

Diagnostic issues

Obsessive–compulsive disorder should not be confused with obsessive–compulsive personality disorder. The latter constitutes an enduring pattern of mental inflexibility where the person is overly concerned and preoccupied with perfectionism, orderliness, and control, in the absence of true obsessions and compulsions (American Psychiatric Association, 1994). It may also be worth considering the different effects of these respective disorders: persons with obsessive–compulsive disorder experience significant anxiety in response to obsessions, whereas in obsessive–compulsive personality disorder, those around the person might actually experience the brunt of the discomfort, as a result of the person's inflexible behavioural patterns. There is also considerable potential for

overlap between some symptoms of obsessive–compulsive disorder and traumatic brain injury. For example, the apathy common to
traumatic brain injury can bear an uncanny resemblance to obsessional slowness, and the cognitive impairment that forms part of
the well-described symptomatology of traumatic brain injury, especially impaired memory, can result in behaviours that are difficult
to distinguish from the compulsions that form part of obsessive–
compulsive disorder. For example, patients who cannot remember
if they switched off the toaster or locked the front door may go back
repeatedly to check if they did indeed perform these actions. It can
be difficult to rely on the presence of anxiety to try to distinguish
these behaviours from checking behaviour, as most people would
experience a sense of discomfort if in doubt as to whether they
performed some important task.

Some patients with traumatic brain injury do also present with
cognitive inflexibility, which may make their behaviour appear as
being possibly somewhat obsessional in nature. However, this
inflexibility in their approach to everyday problem solving may
actually be more representative of an impairment of executive
control function. Impaired executive control function can present as
a rigidity of behavioural patterns, which, in turn, may be mistaken
for compulsions. Indeed, Williams, Evans, and Fleminger (2003)
remind us that obsessive–compulsive symptoms must not be
confused with "organic orderliness", constituting rigidity and poor
tolerance of disruption to routines commonly seen in persons with
traumatic brain injury. In fact, this tendency to have everything tidy
and well ordered can also be understood within the context of
compensating for problems related to memory impairment and
difficulties with executive control function, rather than representing
core symptoms of obsessive–compulsive disorder *per se* (*ibid.*).

Likewise, other symptoms common to traumatic brain injury,
such as perseveration, can sometimes be mistaken for obsessions or
compulsions. In these cases, if the perseverative behaviour the
person presents with appears to be more likely to represent, for
example, personality changes after traumatic brain injury, neither a
diagnosis of obsessive–compulsive disorder nor a diagnosis of
obsessive–compulsive personality disorder should be made. The
correct diagnosis, according to the *DSM-IV* (American Psychiatric
Association, 1994) diagnostic criteria, under these circumstances

would most probably be personality change due to a general medical condition, with traumatic brain injury as the relevant specifier. However, while perhaps not as common as some of the other mental disorders, if obsessive–compulsive disorder indeed presents for the first time after a person has sustained a traumatic brain injury, the appropriate diagnosis should be made. Hence, in the presence of traumatic brain injury resulting in obsessive–compulsive disorder, *DSM-IV* specifies that an anxiety disorder due to a general medical condition should be diagnosed.

Symptom differentiation

As already pointed out, it can be extremely difficult to identify obsessive–compulsive disorder in persons who have suffered a traumatic brain injury. Considering the symptoms of traumatic brain injury, diagnostic criteria, and actual observed clinical presentations seen in practice in the specific context of traumatic brain injury, the following general differentiation between symptoms that may either increase the probability or alternatively reduce the probability that an obsessive–compulsive disorder could be the primary diagnosis may assist clinicians during the process of making a differential diagnosis:

The most confusing symptoms potentially related to traumatic brain injury and not necessarily always obsessive–compulsive disorder are likely to include the following:

- memory impairment;
- perseverative behaviour;
- mental inflexibility.

The most telling symptoms indicative of the potential presence of obsessive–compulsive disorder are likely to include:

- clear obsessions or compulsions;
- attempts to suppress obsessive thoughts or images;
- compulsions clearly having an anxiety reduction function.

Nevertheless, it remains extremely difficult to make a diagnosis of obsessive–compulsive disorder in the context of traumatic brain injury. Hence, the above should be seen as merely constituting clinical guidelines or suggestions to assist the clinician in making a differential diagnosis. The working diagnosis and formulation for an individual patient would be based on more comprehensive clinical data, including questionnaires, scans, and neuropsychological test results, among others. Finally, an understanding of how common or not obsessive–compulsive disorder actually is after traumatic brain injury can prove helpful also.

Obsessive–compulsive disorder after traumatic brain injury

Hiott and Labbate (2002), in their review of the literature, conclude that there is an increased frequency of neuropsychiatric sequelae such as anxiety disorders (including obsessive–compulsive disorder) after a traumatic brain injury. More specifically related to obsessive–compulsive disorder, Grados (2003) provided a comprehensive review of the disorder following traumatic brain injury, including aspects pertaining to treatment. Grados concludes that obsessive–compulsive disorder after traumatic brain injury in adults was perhaps rare, with most patients actually presenting with obsessive–compulsive personality disorder (presumably implying personality change due to a general medical condition) rather than obsessive–compulsive disorder or, alternatively, with perseverative behaviours outside of *DSM* categorization. Van Reekum, Cohen, and Wong (2000), in their detailed literature review, pooled the data from three studies and found that about 6.5% (18/282) of these patients presented with obsessive–compulsive disorder after traumatic brain injury. Furthermore, several authors have reported case studies of obsessive–compulsive disorder following traumatic brain injury (Childers, Holland, Ryan, & Rupright, 1998; McKeon, McGuffin, & Robinson, 1984; Stengler-Wenzke, Muller, & Matthes-von-Cramon, 2003; Williams, Evans, & Fleminger, 2003). Williams, Evans, and Fleminger (2003) described a single case of obsessive–compulsive disorder following a severe traumatic brain injury and highlighted the potential interaction between cognitive impairment (memory) and checking behaviour. Interestingly, there is some evidence that obsessive–compulsive disorder after traumatic brain injury may be more transient in nature. For example, Childers, Holland, Ryan, and Rupright (1998) reported four cases of more transient obsessional behaviour occurring during the very early recovery phase from traumatic brain injury.

The diagnosis of obsessive–compulsive disorder after traumatic brain injury can be complex, not least because of a possible overlap between symptoms of obsessive–compulsive disorder and traumatic brain injury. Berthier, Kulisevsky, Gironell, and Heras (1996) reported a group of thirteen patients with a diagnosis of obsessive–compulsive disorder and a brain lesion, where four had sustained a traumatic brain injury. In a later study, Berthier, Kulisevsky, Gironell, and Lopez (2001) evaluated ten patients with obsessive–compulsive disorder following traumatic brain injury and concluded that a specific pattern of behaviour and cognitive impairments may be common to this group of patients, including aggressive, contamination, and sexual obsessions, as well as cleaning, checking, and repeating (ritualistic behaviours) compulsions. Furthermore, these symptoms were accompanied by impairments on measures of general intellectual ability, memory, and executive control function (ibid.). While thought to be specific to obsessive–compulsive disorder following traumatic brain injury, these cognitive impairments may possibly be almost identical to those usually seen in traumatic brain injury without the co-existence of obsessive–compulsive disorder, especially with regard to impairment of memory and executive control function.

Another potentially confounding factor in the diagnosis of obsessive–compulsive disorder in this clinical population may be the period of time that has elapsed since the person sustained the traumatic brain injury. Almost any combination of symptoms, often changing rapidly, may present in the early days following traumatic brain injury, and, indeed, Childers, Holland, Ryan, and Rupright (1998) reported on the possible transient nature of obsessional symptoms after traumatic brain injury. Furthermore, given the temporal instability of obsessive–compulsive disorder after traumatic brain injury, it is possible that obsessive–compulsive disorder merely represents a stage in the progression of other mental disorders. For example, Kant, Smith-Seemiller, and Duffy (1996) proposed that as depression is often associated with obsessive–compulsive disorder symptoms, and especially in their case series of four patients, this may actually mean that obsessive–compulsive disorder is merely a variation of the presentation of depression after traumatic brain injury. These and other factors are likely to substantially increase the risk of incorrect diagnoses being made. Coetzer and Stein (2003) provide an overview of the clinical issues and resulting difficulties surrounding the diagnosis of obsessive–compulsive disorder after traumatic brain injury. Below follows a case report highlighting some of the clinical issues related to obsessive–compulsive disorder in a person with a history of traumatic brain injury.

Case report

The patient, Mr A, was a twenty-one-year-old student at the time he sustained multiple injuries following a road traffic accident as a motorcyclist. He sustained multiple fractures, injuries to his internal organs, and a severe traumatic brain injury. He was instantaneously rendered unconscious and his period of post trauma amnesia extended over a period of at least four weeks. His retrograde amnesia was approximately ten minutes. The total period of loss of consciousness or coma was not possible to determine with complete accuracy because, in view of his orthopaedic injuries, Mr A was sedated while in intensive care. A computed tomography (CT) scan of the brain performed on the day of the accident revealed a fracture of the left frontal bone extending into the floor of the anterior fossa as well as a left frontal contusion. A basal skull fracture was present also. The remainder of the brain, including the ventricular system, was reported as being normal in appearance. By using the Mayo Traumatic Brain Injury Severity Classification System (Malec et al., 2007) the patient's traumatic brain injury was retrospectively classified as moderate–severe (definite).

The patient was first seen for brain injury rehabilitation in the community about five years after his accident, when he moved into an area where a community-based brain injury rehabilitation service existed. He did not receive any community-based brain injury rehabilitation prior to this. Thus, his family doctor at this point referred him for further rehabilitation. An initial clinical assessment revealed the following. Mr A had no pre-accident psychiatric history, his development and scholastic performance was satisfactory, and there was no history of substance abuse. He completed his schooling without any difficulty and enrolled at university. Of further relevance, there were no illnesses or surgery of note or significant head injuries predating the accident. There was no family history of obsessive–compulsive disorder or, indeed, any other mental health problems. During this initial clinical assessment, Mr A reported suffering from poor memory, personality change, anosmia, fatiguability and reduced mobility (due to orthopaedic injuries). The onset of these all followed his accident. He was not on any psychotropic medication at the time he was referred for community rehabilitation, but was taking painkillers on a daily basis.

Mental status examination revealed the patient to be right handed. His mini-mental state examination (Folstein, Folstein, & McHugh, 1975) was 29/30. He was not depressed. Mr A's thought processes and perceptual functions were normal. His speech was normal and he did not appear to have any obvious severe cognitive impairments. The patient provided a clear description of obsessions. These, he reported, presented as visual images, resulting in almost immediate and significant anxiety. The most frequently encountered and anxiety-provoking obsessions related to horrific images about catastrophic incidents: for example, having run down someone while driving or seeing a car leave the road and crash or fall off a bridge. He also reported at times ruminating about the possible meaning of social interactions, again resulting in significant anxiety. These obsessions were time consuming and he tried unsuccessfully to use techniques such as distraction to terminate the obsessions. There was no robust evidence for the presence of compulsions. While there were episodes of repetitive behaviour, for example, counting or ordering, these behaviours were unrelated to the obsessions and were not aimed at reducing anxiety, but rather intended to organize his environment in an attempt to compensate for his subtle memory difficulties.

To augment the clinical diagnosis (and considering how difficult it is to make this diagnosis in the presence of traumatic brain injury), it was decided to administer a questionnaire to obtain more information about the potential presence of obsessive–compulsive disorder. The results revealed the patient's Florida Obsessive–

Compulsive Inventory scores to be eight (Part A) and ten (Part B), respectively. The Florida Obsessive–Compulsive Inventory is a self-report questionnaire developed by Wayne Goodman and, according to recent findings (Storch et al., 2007), is highly correlated with the total score of the Yale–Brown Obsessive Compulsive Scale (Goodman et al., 1989). The strengths of the Florida Obsessive–Compulsive Inventory were considered to be the ability to provide a quick assessment of the presence and severity of symptoms in obsessive–compulsive disorder. Part A of the Florida Obsessive–Compulsive Inventory assesses the presence of symptoms, while Part B assesses the intensity of symptoms. The results for Mr A on this questionnaire appeared to further confirm the presence of first onset obsessive–compulsive disorder after traumatic brain injury. In addition, neuropsychological testing was performed to identify any relevant cognitive impairment that may have impacted on the patient's symptoms of obsesssive–compulsive disorder.

The neuropsychological test results for Mr A revealed general intelligence to be in the superior range, with visio-spatial performance modestly better than verbal performance. Regarding the remainder of the neuropsychological tests, memory for visual stimuli was excellent for both immediate and delayed recall. While recall for a word list was quantitatively in the normal range for both immediate and delayed recall, qualitative analysis revealed a very high number of repetitions during recall. Very robust performances were seen on two commonly used tests of executive function, the Tower of Hanoi (Goel & Grafman, 1995) and the Wisconsin Card Sorting Test (Heaton, 1981). However, a clear and significant impairment (percentile one) was observed on Part B (set shifting) of the trail-making test (Reitan & Wolfson, 1985). All the other tests that were administered revealed normal performances. From a phenomenological perspective, it was interesting to note that the patient described the cognitive impairment to manifest as follows in his everyday life. "Not remembering what I remember" (repetitions on word list recall) and "I remain too focused on one event in an effort to help me avoid distraction" (set shifting). These qualitative data, almost more effectively than the quantitative data, illuminate how the patient's cognitive impairment relates to (or does not relate to) some of the symptoms of obsessive–compulsive disorder.

Psychological approaches to management

For adults without traumatic brain injury, cognitive–behaviour therapy and its derivatives or behaviour therapy have been found to be effective in the treatment of obsessive–compulsive disorder (Gava et al., 2007). According to Hiott and Labbate (2002), the treatment of obsessive–compulsive disorder after traumatic brain injury should, in the first instance, be psychotherapy, possibly also including behaviour therapy. Grados (2003) suggested that pharmacological approaches can be effective to reduce obsessive–compulsive disorder symptoms, and that cognitive–behavioural approaches, supportive psychotherapy, or behavioural management programmes might also prove useful. Arco (2008) described how a neuro-behavioural intervention for compulsive behaviour in a twenty-four-year-old male with traumatic brain injury resulted in a significant reduction of symptoms, including counting and compulsive bladder voiding. The intervention, which was provided in the home environment, consisted of self-regulation procedures, anxiety management, errorless remediation, and social reinforcement, and eventually faded, resulting in gains being maintained at six month follow-up (*ibid.*). Furthermore, Williams, Evans, and Fleminger (2003) reported a case (DC) of obsessive–compulsive disorder after traumatic brain injury where a combination of cognitive rehabilitation and cognitive–behaviour therapy resulted in significant improvement in symptomatology and achievement of rehabilitation goals. The patient received cognitive rehabilitation for problems of attention and memory impairment, the latter by developing external strategies to compensate for these difficulties, whereas his psychological therapy included management of automatic negative thoughts, relaxation skills, and a graded exposure programme (*ibid.*).

Some authors have suggested that treatment should perhaps not focus too narrowly on specific symptoms (for example, related to obsessions or compulsions), but, rather, address more general issues pertaining to adjustment and coping. For example, obsessive–compulsive disorder symptoms may represent a manifestation of the patient's attempts to cope with the general anxiety and depression resulting from having sustained a traumatic brain injury (Kant, Smith-Seemiller, & Duffy, 1996). However, the treatment of depression in these authors' case series of four patients did not generally have a positive impact on obsessive–compulsive disorder symptoms (*ibid.*). Generally speaking, psychological therapy has a very important role in the management of obsessive–compulsive disorder after traumatic brain injury, but it should be noted that pharmacological treatment approaches probably have an equally important role, at least for some patients. For those interested in this aspect of the treatment of obsessive–compulsive disorder, Gava and colleagues (2007) describe some of the pharmacological approaches to the management of this disorder and its effectiveness in the context of traumatic brain injury.

In summary, based on the literature as well as clinical practice, the main psychological therapies to consider in the presence of obsessive–compulsive disorder after traumatic brain injury appear to include the following:

- behaviour therapy, including graded exposure;
- cognitive–behaviour therapy;
- anxiety management, including relaxation skills;
- supportive psychotherapy.

The next section explores the qualitative nature of patients' beliefs, behaviours, and feelings as they may present during psychotherapy, as well as making suggestions for more general or generic therapeutic strategies or factors that may be useful for therapists to consider.

Strategies and themes in psychotherapy

Some patients describe a sense of disbelief and confusion when trying to make sense of why they are experiencing obsessions and compulsions. There is often also an interference effect because of poor memory, with patients reporting that perhaps these (particularly the compulsions) serve a function in compensating for their forgetfulness, almost like a safety net. Sometimes, patients may report that they have never before been controlling, but that, since sustaining a traumatic brain injury, it has become almost impossible for them not to spend huge amounts of time trying to control every aspect of their environment. From a more psychodynamic perspective this may be seen partially as an attempt to control the environment after experiencing an event (traumatic brain injury) which was not only beyond the person's control for preventing, but also resulted in a serious loss of control in many areas as a result of the impairment or disability stemming from the injury. While the clinician may not, early on, wish to put this forward to the patient as an interpretation, it can sometimes be an elegant strategy to communicate an understanding of the patient's feelings of loss of control and perhaps encourage them, or gently probe to try to further explore hypotheses such as these.

Potentially helpful strategies within the psychotherapeutic encounter may include not being judgemental regarding the nature of obsessions or compulsions, but rather to provide information about the nature of obsessive–compulsive disorder, emphasizing that it is a well-recognized condition that in some cases can be associated with traumatic brain injury. It can be important to identify whether there are any cognitive difficulties, such as poor short-term memory, contributing to obsessions or compulsions and, accordingly, to help the patient with compensatory strategies to minimize the potential effect of these cognitive impairments. Exposure and response prevention may be useful for some, but these techniques should be adapted for persons with traumatic brain injury. The main generic component of cognitive–behaviour therapy that I find useful in this population is probably that it increases the person's understanding of how his or her thought-based obsessions relate to compulsions, correspondingly interfering with its ongoing mediation. However, sometimes it may be necessary to be cautious that a cognitive therapy strategy does not result in excessive rumination or perseveration in itself, especially in a person with more significant cognitive impairment, meaning that the patient may actually "use" the tools from cognitive therapy to endlessly try to ascertain if a belief is rational or irrational (functional or dysfunctional). Hence, other psychotherapeutic approaches may be worth considering also.

Some of the more mindfulness-based psychotherapeutic strategies may be particularly suited to managing obsessive–compulsive disorder after traumatic brain injury. The generic factors underpinning many of these psychotherapies are probably twofold. It helps patients to be more aware of thoughts and emotions in the moment, thereby helping to take the edge off these problematic feelings and thoughts. Second, some of these therapies help patients by teaching them to avoid the struggle with, or evaluation of, these difficult thoughts and feelings (for example, as in acceptance and commitment therapy, as described by Hayes, Strohsal, and Wilson, 2004). This approach feels intuitively sensible for managing obsessions and, to a lesser degree, compulsions. Indeed, in the case of Mr A, while some principles of cognitive–behaviour therapy were used, some of the psychotherapeutic work also explored loss related to his injury, as well as helping him recognize obsessions or difficult thoughts in the moment, but not to be drawn into necessarily and always disputing or challenging these thoughts. Last, it is worth clinicians remembering that acute obsessive–compulsive disorder in the context of traumatic brain injury has a high potential for negative transference and countertransference. Both patient and therapist can experience strong negative emotions towards each other, most notably frustration in response to real or perceived lack of progress, during the course of therapy. In view of this, the therapeutic relationship can be fragile and should be preserved at all costs. One of the most valuable resources therapists can access in this regard is supervision with an experienced colleague.

Summary points for this chapter

1. Definite obsessive–compulsive disorder is rare after traumatic brain injury.
2. Memory impairment, in particular, may confuse the clinical picture of obsessive–compulsive disorder.
3. In the presence of traumatic brain injury, an obsessive–compulsive disorder should be categorized as an anxiety disorder due to a general medical condition.
4. Obsessive–compulsive disorder may sometimes coexist with major depressive disorder.
5. Supportive psychotherapy, behaviour therapy, cognitive–behaviour therapy, and a combination of cognitive–behaviour therapy and cognitive rehabilitation may be helpful for some patients.

CHAPTER EIGHT

Post traumatic stress disorder

Introduction

At times controversial and at other times possibly grossly misunderstood, post traumatic stress disorder has periodically, most notably during periods of military conflict (for example, the Vietnam war), found itself at the centre of public, political, and academic debate. Perhaps as a consequence, post traumatic stress disorder has been portrayed and explored widely in books, films, and other popular media, as representing a particularly disabling emotional consequence specifically related to combat experiences. And perhaps some of these portrayals have rather unrealistically or unfairly concentrated on vividly illustrating symptoms such as nightmares and behavioural changes, at the cost of some of the other very disabling core symptoms of the disorder. Furthermore, post traumatic stress disorder can, of course, also follow exposure to experiences other than war. Not acknowledging this fact may do a great disservice to persons who have been exposed to traumas unrelated to combat, such as grievous bodily assault, torture, severe accidents, or natural disasters, to name but a few. These people can and do, under certain circumstances, present with features of post traumatic stress disorder also.

Post traumatic stress disorder is perhaps unique among the anxiety and mood disorders in that, more so than with almost all the other disorders (perhaps excluding simple phobias), the major (but not the only) factor involved in its onset appears to be the exposure to a clear, non-biological event that acts as a trigger. As such, it is perhaps one of a few mental disorders that really lend themselves specifically to investigating the contribution of environmental and psychological factors to the onset of mental health difficulties. For this reason, this chapter places an emphasis on the possible role that special environments, such as theatres of conflict and war, that have a higher probability for an increased incidence of the disorder as well as traumatic brain injury, might have in furthering our knowledge and creating unique research possibilities. Studying populations or case reports from these environments could have the potential to increase our understanding of the onset and subsequent evolution over time of this complex disorder, and especially so in the context of co-existing traumatic brain injury.

With regard to formal definitions, post traumatic stress disorder is defined in *DSM-IV* (American Psychiatric Association, 1994) as the development of intense anxiety symptoms following exposure to a traumatic event of a magnitude outside the normal range of human experience. Examples of traumatic events can include military combat, violence against the person, kidnapping, torture, and others. Furthermore, the traumatic event is continuously re-experienced in several ways, including dreams (nightmares), intrusive anxiety-provoking recollections, and intense anxiety in response to internal or external cues associated with the event. There is also ongoing avoidance of stimuli associated with the traumatic event and some numbing of responsiveness, for example, avoidance of thoughts and places, memory loss for aspects of the event, restricted range of feelings, and a sense of a shorter future. In addition, there is also, in many cases, ongoing hyper-arousal: for example, difficulty falling asleep, irritability, hyper-vigilance, and an exaggerated startle response. Post traumatic stress disorder is distinguished from acute stress disorder in that this disorder must occur and resolve within four weeks of exposure to the traumatic event (American Psychiatric Association, 1994). Finally, *DSM-IV* (*ibid.*) specifies that the duration of post traumatic stress disorder is more than a month and distinguishes between early and late onset.

Diagnostic issues

Strictly following *DSM-IV* guidelines, new onset post traumatic stress disorder associated with traumatic brain injury technically should be diagnosed as an anxiety disorder due to a general medical condition. Post traumatic stress disorder should not be confused with other anxiety disorders where there is no exposure to an extraordinary traumatic event. And, at its core, the disorder represents re-experience and avoidance; the former, under most circumstances, requiring a memory of some sort of the exposure to exceptional personal trauma. Post traumatic stress disorder should not be confused with normal human reactions in response to exposure to trauma. It should also be remembered that exposure to extreme trauma, including war situations, does not always result in post traumatic stress disorder. One merely has to remember how during the Second World War bombing of London, many of its citizens presented with what has become known as the "Blitz spirit", demonstrating extreme resilience under catastrophic circumstances. And there are many similar historical examples further illustrating possibly the opposite of extreme trauma necessarily always resulting in emotional maladjustment, in as much as post traumatic stress disorder may be less common than we might suspect.

With regard to symptoms following both traumatic brain injury and post traumatic stress disorder, many of the anxiety symptoms associated with the latter may be obscured by some of the physical symptoms that normally form part of traumatic brain injury (see also Chapter Three). Some of these potentially confusing symptoms of post traumatic stress disorder include irritability, memory loss, sleep problems, and poor emotional expression. While these may superficially appear similar to those seen as part of traumatic brain injury, there are quite significant differences. For example, the poor emotional expression in post traumatic stress disorder represents emotional blunting rather than the apathy (or lack of initiation) of traumatic brain injury. Furthermore, the memory loss of post traumatic stress disorder pertains to the traumatic event, not everyday events (or problems of new learning), as is the case in traumatic brain injury. Finally, sleep disturbances in post traumatic stress disorder tend to be in response to anxiety, rumination, and nightmares, whereas in traumatic brain injury there can be hypersomnia or hyposomnia, sometimes related to pain or other biological factors. Clearly, the diagnosis of post traumatic stress disorder in the presence of traumatic brain injury is complex, and Parker (2002) reasoned that *DSM-IV* definitions do not reflect the considerable overlapping symptomatology. How, then, can we disentangle genuine post traumatic stress disorder from the common symptoms of severe traumatic brain injury?

Symptom differentiation

Questionnaires can be entirely unhelpful when it comes to this disorder, except when used as a screening device. Rather, based on diagnostic criteria and observed clinical presentation of actual patients in the specific context of traumatic brain injury, the following general differentiation between symptoms that may either lend weight to, or, alternatively, reduce the index of suspicion of post traumatic stress disorder, may assist us during the process of making a differential diagnosis:

The most confusing symptoms more likely to be related to traumatic brain injury, and not necessarily always post–traumatic stress disorder, may include the following:

● memory loss;
● sleep disturbances;
● irritability.

The most telling symptoms indicative of the potential presence of a post traumatic stress disorder are likely to include the following:

● history of exposure to, and some recall of, the event (which should be outside the normal range of human experience);
● recurrent re-experiencing of the event including nightmares, flashbacks, etc.
● avoidance of stimuli associated with the traumatic event.

Clearly, the above should be seen as merely constituting suggestions or practical clinical guidelines to assist the clinician attempting to make a differential diagnosis. As is invariably the case, the actual working diagnosis and formulation of a given patient would be based on a thorough assessment, data from other investigations, and medical records. Furthermore, these data would ultimately have to be weighed and considered against findings from the literature with regard to the frequency with which post traumatic stress disorder actually occurs after traumatic brain injury.

Post traumatic stress disorder after traumatic brain injury

While anxiety disorders after traumatic brain injury are common, especially panic disorder and generalized anxiety disorder (Hiott & Labbate, 2002), there remains some controversy regarding post traumatic stress disorder more generally (for example, Rosen, Spitzer, & McHugh, 2008) and specifically in the context of traumatic brain injury (see, for example, Bryant, 2001; King, 2008). Due to reasons already mentioned, such as overlapping symptoms and meeting the diagnostic criterion of exposure to a stressor outside the normal range of human experience, some clinicians perceive as quite limited the confidence with which post traumatic stress disorder can be diagnosed in the context of traumatic brain injury. One way around this dilemma might be for researchers to consider conducting more research with participants from environments with a high potential for traumatic brain injury and extraordinary trauma co-occurring. Other problems with the diagnosis of post traumatic stress disorder have included the not insignificant difficulties associated with using questionnaires to make the diagnosis, as discussed earlier (Chapter Three). There are also problems related to co-morbidity. For example, Bombardier and colleagues (2006) reported a high co-morbidity of post traumatic stress disorder with major depressive disorder, in as much as seventy-nine per cent of their sample with post-traumatic stress disorder also presented with major depressive disorder.

The real incidence of post traumatic stress disorder after traumatic brain injury is, understandably, very difficult to determine. Earlier studies reported rather high incidences of post traumatic stress disorder after traumatic brain injury (e.g., Williams, Evans, Wilson, & Needham, 2002), but some researchers have thought that there may be difficulties with incidence figures from studies using questionnaires to identify the disorder in this clinical population (e.g. Sumpter & McMillan, 2005). Van Reekum, Cohen, and Wong (2000), in their comprehensive review, pooled the data from six studies and found that about fourteen per cent (62/441) of patients presented with symptoms of post traumatic stress disorder. Having addressed some of the problems of overlapping symptomatology and also the criterion of exposure to a severe stressor, Bombardier and colleages (2006) reported an incidence of about 5.5% for patients meeting the full criteria for post traumatic stress disorder six months after traumatic brain injury. It should be kept in mind that a particular strength of this study was the inclusion only of participants who had definitely sustained a moderate to severe traumatic brain injury and, conversely, the exclusion of those with a mild injury, as persons with a mild injury may be less well protected by amnesia for the event.

There are also other issues to consider. Several pre-injury factors that may increase the person's vulnerability may be important to consider in this population. For example, Bombardier and colleagues (2006) reported that twenty-nine per cent of the persons in their sample who met the criteria for post traumatic stress disorder after traumatic brain injury, reported a pre-injury history of the disorder. Furthermore, there was a very high co-morbidity with other anxiety disorders in this sample, perhaps suggesting a more general vulnerability to the development of anxiety disorders (*ibid.*). Other factors to consider, according to Bombardier and colleagues (*ibid.*) included below average school years completed and the use of drugs at around the time the injury was sustained. More recently, Koenigs and colleagues (2008) reported a fascinating finding from their study that investigated lesion locality and post traumatic stress disorder among Vietnam veterans who were exposed to traumatic events. These authors found that participants, who had focal lesions to either the ventromedial prefrontal cortex and an anterior temporal area, including the amygdala, did not present as frequently with post traumatic stress disorder as did the other participants in the study. With the above issues in mind, the question still remains, for some, whether a person can really suffer new onset post traumatic stress disorder after sustaining a traumatic brain injury.

King (2008) provides an excellent overview of some of the controversies and issues surrounding post traumatic stress disorder after traumatic brain injury and concludes that essentially traumatic brain injury and post traumatic stress disorder can co-exist. But there is a caveat, in that mild traumatic brain injury offers no protection against post traumatic stress disorder, whereas severe traumatic brain injury provides significant but not complete protection against the development of the disorder (*ibid.*). Generally, inability to recall the traumatic event after more severe traumatic brain injury has, in the past, been thought to be the most important protective factor for preventing the onset of post traumatic stress disorder. Hence, post traumatic stress disorder after severe traumatic brain injury has been considered by some practitioners to be perhaps rather rare. There are significant difficulties related to diagnosing post traumatic stress disorder after traumatic brain injury (e.g., McMillan, 2001). Hence, it is possible that patients with traumatic brain injury are mistakenly diagnosed with post traumatic stress disorder, artificially increasing the reported incidence and prevalence. For example, some case reports of this mistaken diagnosis exist (e.g., Tobe, Schneider, Mrozik, & Lidsky, 1999) and empirical research supporting this has been published also (Sumpter & McMillan, 2005). Are there innovative ways to study or increase our understanding of post traumatic stress disorder following traumatic brain injury?

Special environments

Let us now return to the point that exposure to an experience outside the normal range of human experiences constitutes one of the core diagnostic criteria for post traumatic stress disorder. Accordingly, it would be fair to reason that certain environments, such as war zones or disaster areas, perhaps pose a greater risk to the development of post traumatic stress disorder. What, then, if there were environments that posed a high risk to both post traumatic stress disorder and traumatic brain injury? Could this provide a unique opportunity for observing co-existing post traumatic stress disorder and traumatic brain injury? For example, it is known that there is a high incidence of traumatic brain injury during military conflict (Keltner & Cooke, 2007; Warden, 2006). Likewise, there is a high incidence of post traumatic stress disorder in these environments (Milliken, Auchterlonie, & Hoge, 2007) also, especially, for example, when accompanied by early symptoms of severe physical injury (Grieger et al., 2006) or when the person has been exposed to actual combat as opposed to deployment only (Smith et al., 2008). Clearly, then, traumatic brain injury and post-traumatic stress disorder, in view of the higher frequency of occurrence after military combat, can both be present in the same patient. For example, Keltner and Cooke (2007) described cases where ex-servicemen presented with both diagnoses. Indeed, where both conditions exist in the same patient, both would require treatment (Warden, 2006). However, the nature of traumatic brain injury sustained in combat can have important differences to civilian traumatic brain injury resulting from, for example, car accidents or assaults.

In combat situations traumatic brain injury can be sustained by different mechanisms, including, but not limited to, missile wounds and blast injuries. Missile wounds would, of course, usually result in much more focal damage and, as a result, more circumscribed impairments (see Chapter One). Taber, Warden, and Hurley (2006) reviewed the mechanisms involved in blast injuries. Blasts can produce traumatic brain injury in a few different ways, including blast wave-induced pressure changes (primary injury), objects hitting the person's head (secondary injury), and the force of the blast moving the person (tertiary injury) and in this way transferring energy or momentum to the person (*ibid.*). The most common forms of non-penetrating traumatic brain injury stemming from explosions are contusions, diffuse axonal injury, and haemorrhage (*ibid.*). The authors pointed out that the most common areas involved as a result of diffuse axonal injury were the cortico-medullary junction, internal capsule grey matter, corpus callosum, and upper brainstem. This pattern of injury appears to differ in some important aspects to the more usual pattern seen with acceleration, deceleration, or rotational traumatic brain injury typically sustained by civilians.

In summary, post traumatic stress disorder after traumatic brain injury is probably rare and we may need to look towards special populations to study and better understand persons with this unusual co-morbidity. Post traumatic stress disorder and traumatic brain injury are common in military populations. But post traumatic stress disorder presents in civilian populations also, following a wide variety of stressors, including natural disasters, assaults, or torture, to name but a few. However, in these cases, there may not always be substantial numbers of persons with co-morbid traumatic brain injury and there is, of course, also great heterogeneity in the nature of the stressor these persons may have been exposed to. Furthermore, it may be more difficult to recruit substantial numbers of similar (for example, with regard to age) participants for research from such heterogeneous sub-groups of patients. Military populations may have a high incidence of co-morbid post traumatic stress disorder and traumatic brain injury, and, as such, may provide both opportunities for research and chal-lenges to develop and provide more complex models of clinical care. Below, a case is presented of a soldier without pre-existing post traumatic stress disorder who sustained a severe traumatic brain injury as a result of being injured in an explosion. Although he had no explicit recall of events, and one accordingly would have expected considerable protection against the development of post traumatic stress disorder, he subsequently presented with classic symptoms of the disorder.

Case report

Mr D was an eighteen-year-old professional soldier when he was injured during a bomb explosion. Fellow soldiers almost immedi-ately freed Mr D from the debris and rubble resulting from the explosion. He was treated at the scene as a "walking wounded". However, when he was picked up by an ambulance to be taken to hospital, it was discovered that his injuries, especially to the head, were probably much more severe than initially thought. Indeed, it transpired that he suffered a total loss of vision. Later, it was deter-mined that he had suffered an open traumatic brain injury and burns to his arm and trunk. Mr D was taken to hospital, where neurosurgery was performed to insert a plate to the occipital region of his skull. He had no recollection of the explosion, subsequent events, the journey to hospital, or being admitted to hospital. His first memory was of waking up in hospital several days later. He was overwhelmed by confusion and anxiety, as he could not see anything. Gradually, though, his vision returned, and he was told that he had been injured in an explosion. He was discharged from hospital and had a period of convalescence.

After a few months, Mr D was assessed and deemed to be unfit for further military service and subsequently discharged on medical grounds. He returned to a civilian job but, after a few years, realized that he was unable to cope with the demands of the work environment. Mr D knew he was not right, but reminded himself of being told that he had made a good (physical) recovery. This increasingly resulted in feelings of guilt and confusion about his ongoing symptoms. He started self-harming by cutting himself. Because of his ongoing difficulties, he eventually came to the attention of local psychiatric services. Here, he was diagnosed with, and treated for, post traumatic stress disorder, as well as chronic depression and anxiety. The psychiatric service decided to refer Mr D for a neuropsychological opinion in view of the history of a head injury he sustained two decades earlier. Applying the Mayo Traumatic Brain Injury Severity Classification System (Malec et al., 2007) to the information provided by the referrer, the patient's traumatic brain injury was retrospectively classified as moderate–severe (definite) and the referral was accepted.

Clinically, Mr D presented as follows. He was right-handed. His attention appeared to be reasonable. His speech was normal. His level of co-operation was excellent. Mr D was fully orientated for time and place. His mini mental state examination was 29/30 (Folstein, Folstein, & McHugh, 1975). His mood was depressed. Symptoms of severe anxiety were present. Mr D reported ongoing and severe difficulties, including inability to sleep in the dark, being startled by sudden noise, being disturbed by burning smells, and generally blaming himself for not being able to cope. He avoided many everyday activities and, in fact, preferred solitary activities away from noisy environments. He would frequently be overcome by severe anxiety in response to perceptual stimuli such as noise or darkness. Mr D told the clinician that he was having nightmares, somewhat vague in nature, about being unable to move or see, and experiencing a sensation of smelling fire, smoke, or something burning. For example, once, upon waking up at night in severe panic thinking that he could not see, he ripped off the curtains in front of the windows to let some light in. Furthermore, while out and about, he would, for example, dive for cover when a car back-fired near him. Mr D found these difficulties extremely difficult to come to terms with, especially as he could not figure out why he was suffering from these symptoms.

Mr D's pre-injury medical and developmental history was unre-markable. He had a happy childhood and did not encounter any significant difficulties while at school. Up to the point of being injured, he was thoroughly enjoying being in the army. A shortened and focused neuropsychological test battery was performed to complete the clinical assessment and test the hypothesis that he may have cognitive impairment compatible with traumatic brain injury, potentially further informing rehabilitation approaches. These revealed significant memory impairment and problems related to executive control function. This pattern of impairment was thought to be clearly compatible with the expected effects of severe traumatic brain injury, rather than being representative of post traumatic stress disorder. Indeed, Crowell, Kieffer, Siders, and Vanderploeg (2002) found that Vietnam veterans (without a history of traumatic brain injury) suffering from post traumatic stress disorder perform similarly to controls on neuropsychological tests. With regard to other data, Mr D's baseline European Brain Injury Questionnaire (Teasdale et al., 1997) scores were as follows. His self-rating was 168, whereas the relative-rating was 133. The Post Trau-matic Stress Diagnostic Scale (self-report version) (Foa, Cashman, Jaycox, & Perry, 1997) was administered later (to further investigate the possibility of a diagnosis of post traumatic stress disorder), and revealed a total score of 38. The Post Traumatic Stress Diagnostic Scale covers *DSM-IV* (American Psychiatric Association, 1994) symptoms as well as severity. Because of the metal plate in his head, no brain scan data were available.

Mr D was offered psychotherapy as part of his neuropsycho-logical rehabilitation. He continued to attend follow-up with the mental health service also, where his treatment included pharmaco-therapy, counselling, and periodic respite care in a facility for veter-ans. The initial focus of his brain injury rehabilitation was the provision of feedback from the neuropsychological assessment and the provision of information about traumatic brain injury. This resulted in an increased understanding of some of his symp-toms, which Mr D reported finding helpful. Furthermore, practical strategies were employed, including compensatory strategies for poor memory and advice to avoid perceptual over-stimulation. Concurrent with the aforementioned, elements from behavioural activation (for a description of this approach, see, for example, Veale, 2008) were utilized to increase activity levels. However, he continued to question the relationship between his symptoms and his brain injury. He found it difficult to believe that he was actually injured in an explosion and his cognitions reflected disbelief that he should be continuing to experience profound difficulties in the absence of obvious scars or physical disability (for example, an amputated limb) as other veterans could indeed show. In response, during this stage of psychotherapy, reports of the explosion, including photographs, were obtained by the patient from a book published by the military unit he served with. These data had a powerful effect in reassuring him that he was not imagining events. This also provided a platform for the next stage of psychotherapy, to explore in depth some of his emotions surrounding the event, including guilt and anger. By this point the episodes of self-harm had ceased.

After some time Mr D reported that dwelling on emotions related to the past was now not particularly helpful any more. Strategies from cognitive–behaviour therapy were introduced at this point to address specific dysfunctional cognitive patterns about his own perceived role in his injury, for example, that he should have spotted the explosive device and hence that it was his own fault. The connection between not being able to recall the event, but the fact that undifferentiated perceptual stimuli similar to those experienced during (for example feeling trapped, smell of fire, general confusion) and after (temporary blindness) the explosion, continued to trigger severe anxiety, was explored and explained in much greater depth. While his anxiety continued, Mr D was able to significantly increase his functional independence, including an increase of his engagement in pleasurable activities: for example, including substantial involvement in raising his children. After approximately three years, repeated European Brain Injury Questionnaire (Teasdale et al., 1997) scores revealed the following scores: self-rating 138, relative-rating 149. Self-harm had completely ceased and this outcome was maintained for at least six years, up to and including the time of writing this case report. Nevertheless, though decreased in frequency, intense anxiety under certain conditions continued to be present. Long-term employment outcome remained poor and Mr D did not return to work. During later stages, Mr D accessed group psychotherapy and was able to play an active role, sharing with other patients in the group some of the insights he gained during his individual psychotherapy. He continued to be seen for review at the brain injury service but was discharged by the mental health service.

Psychological approaches to management

Let us first discuss the case of Mr D described above. Case reports of new onset post traumatic stress disorder after a severe traumatic brain injury sustained in an explosion during combat, and accompanied by total amnesia for the event, are probably rare at present. Interestingly, Mr D's anxiety was associated with vague perceptual stimuli and not specific events. Berthier, Posada, and Puentes (2001) described a patient with flashbacks of military experiences emerging for the first time after he had sustained a traumatic brain injury as a civilian, but the traumatic brain injury was sustained years later and the anxiety was associated with specific events, as opposed to undifferentiated perceptual stimuli. This chapter focused on post traumatic stress disorder after severe traumatic brain injury sustained in the military. Whereas a clear role for neuropsychology in the assessment and rehabilitation of veterans with mild traumatic brain injury and post traumatic stress disorder following combat has been outlined (McCrea et al., 2008), treatment for post traumatic stress disorder after severe traumatic brain injury is essentially still uncharted waters. While this chapter focused on the onset of post traumatic stress disorder in the military, it is well known that civilians also present with this disorder after traumatic brain injury and concurrent exposure to traumatic events, and equally require complex rehabilitation input also.

While there is clearly a need for the rehabilitation of persons with post traumatic stress disorder following traumatic brain injury, there are significant difficulties in finding clear guidelines to help with the provision of rehabilitation interventions, including, specifically, psychological therapy. King (2008), in his review, concludes that there are no evidence-based treatments specifically designed for this clinical population and that clinicians generally tend to adapt existing treatments, for example, cognitive–behaviour therapy strategies. For example, Williams, Evans, and Wilson (2003) reported using cognitive–behaviour therapy successfully with two patients who presented with post traumatic stress disorder after they had sustained a traumatic brain injury. While, at present, there are limited studies available, psychological therapy for post traumatic stress disorder nevertheless appears to be at least one of the treatments of choice, or, some might say, by default, one of only a few treatment options available to clinicians. Let us now review the limited evidence for the appropriateness of psychological therapy for this disorder.

With regard to treatment of post traumatic stress disorder in persons without traumatic brain injury, trauma focused cognitive–behaviour therapy, stress management, and eye movement desensitization and reprocessing (EMDR) have been found to be effective in the treatment of post traumatic stress disorder (Bisson & Andrew, 2007). Furthermore, according to Ehlers and Clark (2000), memory for the trauma and cognitive appraisal (in persons without traumatic brain injury) play an important role in the maintenance of post traumatic stress disorder. More specifically, incomplete memory has an important aetiological role in the development and maintenance of post traumatic stress disorder and many of the trigger stimuli can be perceptual cues that do not have a clear semantic relationship to the traumatic event (Ehlers & Clark, 2000). Ehlers and Clark propose that there is very strong perceptual priming for traumatic events, meaning that there is a reduced threshold for these stimuli to trigger anxiety. Applying these points to the treatment of post traumatic stress disorder, Ehlers and Clark (*ibid.*) suggest three areas of focus: the trauma memory needing to be elaborated, dealing with problematic appraisals, and reducing dysfunctional cognitive and behavioural strategies.

Returning to post traumatic stress disorder after traumatic brain injury, King (2008) posits that psychoeducation is an important component of treating post traumatic stress disorder and traumatic brain injury. Elbaum (2007), on the other hand, suggests that the expression and working through of emotions about the injury, describing memories, and learning how to control their anxiety might also be helpful to persons. In their review of the mechanisms underlying post traumatic stress disorder after traumatic brain injury and its treatment, McMillan, Williams, and Bryant (2003) suggest that cognitive–behaviour therapy is well suited as a psychological therapy for this group of patients. Indeed, one of the first cases of post traumatic stess disorder following traumatic brain injury, who was treated with cognitive–behaviour therapy, was described by McMillan (1991) almost two decades ago. Furthermore, Williams, Evans, and Wilson (2003) report that the cognitive–behaviour therapy they provided to their two patients, including stress inoculation training and graded exposure, was provided as a component of a specialist neuro-rehabilitation programme. It is important to note that the psychotherapy here was provided as part of a more comprehensive brain injury rehabilitation programme as opposed to a stand-alone treatment.

Finally, returning to the case of Mr D reported in this chapter, the psychotherapeutic approach appears to have benefited from employing some of the strategies proposed by King (2008) and Ehlers and Clark (2000). First, the role of psychoeducation (covering both traumatic brain injury and post traumatic stress disorder) appears to have been particularly useful for Mr D. Understanding that perceptual stimuli can easily trigger anxiety in the absence of any explicit memory of the explosion was particularly important for him. Second, elaboration of the trauma memory through historical resources, in view of the patient's amnesia, proved very helpful. This served as reassuring evidence to the patient that events really did happen and reduced his confusion. Third, the use of cognitive–behaviour therapy strategies to break some of the dysfunctional beliefs about the explosion and his symptoms helped move things forward also. In addition, the commonly employed approaches from neurorehabilitation played an important role also. First, the role of neuropsychological assessment, including neuropsychological testing, cannot be over emphasized. Furthermore, compensatory strategies (for example, to help compensate for his poor short-term memory) can have important positive effects on the everyday tasks patients have to perform. Finally, behavioural strategies were employed to increase activity levels. Extremely limited guidance on the treatment of coexisting post traumatic stress disorder and severe traumatic brain injury is available, and it is hoped that future research may improve our understanding of post traumatic stress disorder in this unique clinical population.

To conclude, based on the current literature as well as clinical experience, the main psychological therapies to consider in post traumatic stress disorder after traumatic brain injury appear to include the following:

- cognitive–behaviour therapy (trauma focused);
- graded exposure;
- psychoeducation;
- behavioural activation.

In addition to the psychological approaches discussed above, the section below attempts to further explore the qualitative nature of patients' thoughts, behaviours, and emotions as they may present during the course of psychological interventions. Potential generic factors underlying psychotherapeutic strategies that may be of use when working with post traumatic stress disorder in the context of traumatic brain injury are explored also.

Strategies and themes in psychotherapy

Some of the themes I have encountered include the following. Persons tend to ruminate over thoughts like "Why did this happen to me?", or "Am I being punished?", to "If only I never went out that evening". Patients under some circumstances describe thoughts indicative of a loss of trust in their fellow human beings, especially if the traumatic brain injury was sustained as a result of an assault or the careless attitude of a drunk driver, for example. Where there are issues surrounding trust, the therapist should be sensitive to the very important generic role of the development of the therapeutic relationship. Other persons may express feelings of anger, sometimes related to being an innocent victim, and at other times where the punishment (by the criminal justice system) of, for example, an assailant or guilty driver, is perceived as too lenient. Under these circumstances, it is not uncommon for patients to express the thought that while the perpetrator will serve his or her limited custodial sentence and pay a modest fine, the patient will have to suffer the consequences of the injury for an unlimited (meaning forever) period. Persons describe experiencing this as a huge injustice and, accordingly, experience feelings of bitterness, anger, and resentment that can sometimes linger for years. As a generic therapeutic strategy, it can, under some conditions, be productive to explore how these events can never be rationalized or made sense of and that, as a consequence, the strong associated feelings have persisted. Accordingly, strategies that avoid struggling with these almost incomprehensible thoughts can bring relief for some persons. At other times, patients spontaneously start to explore the complex area of forgiveness. Here, it is perhaps more crucial than ever during the therapeutic relationship to never impose one's own views, but rather let patients, over time, come to their own insights.

Loss and grief are more commonly expressed following post traumatic stress disorder than is perhaps thought. In my experience, this tends to occur later during the therapy process, usually after some insights have taken place or following an increase in self-awareness. As an example, a person might move from expressing intense anger and resentment following a violent, unprovoked assault, to revealing profound feelings of grief and loss related to how life and the person have been changed by the fateful event. As such, grief can be one of the core emotional symptoms of post traumatic stress disorder. Grief is a complex phenomenon, though, and there has been much debate about whether it constitutes a mental disorder in its own right or if it is in effect, subsumed by other disorders. Interestingly, Parkes (2006), summarizing the contributions to a special symposium that explored this question, concludes that complicated grief probably qualifies for inclusion as a separate disorder in future diagnostic systems, such as *DSM-V*. Nevertheless, therapists in the meantime need to be aware that loss and grief can, in many cases, constitute an important part of the phenomenological experience of patients with post traumatic stress disorder.

Summary points for this chapter

1. Post traumatic stress disorder after severe traumatic brain injury is controversial and probably relatively rare.

2. It has been thought that extended and complete post trauma amnesia after severe traumatic brain injury provides protection against post traumatic stress disorder in most cases.

3. In cases where post traumatic stress disorder follows severe traumatic brain injury, for example, where there has been non-continuous post trauma amnesia, a diagnosis of anxiety disorder due to a general medical condition should be made.

4. While post traumatic stress disorder after traumatic brain injury clearly can occur in any traumatized population, some homogenous populations may provide opportunities for increasing our understanding of this complex co-morbidity.

5. With regard to psychological approaches to management, cognitive–behaviour therapy, graded exposure, and psycho-education can all be beneficial for some patients.

6. In addition to cognitive therapy approaches, clinicians need to be alert to the possibility of patients experiencing loss and grief and allow for these to be explored during therapy.

CHAPTER NINE

Generalized anxiety disorder

Introduction

Most people worry about current and future events, and probably on a regular basis. This is normal and part of life and the human condition, perhaps. In some situations, anxiety can even serve as a motivational drive for changing our circumstances. However, what we need to know is how are these normal and rather common emotions of anxiety distinguished from more problematic, enduring, or pathological anxiety symptoms? According to *DSM-IV* (American Psychiatric Association, 1994), the diagnostic criteria for a generalized anxiety disorder include excessive anxiety regarding a number of activities that the person finds difficult to control. Some of the consequent symptoms may include restlessness, fatigue, irritability, muscle tension, and difficulty falling asleep, among others. Furthermore, this anxiety causes significant distress and may interfere with the person's social or occupational functioning. With regard to the diagnosis of the disorder in the presence of traumatic brain injury, once again, *DSM-IV* specifies that the disturbance is not due to a general medical condition and, where this is thought to be the case, technically speaking, an anxiety disorder due to a general medical condition should be diagnosed.

One of the core psychological concepts regarding generalized anxiety disorder that is perhaps very relevant to persons with traumatic brain injury is the issue of control. Because of the unique impairments associated with traumatic brain injury, for example, cognitive problems, many persons may experience a reduced ability to control their environments or to solve problems that may have appeared straightforward or even trivial to deal with in the past. An example here might include an inability to figure out how to pay a bill at the Post Office or withdraw cash at a machine. This reduced ability to solve or figure out everyday problems can, in some cases, prove to be fertile ground for the development of general anxiety after traumatic brain injury. Also, some of the physical symptoms common to traumatic brain injury, for example, dizziness or visual disturbances, can, in themselves, make some patients anxious anyway. Perhaps reasoning from a more psychological perspective, Epstein and Ursano (1994) point out that traumatic brain injury represents a major impact on the person's sense of awareness, existence, and identity, and that it is, therefore, not surprising that, in response, they regularly present with anxiety. Clearly, persons presenting with general anxiety symptoms after traumatic brain injury present us with a potentially complex area, and diagnosis may not be as simple as might appear. How do we reconcile these points into a systematic diagnostic system?

Diagnostic issues

According to the guidance provided by *DSM-IV* (American Psychiatric Association, 1994), new onset generalized anxiety disorder after traumatic brain injury should, strictly speaking, be diagnosed as an anxiety disorder due to a general medical condition and the medical condition specified as traumatic brain injury. While this may seem a straightforward process, there are some issues of potential clinical relevance to be considered by practitioners before making this diagnosis. Even if the diagnostic category remains unchanged after weighing up the list constituting the differential diagnosis, the process of considering the potential psychological and other factors underpinning the individual's presentation may prove to have more important implications for the management and rehabilitation of the patient. It is essential that, on each occasion, we attempt to understand why the individual with traumatic brain injury presents with general anxiety symptoms on this occasion and under these specific circumstances. It is not only the clinical symptoms that are important, but also the triggers and maintaining factors that need to be considered in each case.

Clearly, anxiety can be present for many reasons, and, because of this, it can sometimes be particularly difficult to disentangle anxiety from other symptoms. For example, Rao and colleagues (2008) investigated fifty-four patients with traumatic brain injury within three months after injury and found that there was an association between first onset anxiety symptoms and sleep disturbances, and, in particular, where there were generalized anxiety features. In these type of situations, how do we know what came first? Sleep deprivation gradually increasing the person's anxiety, or anxiety resulting in chronic insomnia? Furthermore, Epstein and Ursano (1994) pointed out the importance of accurate diagnosis and providing information, as, in the absence of this, patients may be sucked into a cycle of uncertainty, worry, and pain that may, at least to some degree, be accentuated when clinicians are unable to adequately explain their symptoms to them. However, somatic symptoms are not the only source of worry to persons with traumatic brain injury. Often, there may be psychological mechanisms involved in the onset of anxiety. For example, Fleminger (2008) points out that some persons may, upon returning to work, discover that they now have cognitive problems and experience an increase in anxiety, which, in turn, may have a negative effect on other symptoms such as headaches and fatigue. Does this constitute generalized anxiety disorder or a normal psychological reaction to loss of function? How can we differentiate generalized anxiety disorder from traumatic brain injury symptoms?

Symptom differentiation

It is important to observe the patient for objective or qualitative indicators of anxiety. Moreover, considering both diagnostic criteria and observed clinical presentation of patients, in the specific context of traumatic brain injury, the following general differentiation between symptoms that may either lend weight to, or, alternatively, reduce the index of suspicion of generalized anxiety disorder may prove helpful during the process of making a differential diagnosis:

The most confusing symptoms potentially related to traumatic brain injury, and not necessarily always generalized anxiety disorder, are likely to include:

- realistic worries about the future in response to disability and loss of role or function;
- fatigue and poor concentration;
- irritability,

The most telling symptoms indicative of the potential presence of a generalized anxiety disorder, are likely to include the following:

- worries about future events most days, not related to disability *per se*;
- muscle tension;
- difficulty in falling asleep.

As always, the above are merely clinical suggestions or guidelines to assist the clinician who is trying to make a differential diagnosis. Making an actual working diagnosis and formulation for an individual patient would require much more comprehensive information, typically obtained during the clinical assessment and consideration of medical records, scans, and other sources of information. Furthermore, it is also necessary to understand more clearly how commonly generalized anxiety disorder is encountered in the context of traumatic brain injury.

Generalized anxiety disorder after traumatic brain injury

Given the nature of the symptoms associated with traumatic brain injury, the presence of some anxiety should be common and to be expected post-injury. However, and rather counter-intuitively perhaps, generalized anxiety disorder, as defined in *DSM-IV*

(American Psychiatric Association, 1994), appears to be slightly less common according to the available research reports. For example, Epstein and Ursano (1994), following an early overview of the literature, conclude that while about twenty-nine per cent of persons with traumatic brain injury did indeed present with clinical symptoms of general anxiety of some sort, this was not necessarily specifically generalized anxiety disorder in the strict sense of the diagnosis. Similarly, Whelan-Goodinson, Ponsford, and Schonberger (2009) report anxiety disorders or symptoms to be present in thirty-six of their 100 persons with mild to severe traumatic brain injury. There might, though, be a problem with applying the diagnostic criteria of this specific anxiety disorder to persons with traumatic brain injury. The main culprit may well be criterion A of the disorder in *DSM-IV*, specifying excessive worrying about activities such as work (American Psychiatric Association, 1994). In most cases, it would be considered entirely normal for a person who has suffered a traumatic brain injury to worry about work, school, or other personally relevant areas. While many persons are likely to meet the diagnostic criteria for the more physical symptoms of generalized anxiety disorder, it is unlikely that many would meet criterion A on grounds not related to the injury. Perhaps this is one of the factors contributing to the surprisingly low incidence and prevalence figures in the literature.

Nevertheless, there is some evidence for specifically generalized anxiety disorder presenting as a consequence of traumatic brain injury. For example, Hiott and Labbate (2002), in their more recent review of anxiety disorders after traumatic brain injury, combined the results from four separate studies and found a cumulative prevalence of generalized anxiety disorder following traumatic brain injury of just over ten per cent. In addition, perhaps reassuringly, similar findings were reported by Van Reekum, Cohen, and Wong (2000), who pooled the data from five studies and found that just over nine per cent (36/398) of these patients presented with generalized anxiety disorder after traumatic brain injury. Thus, generalised anxiety disorder is a relatively common complication of traumatic brain injury. However, rather surprisingly, it appears to be not as common as some of the other emotional difficulties following traumatic brain injury. Nevertheless, a figure of around nine per cent is still somewhat higher than the lifetime prevalence of five per cent quoted by *DSM-IV* (American Psychiatric Association, 1994). We shall now turn to a case study to illuminate the qualitative nature of the presentation of generalized anxiety disorder as a result of traumatic brain injury.

Case report

Ms A was a lady in her late fifties who was run over as a pedestrian by a careless driver who failed to stop at a junction. The accident occurred almost two decades prior to her referral to a community-based brain injury rehabilitation service. She was referred to the brain injury service by the local community mental health team. It transpired that, during the accident, she suffered fractured limbs and a traumatic brain injury. While her period of post trauma amnesia extended over a considerable period, she did have some islands of memory of the event: for example, being aware that she was lying in the road, with people's legs, but not the rest of their bodies, visible to her. Ms A spent a considerable period of time in hospital, mainly as a result of her orthopaedic injuries. After she was discharged, her emotional difficulties came more to the fore and she was picked up by local mental health services. Prior to her injury, Ms A was confident and outgoing. She held down a responsible position as a government official, which she was unable to return to after the injury.

Clinically, Ms A presented with no obvious cognitive impairment. Nevertheless, neuropsychological testing did identify problems of attention. This generally manifested as distractibility and, at times, an overly detailed description of events or topics, the latter perhaps representing a compensatory strategy to prevent her from losing track of the topic she was talking about. She had moderate problems related to mobility, stemming from her orthopaedic injuries. Most noticeable, though, was the high levels of generalized anxiety she experienced. The anxiety almost always related to future events and, as soon as these perceived disasters had failed to materialize, their places would be taken by new worries. For example, Ms A often had to see her doctor about difficulties (of which only some were actually related to her physical injuries) and would assume that she would have to spend a significant period in hospital as a result (which never materialized), or that any social or recreational activity would prove to be disastrous. Moreover, she would tend to ruminate and be unable to shift her thoughts or feelings about her latest worry, despite her best efforts. However, most of her worries were about trivial matters that were quite obviously unrelated to her injury and its direct effects *per se*. These worries significantly interfered with her sleep pattern, and, at times, her anxiety would psychologically paralyse her, making it impossible for her to enjoy activities that she would on other occasions derive great pleasure from.

Due to staff changes, Ms A was seen for psychotherapeutic follow-up by two different clinical neuropsychologists. The first neuropsychologist followed an acceptance and commitment therapy (Hayes, Strosahl, & Wilson, 2004) approach, which resulted in Ms A being more aware of her emotions and perhaps less caught up in trying to "fight" her feelings of discomfort. Rather, she was encouraged to set herself goals based on values. The second neuropsychologist, who took over Ms A's care when her regular therapist left, followed more of a cognitive therapy (along the lines of Maultsby, 1984) approach to try to help equip Ms A to better manage some of the clearly inaccurate thoughts and unhelpful styles of thinking she continued to present with. Ms A was able to apply the principles from cognitive therapy and did gain some control over her anxiety in this way, but was mostly not quite able to apply the techniques "in the moment", preferring a *post hoc* analysis (mostly in written homework assignments) of her thoughts and feelings. Interestingly, with regard to generic factors, Ms A reported that she found the therapeutic relationship she had with both therapists to have been the most useful agent of change. Moreover, it is perhaps the case that the therapists were almost subconsciously aware of this factor, as much more than usual care was taken during handover to preserve the therapeutic bond, by seeing Ms A together on a couple of occasions before the first neuropsychologist left.

Psychological approaches to management

Psychotherapy can potentially be useful for some patients presenting with generalized anxiety disorder, and there is possibly a role for drug treatments also. People clearly have the potential to experience positive psychological development after traumatic brain injury. For example, Hawley and Joseph (2008) reviewed survivors of traumatic brain injury on average 11½ years after injury and found an inverse relation between positive growth and anxiety. This finding seems to support the notion that some survivors can and do adjust to disability with the passing of time, and that in some cases, something meaningful or positive might also come from the tragedy, albeit in most cases probably many years down the line. Moreover, this appears to suggest that if there were potential for development after traumatic brain injury and that, as a result, ultimately anxiety could be reduced, psychotherapeutic approaches to rehabilitation for at least some patients might serve as a further catalyst to facilitate the longer-term process of adjustment.

In clinical populations without a history of traumatic brain injury, cognitive–behaviour therapy and possibly supportive psychotherapy have demonstrated efficacy for the management of generalized anxiety disorder (e.g., Borkovec & Ruscio, 2001; Hunot, Churchill, Silva de Lima, & Teixaira, 2007). Survivors of traumatic brain injury can experience a huge amount of anxiety stemming from changes in role and function, and the life-threatening experience of sustaining an injury can make persons feel vulnerable and weak (Elbaum, 2007). Regarding psychological therapy for persons with traumatic brain injury, according to Epstein and Ursano (1994), an empathic approach to assist the patient to understand the changes stemming from their injury and to help them develop strategies for compensating for, and coping with, these changes, can be effective for some. Elbaum (2007) suggested the use of relaxation therapy and stress management techniques. More specifically, Ponsford (1995) suggested the use and adaptation (for cognitive problems and fatigue) of muscle relaxation as a treatment. However, clinicians should be aware that persons with anxiety could be vulnerable, and possibly also become dependent on the psychotherapist. For this reason, there should always, within a robust therapeutic relationship, be a clear focus on rehabilitation goals. Sometimes pursuing these goals can, by their very nature, be anxiety provoking for patients. However, prevention of avoidance of potentially stressful situations on the part of the patient may be a goal in itself.

There are other approaches to managing symptoms of general anxiety after traumatic brain also. Ponsford (1995) provides an overview of these, including the already mentioned use of muscle relaxation therapy. Other approaches, according to Ponsford (1995), include breathing as an augmentation to muscle relaxation, biofeedback, using visual imagery, dealing with avoidance as well as the implementation of distraction and cognitive restructuring to address the thoughts underlying symptoms of anxiety. With regard to cognitive restructuring, records may be kept by the patient to use as a strategy to challenge the thoughts that contribute to anxiety, or cue cards may be useful in initiating self-talk exercises intended to address problems related to thoughts possibly triggering an increase in anxiety (Ponsford, 1995). Avoidance may be addressed by devising a hierarchy of anxiety-provoking situations and, working in small steps, prevent the avoidance of these situations, sometimes making use of the support of a friend or family member (*ibid*.). These strategies clearly draw upon techniques from cognitive–behaviour therapy, as well as behaviour therapy more generally. Curren, Ponsford, and Crowe (2000) investigated patients' coping strategies after traumatic brain injury and reported that strategies emphasizing problem solving and developing a positive outlook were associated with reduced anxiety. Moreover, coping characterized by patients actively working on problems, pursuing enjoyable activities, and utilizing humour may be associated with better self-esteem and reduced anxiety (Anson & Ponsford, 2006).

There have also been suggestions for treatments based on, for example, a psychoanalytic viewpoint. Freed (2002) suggests that traumatic brain injury can result in disturbances of intrapsychic function, and that therapists aiming to facilitate ego reintegration should be aware that anxious patients may need others who are comfortable in providing auxiliary functions, specifically to help them better manage their symptoms of anxiety. Moreover, O'Gorman (2006), from a psychodynamic perspective, described a male in his early forties (Mr A) who presented with cognitive impairment, anxiety, and confusion, after he sustained a traumatic brain injury when he was run over by a car. Mr A had fears related to the (unknown to him at the time) extent of his injuries as well as anxiety and panic about not knowing the extent of the losses he had suffered (O'Gorman, 2006). O'Gorman concludes that the provision of psychodynamic psychotherapy assisted Mr A to make sense of his experience, accept his condition, and mourn losses so that he could live his life again, although not necessarily always as it was in the past.

Reassurance is, of course, also an important strategy for helping persons with chronic general anxiety symptoms after traumatic brain injury. Sometimes, patients who experience unpleasant symptoms such as emotional lability, feelings of detachment, or severe fatigue need reassurance that they are not, in fact, losing their minds or going mad (Epstein & Ursano, 1994). Memory compensatory strategies may have an important emotional benefit to patients also. For example Kim, Burke, Dowds, Boone, and Park (2000) report a significant reduction in anxiety in their small group of patients who used handheld computers to compensate for poor memory. Aniskiewicz (2007) suggests a mindfulness approach to general anxiety that was intended to help patients change their relationship to anxiety symptoms. More specifically, in this approach patients are helped to maintain an open mind, are encouraged to have a more active orientation, pursue a balanced view to help accept uncertainty, and to strive to return to the present moment with a view to avoiding worries about future events (Aniskiewicz, 2007). It appears that, in this approach, some psychotherapeutic work is also aimed at the level of cognitive processes, with patients being helped to notice distressing thoughts and feelings, but then to let it go. This is, however, somewhat different from a more classical cognitive–behaviour therapy approach where the thoughts would be disputed or challenged in an attempt to change emotions.

In summary, based on the above overview of the literature as well as clinical practice, it appears that the most relevant psychological therapies to consider for the management of generalized anxiety disorder after traumatic brain injury include the following:

- reassurance and provision of information;
- supportive psychotherapy;
- cognitive–behaviour therapy;
- mindfulness approaches;
- psychodynamic psychotherapies.

The following section, in addition to the above overview, draws on my clinical work to address the qualitative nature of patients' thoughts, behaviours, and emotions, as these may present during the process of providing psychological interventions. Furthermore, some potentially useful generic factors (see Chapter Four also) pertaining to, for example, psychotherapeutic strategies, the therapeutic relationship, and self-awareness are discussed also.

Strategies and themes in psychotherapy

Uncertainty about the future represents a major theme for many presenting with generalized anxiety disorder following traumatic brain injury. From a cognitive–behaviour therapy perspective, we can perhaps expect that patients may present with several beliefs that might trigger and maintain their high levels of general anxiety. Some examples of beliefs seen in clinical practice include the following: "I never used to be anxious, there must be something seriously wrong with me", or "Why is this happening to me?", and "I think it will get worse", or "I will forget to do it and then I will be so ashamed of myself". It is, as already mentioned earlier, important to distinguish between realistic and more trivial worries, or risk seriously adversely affecting the therapeutic relationship. If patients even slightly suspect that their worries are not taken seriously by the therapist, serious negative transference can occur, putting further therapeutic progress at risk. As a first port of call, rather, acknowledge patients' worries and allow them to freely express these emotions before even considering which belief(s) may underlie or contribute to their anxieties.

With generalized anxiety disorder, clinicians are well advised to always keep an open mind as to the potential role of psychodynamic factors. People's pre-injury psychological development and history can substantially colour their post-injury presentation. "Know the person who sustained the traumatic brain injury and not only the injury" would seem to be a good mantra and task for investment of psychotherapeutic time. For example, Ms A, described earlier on in this chapter, presented with generalized anxiety especially surrounding perceived male authority figures. She actively denied that this was a problem prior to the accident, and, in fact, provided evidence to support this, stating that she used to work in a very male dominated environment without any difficulty whatsoever prior to the accident. However, her awareness regarding this developed, and during one session she rather dramatically reported having made a connection between the complicated relationship she had with her father and now experiencing exactly the same feelings of anxiety when in the presence of certain males who subconsciously reminded her of her father. Once this insight occurred, Ms A reported a significant reduction in worries pertaining to these specific situations. Interestingly, this did not generalize to other situations, and she continued to experience worries and anxiety related to other matters.

Another factor to be aware of is the possibility that a loss of self-confidence may, in some cases, also make a significant contribution to the onset of anxiety and worries. Here, cognitive–behaviour therapy may be particularly useful, especially when coupled with activities that will have a high potential for successful completion, or at least constituting a pleasurable experience. Occupational therapy can be a hugely important adjunctive therapy under these circumstances. Working on changing beliefs related to confidence will almost certainly have no effect unless accompanied by behavioural assignments or tasks to reinforce new, more functional beliefs. Where worries are about very realistic matters, for example, financial problems such as paying a mortgage while not in employment, the assistance of a social worker should be obtained before attempting to help the patient with cognitive strategies or anxiety management techniques. Finally, as with many difficulties following traumatic brain injury, it is so important to ensure the patient's understanding of the nature of his or her symptomatology. This should always be done with the patient's level of self-awareness in mind, as well as trying to strike a balance between truthfulness and not painting too bleak a picture, destroying the person's hope for progress in the process, or unnecessarily increasing further their anxiety.

Because many persons find the excessive and out of character worrying almost alien to their pre-injury personality, issues surrounding identity can be important to address here also. Coetzer (2008) discussed the potential importance of long-term community-based follow-up when attempting to address more chronic behavioural alterations manifesting as identity change. For example,

Ms A's deeply ingrained pattern (over many years) of worrying about many matters was in great contrast to her ability to deal with substantial pressure in the workplace prior to sustaining her injury. Understandably, she often commented that it felt as if she were not the same person any more. When working with generalized anxiety disorder, one of the aims might well be to get the person more involved in the pursuit of personally salient goals. In this regard, it is worth being aware of the interesting work conducted by Ylvisaker, McPherson, Kayes, and Pellett (2008), where they proposed a strategy of using metaphoric identity mapping to jointly set personally meaningful goals with the patient, especially with regard to work related to identity after traumatic brain injury. According to the authors, this technique, which uses patient-generated metaphors related to identity to pursue rehabilitation goals, has generally been well received by patients, but may require some adjustment to practice and draw on more unusual clinical skills for many practitioners (Ylvisaker, McPherson, Kayes, & Pellett, 2008). These and other novel strategies may be very useful for clinicians to consider, either on their own or as part of other therapeutic approaches when managing generalized anxiety disorder.

Summary points for this chapter

1. Generalized anxiety disorder is relatively common after traumatic brain injury.
2. Realistic worries about the future after traumatic brain injury should not be confused with generalized anxiety disorder.
3. In the context of traumatic brain injury, generalized anxiety disorder should technically be diagnosed as an anxiety disorder due to a general medical condition.
4. As regards psychological approaches to management, an empathic approach and reassurance have been thought to be potentially useful.
5. Other potentially useful psychotherapy techniques include cognitive–behaviour therapy and mindfulness approaches.

CHAPTER TEN

Major depressive disorder

Introduction

I n our everyday language or social conversations, it would be
fair to conclude that depression is more likely to be understood
as being synonymous with the concept of unhappiness. For
example, someone might say that something (say, the weather)
made him or her depressed, or that the news was depressing. This
is likely to imply unhappiness about something or some situation.
However, from a clinical perspective depression is more than the
unhappiness experienced by most people at some point in their
lives. The *DSM-IV* (American Psychiatric Association, 1994) defines
a depressed mood or loss of interest and pleasure in nearly all activities as the essential feature of a major depressive episode. It also
specifies that the duration of the depressed mood should be for at
least two weeks. Some of the other criteria for a major depressive
episode include significant weight loss or weight gain, insomnia,
psychomotor agitation or retardation, feelings of worthlessness or
guilt, poor concentration, and, in some instances, suicidal ideation.
These symptoms should result in significant distress or impairment
of social and occupational functioning. Finally, a bereavement

process cannot better explain the aforementioned symptoms. *DSM-IV* specifies that the symptoms should not be due to a general medical condition, and that where this is the case, a mood disorder due to a general medical condition should be diagnosed. Major depressive disorder should also not be confused with, for example, an adjustment disorder, which is a time-limited response to a stressor.

As already mentioned, feeling unhappy in response to some event or environmental stimulus is probably common and is quite obviously not ever to be confused with clinical depression. While sometimes the differences can possibly be difficult to pinpoint, it is perhaps the intensity of mood disturbance, duration, and physiological symptoms that distinguishes clinical depression from the more everyday negative fluctuations in mood experienced by most people. Nevertheless, in view of the rather extensive and profound life changes that often result from a traumatic brain injury, it seems plausible that depression may be one of the most common complications associated with it. Indeed, many persons with traumatic brain injury experience major changes and stressors in their lives, including in the areas of finances, employment, education, and relationships, to name but a few. Considering some of the symptoms commonly seen after traumatic brain injury, it is likely that it may, at times, prove really challenging for clinicians to make a definite diagnosis of a major depressive episode in patients with traumatic brain injury. Furthermore, some might argue that it would seem absolutely normal to feel low in mood in response to the changes associated with traumatic brain injury and that surely it is not necessary, or indeed even desirable, to formally diagnose or medicalize a normal human reaction to trauma. If it were the case that depression under these circumstances is representative of a normal reaction, how would one diagnose the said condition anyway?

Diagnostic issues

How do we distinguish in an individual patient the clinical symptoms of depression from the other (similar) symptoms common to traumatic brain injury? Some of these symptoms might appear almost exactly the same and therefore difficult to ascribe to one or the other only (Babin, 2003; Ponsford, 1995). Patients with traumatic brain injury often may have an obvious disturbance of their mood, yet not satisfy all the diagnostic criteria for a major depressive episode (Scicutella, 2007). For example, the apathy and lack of initiation so common to traumatic brain injury can easily be confused for poor energy and depressed mood. On the other hand, poor energy and fatigue is common after traumatic brain injury. And, of course, symptoms of apathy and poor motivation in themselves may be indicative of depression (Fleminger, 2008). Indeed, even when using questionnaires and structured clinical interviewing, it remains difficult to distinguish fully the symptoms of depression and apathy, respectively (Al-Adawi et al., 2004). In essence, before concluding that a patient presents with apathy, depression should, in the first instance, be ruled out (Fleminger, Oliver, Williams, & Evans, 2003). However, apathy is only one of many symptoms that can cause diagnostic uncertainty regarding depression in the context of traumatic brain injury. Starkstein and Lischinsky (2002) provide an overview of strategies and techniques for diagnosing depression in the context of brain injury.

Disturbance of sleep pattern, one of the central symptoms of depression, is perhaps of particular interest in this context. Sleep disturbances are common to both traumatic brain injury and depression. Parcell, Ponsford, Redman and Rajaratnam (2008) reported that both subjectively reported disturbances and objective polysomnography in persons with traumatic brain injury were associated with increased levels of depression (and anxiety). In addition, no associations between time since injury or injury severity were observed in this study (Parcell, Ponsford, Redman, & Rajaratnam, 2008). Interestingly, Tobe, Schneider, Mrozik, and Lidsky (1999) reported a more unusual pattern of enduring inability to sleep, despite attempts to treat the insomnia, in a depressed patient with traumatic brain injury. Thus, disturbances in sleep pattern may need to be particularly closely monitored in patients at all times over the course of their rehabilitation and follow-up. In addition, clinicians need to be mindful also of the potential for more unusual clinical presentations. In summary, then, many symptoms such as fatigue or poor concentration are common after traumatic brain injury and, as a result, it is not uncommon for patients to subjectively report several depressive symptoms, although clinically and objectively they are not actually depressed (Flemiger, Oliver, Williams, & Evans, 2003).

Are there differences between the clinical presentations of depression after traumatic brain injury, compared to depression in the absence of a history of traumatic brain injury? While there are certainly many possible false positive symptoms as a result of the physical problems associated with traumatic brain injury, it is not entirely clear if there is actually a core difference once these pseudo-symptoms have been accounted for. Aloia, Long, and Allen (1995) reported that the symptom profiles of depression in patients with traumatic brain injury did not differ from those without traumatic brain injury. Indeed, there is not much empirical evidence that the core symptoms of major depressive disorder are different in patients with traumatic brain injury when compared to those without (Fleminger, 2008). However, the contrary has also been reported. For example, Kreutzer, Seel, and Gourley (2001) reported that irritability, reduced speed of movement, lack of interest, poor memory, and fatigue were all more common after traumatic brain injury. What should practitioners look for when they suspect that their patients may be depressed? It appears that, in the first instance, as with persons without a traumatic brain injury who present with major depressive disorder, the same indicators of a depressed mood are as relevant. While diagnosing depression after traumatic brain injury may, in many cases, be complicated by the presence of physical and cognitive impairments, feelings of hopelessness, worthlessness, and anhedonia may be indicative of the presence of depression in persons with traumatic brain injury (Simpson & Tate, 2007).

To identify depression after traumatic brain injury, we perhaps need to explore patients' subjective description of their mood much more carefully. Specific emphasis should be placed on the qualitative nature of patients' descriptions of mood and their thoughts about their current perceived roles and how they see the future. In some cases, less emphasis should possibly be placed on the classic somatic markers of depression, such as insomnia, changes in appetite, alteration of libido, as well as the cognitive markers including poor concentration, as these can yield false positives in the absence of a clearly depressed mood in a patient with traumatic brain injury. For example, changes in sex drive can be misleading, as these may present as a consequence of loss of confidence, pain, or lack of initiation as part of impaired executive control function. It is, however, not at all suggested that these important symptoms are ignored, but merely that more emphasis is sometimes placed on mood and that these symptoms are interpreted in the contexts of both the presence of traumatic brain injury and the possible presence of a major depressive disorder. Finally, clinicians attempting to diagnose a major depressive disorder after traumatic brain injury may find it helpful to be aware of the research regarding the incidence and prevalence of depression after severe traumatic brain injury when interpreting clinical findings from their assessment of individual patients. This knowledge can, for example, help us to consider more realistically the probability or likelihood of depression being present in some of our patients.

Symptom differentiation

Keeping in mind the diagnostic criteria for a major depressive disorder and also actual observed clinical presentation of patients, in the specific context of traumatic brain injury, the following general differentiation between symptoms that may either lend weight to, or, alternatively, reduce the index of suspicion for the presence of a major depressive disorder, may assist us during the process of making a differential diagnosis.

The most confusing symptoms potentially related to traumatic brain injury, and not necessarily always major depressive disorder, are likely to include:

● apathy or fatigue;
● poor concentration and memory (resulting directly from cognitive impairment);
● sleep disturbances.

The most telling symptoms indicative of the potential presence of a major depressive disorder, are likely to include the following:

● feelings of hopelessness or worthlessness;
● anhedonia;
● thoughts of death or suicide.

Generally speaking, then, it is important to identify the reasons for a symptom; for example, does the person find it difficult to concentrate because of poor information processing or rather because of rumination? The above points should be seen as representing suggestions from clinical practice and are merely clinical guidelines intended to assist the clinician in making a differential diagnosis. The working diagnosis and formulation should always follow from a rigorous assessment, consideration of other clinical data, and an understanding of how common major depressive disorder is considered to be after traumatic brain injury.

Depression after traumatic brain injury

We know that depression is common after traumatic brain injury. Also, across different cultures, we find similar incidences of depression after traumatic brain injury (for example, Al-Adawi et al., 2004). Several authors have found a high incidence of depression in individuals with traumatic brain injury, ranging from thirty-three per cent (Jorge et al., 2004) to forty-six per cent (Al-Adawi et al., 2004), to even as high as fifty-nine per cent (Glenn, O'Neil-Pirozzi, Goldstein, Burke, & Jacob, 2001). Van Reekum, Cohen, and Wong (2000), in their review, pool the data from ten earlier studies and find that about forty-four per cent (289/653) of patients in this combined sample presented with major depressive disorder up to about seven and a half years following traumatic brain injury. This seems to confirm that depression is one of the most common emotional complications of traumatic brain injury. It is well known that traumatic brain injury occurs more frequently among younger adults. To some extent, one would almost expect younger adults, who have to live with major disability through their most productive years, to be at risk for developing depression. While research is lacking specifically with regard to depression after traumatic brain injury in older adults, Menzel (2008), following a recent review of the literature, reports a prevalence of 21–37% in this population also. Clearly, depression after traumatic brain injury is common across the age range. Indeed, based on Van Reekum, Cohen, and Wong's (2000) review, and also the work of Jorge and Starkstein (2005), major depression appears to be the most common neuropsychiatric complication of traumatic brain injury. What exactly causes depression after traumatic brain injury remains open to debate, though.

There have been different findings regarding potential contributing factors to depression after traumatic brain injury. It is likely that environmental, biological, and psychological factors may all contribute to the onset and subsequent maintenance of depression after traumatic brain injury (Jorge & Starkstein, 2005). For example, Rao and colleagues (2006) investigated the biological correlates, including metabolism, of depression after traumatic brain injury. These authors found that reduced levels of N-acetylaspartate in the thalamus, basal ganglia, and frontal cortex were associated with depression in patients with traumatic brain injury (*ibid.*). In addition, there are several studies that have looked at other biological correlates: for example, lesion location or changes in neuro-transmitters in the brain. However, psychological and other non-biological factors are, of course, relevant also. For example, time since injury may also be an important contributor to depression following traumatic brain injury. The reasoning behind this appears to be suggestive of the reality of the person's situation becoming increasingly apparent over time and representing a major contributory factor to the development of depression later on.

Fleminger (2008) posited that psychosocial factors have a major impact on depression at lengthier periods since injury and proposed that depression in this population may be associated with worsening disability over time. Depression can adversely affect an individual's functioning in several important areas and hamper rehabilitation efforts. Causality is difficult to determine, though. An alternative explanation might be that depression in itself may be a causative factor in long-term disability. Lefebvre, Cloutier, and Josee Levert (2008) investigated the long-term (ten years) social integration of twenty-two survivors of moderate to severe traumatic brain injury as well as twenty-one family members and found that different barriers, including episodes of depression, contributed to poor social integration in this group. Hence, episodes of depression may prevent better functional outcomes, resulting in increasing disability over the longer term. Another important factor to consider in the onset and evolution of depression after traumatic brain injury is, of course, the role of self-awareness (e.g., Malec, Testa, Rush, Brown, & Moessner, 2007), and this is discussed in greater detail later in this chapter.

Common symptoms of depression after traumatic brain injury include low mood, poor self-concept, ahedonia, apathy, complaints of cognitive impairment, and behavioural changes, including hyperactivity and disinhibition (Jorge & Starkstein, 2005). Particularly alarming is the finding that the risk for suicide is increased after traumatic brain injury (Teasdale & Engberg, 2001), most probably as a result of depression (Lewis, 2001). Indeed, Fleminger, Oliver, Williams, and Evans (2003), following their review, concluded that the risk was raised over three-fold the standard rate, with some of the excess risk attributable to pre-injury factors. Some of the warning signs for a potentially increased risk of suicide after traumatic brain injury relate to the patient's perception of the impact of the injury, pressure of multiple stressors, work or financial difficulties, social isolation, relationship conflict or breakdown, and self-reported hopelessness (Simpson & Tate, 2005). According to Teasdale and Engberg (2001), there appears to be no particular time point after traumatic brain injury when patients are more at risk, but men are slightly more at risk and suicide was associated with coexisting drug or alcohol abuse. Mainio and colleagues (2007) reviewed all suicides spanning a sixteen-year period in a Finnish region and identified 103 (out of 1877) persons with a history of suicide. Persons with co-morbid traumatic brain injury tended to commit suicide within three years of the injury, were males, suffered more severe injuries, were older, unemployed, and presented with psychiatric disorders and alcohol abuse (*ibid.*, 2007). With these findings in mind, clinicians should remain alert to the possible risk of suicide and be aware that several other social factors may also be associated with the increased risk.

Depression, specifically as defined by *DSM-IV* (American Psychiatric Association, 1994) diagnostic criteria, is common early after traumatic brain injury, occurring in about thirty-three per cent of patients during the initial year after injury (Jorge et al., 2004). In an earlier study, Jorge and colleagues (1993) reported that out of sixty-six patients who had suffered a traumatic brain injury, twenty-seven had a major depression (using *DSM-III-R* criteria) diagnosed during a one-year follow-up period. This was a bit higher than the thirty-eight per cent at six months post-injury figure reported by Bowen, Neumann, Conner, Tennant, and Chamberlain (1998). While depression may be more common during the first two years following a traumatic brain injury, and perhaps relates, to some degree, to the patient's self-awareness, it can persevere for much longer. Indeed, Fleminger, Oliver, Williams, and Evans (2003) concluded that the prevalence of depression after the first year, rather than reaching a plateau, instead increased with time. Even decades after a traumatic brain injury, depression remains a common problem (Holsinger et al., 2002). Furthermore, there is a high co-morbidity with anxiety and aggressive behaviour and it can, for obvious reasons, pose a significant obstacle to recovery (Jorge et al., 2004).

While the *DSM-IV* (American Psychiatric Association, 1994) diagnostic criteria for depression most probably accurately describe the symptoms or changes in a person's mood and functioning after traumatic brain injury, they perhaps do not always illuminate the dynamic, intrapersonal, or psychological factors involved in the development and maintenance of these symptoms. Indeed, Butler and Satz (1999) reasoned that the co-existence of brain injury and depression could result in some diagnostic confusion. It is not always clear what represents depression, adjustment to change, or perhaps even a bereavement process. The emotional changes after brain injury can also be viewed from a loss and grief theoretical perspective (Coetzer, 2004, 2006). Incorporating these perspectives into our thinking may improve our understanding beyond what can sometimes be seen as narrow diagnostic criteria, and, hence, to include or consider also the phenomenological experiences of persons who have suffered a traumatic brain injury seems sensible. Interestingly, some support for this viewpoint has been provided, for example, by the finding that psychosocial disability, rather than physical disability, was associated with depressed mood (Bowen, Neumann, Conner, Tennant, & Chamberlain, 1998). Clearly, though, there are many factors associated with depression after traumatic brain injury and, for example, much depends also on the patient's perception or understanding of the nature of their impairment and disability.

The role of self-awareness

One of the most perplexing and difficult to understand symptoms after traumatic brain injury must be impaired self-awareness, or altered insight. Impaired self-awareness is one of the hallmark symptoms associated with more severe traumatic brain injury. Self-awareness has, in broad terms, been defined as the ability of a person to consciously process information about the self in a way that reflects a relatively objective view, while maintaining a unique phenomenological experience or sense of self (Prigatano, 1997). Thus, impaired self-awareness would represent the inability of the person to perceive the self objectively, as others would, and, by implication, then represents a disturbance of personal identity. An impairment of self-awareness may manifest itself as personality changes, or mediate inexplicable (to observers) changes in behaviour. Examples of how impaired self-awareness can present include a patient denying that anything is wrong (while there may be obvious and spectacular failures in, for example, return to employment), failure to see the need for rehabilitation, not appreciating the consequences of behaviour (including impulsivity or sexual disinhibition), and underestimating the support he or she may need. The effects on everyday life can be subtle and may take a while for observers to fully understand. Indeed, it is possible that many persons with impaired self-awareness may incorrectly be thought to be presenting with a personality disorder.

It is worth noting here that definitely not all people suffer impaired self-awareness after traumatic brain injury and that, likewise, we do not fully understand all the factors contributing to impaired self-awareness. Over the years, much has been written about the neurological basis of impaired self-awareness. Several specific anatomical regions have been postulated to be involved in, or directly responsible for, the mediation of self-awareness. However, keeping in mind the work of, for example, Bigler (2001), we should be reminded of the importance of recognizing the disruption of networks after brain injury as well as the not insignificant limitations of neuro-imaging in identifying specific brain regions functionally involved in human behaviour. Perhaps, then, the finding of Sherer, Hart, Whyte, Nick, and Yablon (2005) that, in their sample of sub-acute traumatically brain-injured adults, impaired self-awareness was not associated with a lesion in a specific area of the brain but, rather, the actual number of lesions, is fascinating. These authors posited that the most likely explanation for their finding was that the disruption of widely distributed networks was more important to self-awareness than a single lesion in a specific region *per se*.

Furthermore, as regards more psychologically orientated work pertaining to this complex area, Ownsworth, McFarland, and Young (2002), in their study of factors underpinning poor self-awareness, conclude that one of the clinical implications stemming from their research was a need to assess both neuropsychological (cognitive) as well as psychological factors. With regard to theoretical models, there are several that have attempted to increase our understanding of self-awareness and how it relates to behaviour after traumatic brain injury. For example, Flashman, Amador, and McAllister (1998) described three dimensions of impaired self-awareness, including the person's ability to identify specific impairments, the emotional response to these impairments, and, finally, the ability to understand the effects of impairments. Indeed, Giacino and Cicerone (1998) point out that problems of self-awareness could have multiple determinants. In effect, these research findings and theoretical models appear, directly or indirectly, to postulate that self-awareness is influenced by biological, psychological, and environmental factors.

The level of a person's self-awareness could have a significant effect on depression. The two main positions among researchers and practitioners have been that impaired self-awareness could either be associated with the onset or, alternatively, prevention of depression after traumatic brain injury, the latter implying that an inaccurate appraisal of one's situation, which is common in persons with impaired self-awareness, may protect the patient from developing depression. However, the relation between depression and self-awareness is not simple; neither is it unidirectional. For example, Anson and Ponsford (2006) found that there are interaction effects with self-awareness, improved mood being associated with greater self-awareness after intervention, among other contributing variables. On the other hand, while impaired self-awareness may initially protect the individual against depression, longer-term repeated failures resulting from poor self-awareness may actually lead to depression (Prigatano, 1999). Malec, Testa, Rush, Brown, and Moessner (2007) more recently investigated this complex area, and reported that patients' self-appraisal of impairment was associated with both late and early onset depression and that impairment of self-awareness, which was more directly related (as a symptom) to traumatic brain injury, could possibly protect the individual from developing depression.

However, the relation between depression and self-awareness has not been viewed exclusively as constituting either a protective factor or a trigger. Another fascinating perspective on the relation between self-awareness and depression after traumatic brain injury was reported by Fleminger, Oliver, Williams, and Evans (2003), following their review of the relevant literature. That is that the association between depression and self-awareness may well be bi-directional, meaning that depression may result from improved self-awareness, but, conversely, depression in itself may cause better self-awareness (*ibid.*). What this means is that the depressed patient becomes more aware of, or insightful with regard to, their impairment and associated disability and, in response becomes perhaps more realistic in their views about the future, including outcome (*ibid.*). Clearly, we still have much to learn about impaired self-awareness associated with traumatic brain injury, including neuro-anatomical structures involved in its manifestation, psychological factors, and the relation of environmental factors with depression. The case report below highlights some of these issues.

Case report

We now return to Mr L, whose case was also discussed earlier (Chapter One). To recap, Mr L was a thirty-year-old male who sustained a severe traumatic brain injury at the age of twenty, following a road traffic collision. During the accident, he was thrown out of the vehicle and sustained a severe traumatic brain injury, but only very minor other injuries. The severity of his injury was evidenced by, for example, his Glasgow Coma Scale (Teasdale & Jennett, 1974), which was six out of fifteen, as well as a period of unconsciousness of at least two weeks. In addition, Mr L's period of post trauma amnesia extended over a period of approximately two months, further evidence that he had sustained a severe traumatic brain injury. The initial (during his stay in an acute care hospital) computed tomography (CT) scan of his brain revealed generalized cerebral swelling, but no focal lesions such as contusions or intra-cerebral bleeding. Mr L spent a couple of months in the acute hospital where he was initially admitted before being transferred to a rehabilitation unit. Here he stayed for a period of ten weeks. Interestingly, for this period of inpatient rehabilitation, Mr L reported that he had no recollection whatsoever. Eventually, Mr L made what was thought to be an almost complete physical recovery. However, as time moved on, others who knew him well increasingly became aware that his personality had changed significantly following the accident.

More than ten years after Mr L originally sustained his injury, he was referred for assessment with a view to further community-based brain injury rehabilitation. The initial clinical assessment revealed the presence of frustration, poor self-awareness, anxiety, and loss of confidence. Neuropsychological testing revealed subtle cognitive impairments in the areas of verbal memory as well as executive control function. These cognitive impairments were thought to be compatible with the expected effects of a traumatic brain injury. With regard to his history since sustaining the injury, the main theme here represented the presence of numerous failures to resume his studies or return to gainful employment. Rather strikingly, Mr L had poor self-awareness of how his impairments affected his outcome, and had no clear ideas as to why he could not hold down a job. At this point, CT and magnetic resonance imaging (MRI) scans of the brain were requested by the neurologist of the service where Mr L was seen. These were reported as normal (more than ten years post-injury). Mr L received multi-disciplinary neuro-rehabilitation, including neurology review, occupational therapy input, psychological therapy, and social work support and assistance.

Despite, over time, receiving substantial amounts of information about traumatic brain injury, feedback of neuropsychology results, and brain scan findings, Mr L's poor self-awareness and, possibly, the fact that the findings from his most recent brain scans were normal did not positively affect his understanding of what appeared to be rather obvious long-term effects resulting from his injury. Frankly, his outcome remained poor after several years of rehabilitation. While Mr L could acknowledge that he had indeed sustained a severe traumatic brain injury and he could report accurately on a factual level about his impairments, he failed to see the link between his impairments and his poor social and occupational performance. Over time, his inability to return to employment, as well as to understand why this was, resulted in Mr L feeling more and more depressed. For example, two Beck Depression Inventories (Beck, Steer, & Brown, 1996) administered revealed scores of twenty-five and twenty-eight, respectively, whereas at the same time, rather tellingly, he continued to experience poor self-awareness as evidenced by his scores on the Awareness Questionnaire (Sherer, Oden, Bergloff, Levin, & High, 1998) of fifty (self-rating) and thirty-five (relative rating), and also the European Brain Injury Questionnaire (Teasdale et al., 1997) scores of 110 (self-rating) and 148 (relative rating). This case appears to lend some weight to the theory that poor self-awareness coupled with repeated failures can, over the longer term, result in, or at least contribute to, the onset of depression after traumatic brain injury. This patient has also been discussed in some depth elsewhere (Coetzer, 2006).

Psychological approaches to management

It is likely that psychopharmacological approaches to the treatment of depression have a very important role to play. For the interested reader, Alderfer, Arciniegas, and Silver (2005), O'Shanick (2006), and Turner-Stokes and colleagues (2005) provide guidance and overviews on the role of antidepressants in the treatment of depression in the context of traumatic brain injury. Moreover, Fleminger (2008), in a recent paper, provides some general guidance regarding the use of drugs to treat psychiatric complications of traumatic brain injury. In addition to pharmacological treatments, psychological therapy has an important role as an augmentation of drug treatments or, in some cases, as a stand-alone approach. Indeed, some authors have suggested that a psychological approach to managing depression after traumatic brain injury, including work with the family, should take preference (for example, Ponsford, 1995). In yet other circumstances, approaches such as occupational therapy or social work interventions to alleviate or eradicate environmental or social factors contributing to a person's depressed mood may be much more important than psychological therapy. In many cases, a combination of different professionals' input may be what is required to help the depressed patient and stem the often substantial disability that can result from depression. Nevertheless, psychological therapy can often make an important contribution to reducing the impact of depression and possibly equipping the person to better deal with any future relapses in mood.

For persons without traumatic brain injury who present with depression, cognitive–behaviour therapy has been established as an effective psychological treatment (Ekers, Richards, & Gilbody, 2008). Cognitive–behaviour therapy has also been reported to be effective in treating depression after traumatic brain injury (Ponsford, 1995; Williams, 2003). One of the most important symptoms of depression to be aware of is suicidal ideation. Here, general practitioners may be well placed to identify suicidal ideation and refer patients to appropriate mental health services (Simpson & Tate, 2007). Cognitive–behaviour therapy is thought to be well suited to help depressed patients who have suffered traumatic brain injury (Fleminger, 2008; Mateer & Sira, 2006). Khan-Bourne and Brown (2003) proposed that cognitive–behaviour therapy for depression in this population should be client-centred, clearly delineate presenting problems, identify the impact on functioning as well as activating situations, consider pre-injury factors, and, finally, identify the person's appraisal of the injury. Furthermore, cognitive–behaviour therapy should be adapted by using memory aids, shortening consultations, increasing the frequency of consultations, involving relatives or friends to assist with homework assignments such as behavioural activation, and, finally, the clinician should make use of summarizing as a strategy to keep patients focused during the consultation (*ibid.*). Earlier in this chapter, the relation between self-awareness and depression was explored, and it is worth noting that Khan-Bourne and Brown (2003) emphasized the importance of addressing this issue as part of a cognitive–behaviour therapy approach.

There are, of course, other psychological approaches to the management of depression after traumatic brain injury. Psychoanalytic approaches may be useful for some patients (e.g., Kaplan-Solms & Solms 2000; Lewis & Rosenberg, 1990). Changes in self or identity are associated with depression and, hence, may be important to address in psychotherapy (Cantor et al., 2005). We know that positive growth and deriving some sense of meaning after traumatic brain injury have been found to be inversely related to both depression and anxiety (Hawley & Joseph, 2008). Aniskiewicz (2007) proposed a mindfulness approach to the management of depression in this clinical population. He suggested that psychotherapy should aim to reduce suffering and promote an active engagement of life through goals (Aniskiewicz, 2007). This, on some level, appears somewhat similar to a behavioural activation approach (Veale, 2008), known to be an effective technique for treating depression. Aniskiewicz (2007) and Coetzer (2004) also emphasized the need for patients to be helped to accept life as it is now to overcome depressive symptoms in response to loss, and mindfulness meditation can help patients to do this (Aniskiewicz, 2007). Clearly, this approach has the potential not only to have an impact on depression, but, given its nature, is likely to prove beneficial for anxiety-related difficulties as well. This is an important point to consider in view of the very high co-morbidity that exists between anxiety and depression in many patients after traumatic brain injury.

Cognitive difficulties may be related to, and affect, disturbances of mood. Leon-Carrion (1997) asserted that cognitive impairment and mood disorder should be treated simultaneously, because one cannot expect an improvement in a patient's mood simply because of the spontaneous improvement of some of the person's cognitive impairment. The clinician should attempt to support the patient's basic necessities by focusing on providing hope, promoting self-esteem, offering affection, working on awareness, reinforcing the patient's preserved skills, and developing opportunities for expression of emotions (*ibid.*). According to Leon-Carrion (*ibid.*), this can be achieved by providing weekly psychotherapy sessions, encouraging participation in group therapy or group-based rehabilitation activities, ensuring access to family support or therapy, and identifying what is emotionally relevant for the patient to work on. In essence, this approach draws heavily on a more holistic model of brain injury rehabilitation and is probably best provided by post-acute neuro-rehabilitation services with appropriate levels of expertise and staffing.

In summary, considering both clinical practice and the above brief overview, the main approaches to psychological therapies to consider in major depressive disorder after traumatic brain injury include the following.

1. Cognitive–behaviour therapy.
2. Creating a psychotherapeutic environment conducive to the expression of emotions, including feelings related to loss, for example, person-centred therapy.
3. Behavioural activation.
4. Mindfulness approaches.
5. Psychodynamic and psychoanalytic approaches.
6. Combining psychotherapy with cognitive rehabilitation.

The next section very briefly explores the qualitative nature of patients' thoughts, behaviours, and emotions, as these sometimes present during psychological interventions. In addition, drawing upon clinical practice, more generic factors (see Chapter Four), including therapeutic strategies, the therapeutic relationship, and self-awareness, are discussed also.

Strategies and themes in psychotherapy

As is probably to be expected, the theme of loss can feature rather prominently in depression after traumatic brain injury, and may include the following. Patients often talk about and express emotions related to loss of role, financial independence, loss of identity, and loss of the ability to spontaneously take part in activities, among many others. Loss of identity can be a particularly potent factor in the evolution of depression in this population. Some patients report that a clinician's listening skills can play an important role in helping with exploring, expressing, and understanding the losses and grief that can accompany traumatic brain injury. Some other therapy strategies to help to address issues surrounding loss include attempts to derive meaning from the event or to create a new sense of purpose. Uncertainty about the future is often a significant psychological theme associated with depression after traumatic brain injury. From a psychotherapeutic perspective, it may be a useful strategy to look at the impossibility of actually predicting the future and help persons to live more in the here and now. Others may find the converse useful: assistance with setting small goals and actively working towards achieving these.

Some general strategies include the development of a robust therapeutic relationship, providing longer-term follow-up and easy access to the therapist during crises or relapses. Practitioners may also need to be aware that many of the feelings and thoughts patients may express or explore are entirely appropriate and, therefore, should not be tempted to necessarily challenge these or, indeed, expect quick changes to take place. A more useful approach for some patients would be to acknowledge their thoughts and feelings and, over time, more gradually work towards acceptance and new goals to pursue while living life as it is now for the person. A useful practical strategy to facilitate a more gradual therapeutic tempo under certain circumstances might entail spreading consultations out over longer periods of time. In effect, this means favouring length of time over number of sessions. This may be useful, in particular, when working with longer-term dynamic factors related to, for example, identity. Finally, given its relation to depression, clinicians should always be aware of, and actively assess for, problems of self-awareness and adjust their therapeutic strategy accordingly. Nevertheless, therapists should never attempt too vigorously to change impaired self-awareness; this type of approach is bound to fail and ultimately frustrate even the most resilient clinician.

Sometimes, more psychodynamic factors can also be important to consider as well. For example, one of my patients, who presented with enduring depression, reported ongoing feelings of guilt and disappointment. This was, for a long time, seen as being part of a depressed mood in response to loss of function, but it later transpired to be more complex than this. Certainly, some of the disappointment pertained to the losses she suffered, most notably her pre-injury carefree attitude to life and independence. But it later transpired, as the therapeutic relationship evolved, that the patient was her father's only daughter and that she had always felt a special relationship with him because of this. She always worked very hard at school, and, indeed, at most other activities, to earn his approval and to confirm her special relationship to him. The traumatic brain injury unfortunately rendered her unable to achieve to the very high levels she was accustomed to and she felt that she (and the brain injury) must be an ongoing disappointment for him (which was not, in reality, the case at all). It was from these dynamics that her feelings of guilt stemmed, and only through expressing and exploring these thoughts and feelings in psychotherapy could she move towards some form of resolution.

Summary points for this chapter

1. Depression is the most common of the mood and anxiety disorders after traumatic brain injury.
2. Clinicians should be alert to the potential presence of depression in patients with traumatic brain injury at any time point after the injury.
3. Major depressive disorder resulting from traumatic brain injury (where the biological factor of a brain injury is considered to be directly responsible for the mood disorder) should be diagnosed as a mood disorder due to a general medical condition.
4. It is important to recognize suicide potential in the presence of depression after traumatic brain injury.
5. Cognitive–behaviour therapy has been reported to be effective as part of a comprehensive treatment approach to managing depression after traumatic brain injury.
6. Some of the mindfulness-based approaches, as well as strategies to address loss and grief, can be helpful for some patients.

CHAPTER ELEVEN

Bipolar disorder

Introduction

The writer, Ernest Hemingway, was thought to have suffered from a few diagnoses, including bipolar disorder and traumatic brain injury (Martin, 2006). While diagnostic labels change with time, it is likely that difficulties related to mood swings have been around for some time. What is now termed bipolar disorder was previously known as manic–depressive disorder. In essence, *DSM-IV* (American Psychiatric Association, 1994) divides bipolar disorders into bipolar I disorder and bipolar II disorder. Bipolar I disorder represents the occurrence of one or more manic or mixed episodes. In contrast, bipolar II disorder is defined as the occurrence of one or more major depressive episodes, plus at least one hypo-manic episode. There are several other sub-divisions within the bipolar disorder spectrum. None of these is utilized in this chapter, as almost all the (limited) research to date has failed to specify typology. Accordingly, here, the disorder will then also be conceptualized as constituting, in essence, a cyclical fluctuation between episodes of depression and mania in a person. It is acknowledged, though, that in reality this is a much more complex mental disorder than portrayed by this simplistic definition.

A manic episode is defined as a period of unusually and persistently expansive, elevated, or irritable mood, lasting for at least a week (American Psychiatric Association, 1994). The main symptoms include grandiosity, a reduced need for sleeping, increased speech, as well as goal-directed activity, and excessive involvement in enjoyable activities that have a high potential for unpleasant consequences (for example, sexual indiscretions or poor financial investments) (*ibid*.). The disturbance causes impairment in social and occupational functioning. *DSM-IV* specifies that the symptoms are not due to a general medical condition, but that when this is the case, a mood disorder due to a general medical condition should be diagnosed (*ibid*.). A hypomanic episode is essentially the same as a manic episode, but of lesser intensity. A depressive episode has already been defined in the preceding chapter (Chapter Ten) as representing a two-week period of a depressed mood and symptoms such as insomnia and weight loss plus cognitive impairment, including poor concentration, among other symptoms.

Diagnostic issues

A hypomanic or manic episode can sometimes be mistaken for some of the common personality changes associated with traumatic brain injury. For example, increased irritability, reduced need for sleep, and general disinhibition or impulsiveness have all been described as part of the personality changes that can be present in persons with traumatic brain injury. Disinhibition, for example in social situations, including sexual behaviour, is common after traumatic brain injury also. Indeed, as we know, and based on its conceptualization in *DSM-IV* (American Psychiatric Association, 1994), personality change is considered to be common after traumatic brain injury. However, if it becomes clear over time that the patient's presentation actually more accurately reflects personality changes since the traumatic brain injury, rather than bipolar disorder, the correct diagnosis, according to *DSM-IV*, would be personality change due to a general medical condition, with traumatic brain injury in this case specified as part of the diagnosis and additionally recorded on Axis III. The *DSM-IV* specifies that bipolar disorder associated with traumatic brain injury should be diagnosed as a mood disorder due to a general medical condition, with the appropriate specifier (traumatic brain injury).

Returning to the point about the difficulty in disentangling personality changes from manic episodes, it should always be kept in mind, especially in the presence of a complex mental disorder such as bipolar disorder, that personality changes are unlikely to be the direct and sole result of brain damage. Many other factors besides purely biological ones are likely to contribute to what we define as personality changes after traumatic brain injury, including frustration, changes of roles in society, disturbed family or marital relations and identity, to mention only a few. In addition to biological factors, or sometimes even completely independently of the actual damage to the brain, these factors can also have a potent effect on the person's more enduring alterations in behavioural patterns or personality change after traumatic brain injury. Indeed, Yeates, Gracey, and McGrath (2008) asserted that there is not necessarily a direct link between neurological damage and what essentially constitutes personhood, and that "personality change" should rather be conceptualized within a biopsychosocial framework. This is clearly very important generally, and perhaps of particular relevance to bipolar disorder thought to have resulted from traumatic brain injury. A manic episode can easily be confused with personality change and, accordingly, the incorrect assumption made of causality directly due to brain injury.

Do manic episodes present differently in the context of traumatic brain injury? Given the nature of manic or, particularly, hypomanic episodes, and its obvious overlap with traumatic brain injury associated symptomatology as well as more ingrained behavioural patterns or personality traits, this is likely to be extremely difficult to determine. Miller (1993) suggested that post-traumatic mania might present as euphoria, poor insight, sleeplessness, flight of ideas, grandiosity, distractibility, increased libido, and pressured speech, among others. This, however, is remarkably similar to many of the symptoms currently listed for bipolar disorder in *DSM-IV* (American Psychiatric Association, 1994). Nevertheless, Miller (1993) also suggested that an irritable mood, as opposed to a euphoric mood, was possibly more common to manic episodes after traumatic brain injury. Finally, Miller advised that any sudden mood change within the context of traumatic brain injury should also alert the clinician to consider any potential subtle seizure-related activity. Below follow some suggestions pertaining to the identification of mania in the context of traumatic brain injury.

Symptom differentiation

When considering bipolar disorder, clinicians should always keep in mind the possible role of more enduring behaviour patterns that may complicate the presentation. Obtaining a longitudinal picture is essential, manic or hypomanic episodes should represent a change from baseline or usual behavioural patterns. Hence, based on observed clinical presentation, in the specific context of trau-matic brain injury, the following general differentiation between symptoms that may either lend weight to or alternatively reduce the index of suspicion of bipolar disorder, may assist practitioners during the process of making a differential diagnosis:

The most confusing symptoms potentially related to traumatic brain injury and not necessarily always bipolar disorder, are likely to include the following:

- distractibility or poor concentration;
- irritability;
- personality changes, including for example sexual disinhibition or impulsivity, or, for example, spending sprees.

The most telling symptoms indicative of the potential presence of a bipolar disorder, are likely to include:

- elevated mood;
- inflated self-esteem;
- the presence of clear, time-limited manic or hypomanic epi-sodes, representing a change in the person's usual post-injury behaviour patterns.

Bipolar disorder is undoubtedly very complicated to identify in the presence of traumatic brain injury and, therefore, the above should be seen as not representing anything else but suggestions or clinical guidelines to assist the clinician in making a differential diagnosis. Ultimately, the actual diagnosis and formulation in a given case would be based on much more information, including, for example, medical records, family interviews, and a thorough clinical assessment as a minimum. Family reports can be particularly important in identifying a fluctuating pattern in mood as opposed to more stable personality traits. Furthermore, an understanding of how common bipolar disorder actually is after traumatic brain injury can also prove helpful.

Bipolar disorder after traumatic brain injury

Not surprisingly, bipolar disorder appears to be somewhat rare after traumatic brain injury. Koponen and colleagues (2002), in their review of sixty persons with traumatic brain injury over an average of thirty years found that just fewer than two per cent of patients met the *DSM-IV* (American Psychiatric Association, 1994) diagnostic criteria for bipolar disorder. Shukla, Cook, Mukherjee, Godwin and Miller (1987) reported on secondary mania after traumatic brain injury in their patients and found a significant coexistence between mania and post trauma epilepsy. Moreover, a few case reports exist. Sayal, Ford, and Pipe (2000) reported a case of bipolar disorder following head injury in a fifteen-year-old girl, but this was after what was described by the authors as a "mild head injury". However, Handel, Ovitt, Spiro, and Rao (2007) provided an excellent case report of bipolar disorder after severe traumatic brain injury, discussed in greater detail below. Furthermore, Mustafa, Evrim, and Sari (2005) provided a case report of a 35-year old female who presented with a manic episode 23 days after sustaining a severe traumatic brain injury. Mustafa, Evrim, and Sari (2005) used *DSM-IV* (American Psychiatric Association, 1994) criteria to establish the diagnosis of a manic episode in their patient who sustained bilateral temporal lesions and suggest that clinicians need to be aware of this type of presentation after head trauma.

With regard to further group data, Jorge and colleagues (1993) investigated sixty-six consecutive traumatically brain injured patients and found that nine per cent of these patients had secondary mania. These authors used *DSM-III-R* criteria to determine the diagnosis of major affective disorder and manic episode, and reported that the manic episodes tended to be short, lasting, on average, about two months. Furthermore, it appeared that the presence of temporal basal polar lesions was associated with secondary mania in this group of patients. It should be noted that, of the six patients diagnosed with secondary mania in this study, five had a moderate traumatic brain injury and one a mild injury (*ibid.*). Nevertheless, this remains an important study, as it is one of the very few studies using group data to look specifically at bipolar type disorders after traumatic brain injury. Mortensen, Mors, Frydenberg, and Ewald (2003) reported that survivors of traumatic brain injury were approximately one and a half times more likely to develop bipolar disorder compared to persons without a history of traumatic brain injury. Finally, Van Reekum, Cohen, and Wong (2000), in their review, pooled the data from five studies and found that about four per cent (15/354) of patients presented with bipolar affective disorder up to about seven and a half years after suffering a traumatic brain injury.

Case study

Handel, Ovitt, Spiro, and Rao (2007) described a case of a fifty-eight-year-old male who sustained a traumatic brain injury in a motorcycle accident. Computed tomography scan of the brain in this case revealed the presence of a left fronto-parietal haemorrhage. After about four weeks the patient went home for further outpatient rehabilitation, and about one year after his injury he tried to return to his previous employment as a truck driver. It was at this point where the authors saw the patient again and made a diagnosis of depression, but, after somewhat dramatic changes in his presentation, one month later the diagnosis was changed to bipolar disorder when he presented with elevated mood, expansive self-attitude, and increased energy (*ibid.*). The patient was followed up and, over the longer term, presented with what the authors termed personality changes, most probably, in their view, representing an exaggeration of his pre-morbid personality characteristics (*ibid.*).

The case reported by Handel, Ovitt, Spiro, and Rao (*ibid.*) is of considerable interest. It provides a longitudinal perspective on the development of bipolar disorder after traumatic brain injury. Furthermore, it highlights how difficult it can be to disentangle personality changes after traumatic brain injury from some of the symptoms of bipolar disorder. In general, it would be necessary to see patients over a much longer period for follow-up before commenting on possible personality changes and to always consider collateral family accounts of pre-morbid personality characteristics as well as post-injury changes. Indeed, for this reason, it is very important to keep in mind the work of Yeates, Gracey, and McGrath (2008) and, accordingly, to remain alert to the possibility that what is often termed to be "personality changes" may, in some cases, have very little direct biological links to the brain damage the patient suffered. This can be especially relevant where behaviours gradually evolve after traumatic brain injury, implying, perhaps, that factors other than the biological may be contributing to the person's enduring changes in behaviour. The case report by Handel, Ovitt, Spiro, and Rao (2007) also provides some useful suggestions regarding the treatment of bipolar disorder after traumatic brain injury. Finally, this is one of the very few case studies in the literature pertaining to bipolar disorder after traumatic brain injury where the findings from the neuropsychological assessment were included also.

Psychological approaches to management

Unfortunately, the literature pertaining to the psychological management of bipolar disorder after traumatic brain injury is very sparse. It is highly likely that psychological therapy has a more minor or adjunctive role to play in the management of bipolar disorder after traumatic brain injury. Oster, Anderson, Filley, Wortzel, and Arciniegas (2008) provide a description of the pharmacological management of mania secondary to traumatic brain injury. Handel, Ovitt, Spiro, and Rao (2007) reported, in their case of bipolar disorder after traumatic brain injury, that, in addition to pharmacological management, it was important to also provide individual psychotherapy to the patient as well as support and psychoeducation for the relative of the patient. Indeed, family therapy has generally been proposed as constituting an important aspect of neuro-rehabilitation programmes (e.g., Bowen, 2007; Yeates, Henwood, Gracey, & Evans, 2007). As we know, lack of insight or poor awareness can be a real clinical nettle in bipolar disorder after traumatic brain injury, and, in this regard, the work of Yeates, Henwood, Gracey, and Evans (2007) perhaps has particular relevance. These authors linked the important problem of impaired self-awareness and families' accounts of the problems their relatives were experiencing and, accordingly, made suggestions for providing family therapy in this context (*ibid.*). It appeared that, for example, availability of sense-making opportunities and the use of pre-injury meanings accounted for some of the contextual factors related to families' account of their relatives' problems (*ibid.*). Others have suggested that problem-solving training for families may be useful (for example, Rivera, Elliott, Berry, & Grant, 2008). Perhaps some of these, as well as psychoeducation strategies, could be important to consider when working with persons with bipolar disorder after traumatic brain injury.

For persons with bipolar disorder without a history of traumatic brain injury, strategies to improve treatment adherence (Gaudiano, Weinstock, & Miller, 2008), problem solving, and cognitive–behaviour therapy (Miklowitz, Goodwin, Bauer, & Geddes, 2008) have been found to show some promise. Moreover, family therapy, interpersonal therapy, cognitive–behaviour therapy and psychoeducation, when used in conjunction with pharmacotherapy, have been found to lengthen time to relapse (Miklowitz, 2006). With regard to individual psychotherapeutic input for persons with a history of traumatic brain injury, it has been proposed that regular cognitive–behaviour therapy, as well as maintaining routines and structure in the person's everyday life, were important to provide as additional treatment strategies (Handel, Ovitt, Spiro, & Rao, 2007). Indeed, some persons with bipolar disorder following traumatic brain injury can present with problematic cognitions related to especially manic episodes, and it may well be here that an approach such as cognitive–behaviour therapy has a contribution to make. Similarly, maintaining the person's routines can possibly go a long way towards meaningful engagement in activities and so lessen the impact of depressive episodes. Finally, as in almost all neuro-rehabilitation programmes, patient education and provision of information may, one hopes, significantly reduce feelings of confusion and anxiety surrounding the meaning of the person's at times unpredictable clinical presentation.

In summary, based on the very limited guidance from the literature and considering pointers from clinical practice also, the main psychological therapies to consider as an adjunctive to pharmacotherapy in bipolar disorder after traumatic brain injury appear to include the following:

- cognitive–behaviour therapy;
- psychoeducation or family therapy for relatives;
- strategies aimed at maintaining the patient's routines.

The next section again draws upon my clinical practice, and very briefly explores the qualitative nature of patients' thoughts, behaviours, and emotions as they may present during the process of providing psychological interventions. Some generic factors pertaining to psychotherapy (see Chapter Four) are mentioned also, including self-awareness and the therapeutic relationship.

Themes encountered in psychotherapy

In view of the unpredictability and, at times, poor self-awareness associated with bipolar disorder after traumatic brain injury in some persons, two generic factors are perhaps of greater relevance when working psychotherapeutically with this population. First, the formation and maintenance of a strong therapeutic relationship is of utmost importance. In many cases, persons will most probably have to be followed up very long-term, or even for life. Having at least one clinician as a constant feature in their care can be invaluable for many people, especially so in a disorder where relapses can occur at any stage and, unfortunately, often at the most inconvenient times. To have someone to turn to in the aftermath of these episodes to try to make emotional sense of events can be really helpful for some persons. The main role for the clinician here is probably psychological containment. Generally, some of the emotions expressed by patients after manic episodes can include embarrassment, disbelief, and guilt. Guilt can be present especially where indiscreet sexual activity or impulsive spending took place, for example. Moreover, these feelings can perhaps make the person more psychologically vulnerable to experiencing a depressive episode.

Second, self-awareness is of particular importance. For patients, understanding the nature of this complex and very disabling disorder is important for obvious reasons. Not knowing what the disorder is, what may happen, and how it may affect everyday life, can result in serious anxiety or worry for many patients unfamiliar with bipolar disorder after traumatic brain injury. However, psychoeducation should, ideally in the first instance, be provided from a traumatic brain injury background when the disorder clearly has its onset after suffering such injury and, in addition, information should be provided about bipolar disorder. With regard to the latter, for some persons it may be useful to do some work pertaining to the early self-recognition of symptoms which may be signalling an imminent relapse. This strategy is, of course, less likely to succeed where the patient presents with poor insight. From a more psychological perspective, bipolar disorder following traumatic brain injury can, for many, constitute a dramatic change in who they are and some work with identity can be useful. For some persons, it is important to come to the insight that manic and depressive episodes represent constellations of symptoms, and not necessarily the most important or only defining characteristics of their post-injury identities. This, of course, is not unique to bipolar disorder, and most probably is equally relevant to all the anxiety and mood disorders covered in this book

Summary points for this chapter

1. Bipolar disorder is most probably not very common after traumatic brain injury.
2. Personality changes associated with traumatic brain injury may mimic some of the symptoms of bipolar disorder.
3. The concept of personality change after traumatic brain injury, especially in the context of bipolar disorder in this population, is complex and perhaps unlikely to represent only direct biological effects of the injury.

4. If bipolar disorder presents for the first time after traumatic brain injury and the latter is considered to be directly relevant to the aetiology, a mood disorder due to a general medical condition should be diagnosed.

5. Individual psychological approaches to management as an adjunctive to pharmacological approaches include cognitive–behaviour therapy and ensuring structure and routines in the patient's daily life, while providing family therapy could possibly be the most important psychological approach to consider.

CHAPTER TWELVE

Special populations

Introduction

Traumatic brain injury appears to affect all groups of people. Thus, anxiety and mood disorders after traumatic brain injury do not necessarily present in young adults only. While the bulk of patients who come to our attention are young adults (especially males) of working age, many are also much younger, or, indeed, older (see also Chapter One). These patients are most likely to have unique needs. Furthermore, there are many other vulnerable and sometimes "hidden" populations. For example, refugees, who may have come from environments with very high levels of violence, or from war-torn countries, are possibly more likely to have sustained a traumatic brain injury. Poor countries may have less developed roads and infrastructure, perhaps increasing the risk of sustaining a traumatic brain injury while travelling. These countries generally, but not always, tend also to have less developed health-care systems, with patients who have sustained a traumatic brain injury accordingly having less access to appropriate acute care and post-acute rehabilitation. Moreover, residents of these countries may struggle economically, another potent factor to consider in brain injury rehabilitation. These are just a few of the potential special populations or situations clinicians and researchers need to know more about.

There are, of course, other factors that we need to be aware of also. Some of these pertain to language and culture, among other things. Language is, without a doubt, a significant factor. Many of the rehabilitation interventions, including specifically psycho-therapy or speech and language therapy, are heavily dependent upon providers of healthcare being able to speak fluently the lan-guage of patients and their families. Sometimes, this can appear subtle: for example, where a patient is bilingual, being able to speak as a second language the first (only) language of the clinician. But, because a traumatic brain injury often affects language abilities, patients may now struggle to express themselves in what is, after all, their second (or even third) language. This can result in many problems, including misdiagnosis of cognitive impairment, limited chances of assessing with any accuracy more qualitative aspects of anxiety and mood, or the patient simply not being "heard" by the clinical team. While culture can be closely tied to language, it is crucial to be sensitive to this aspect as an entity in its own right. The reason for this is that even where persons speak the same language (say, English) but come from different parts of the world, they quite often have very different customs and ways of doing things. At other times, it may be far more obvious that there are important cultural differences to consider and respect when providing reha-bilitation for the person with traumatic brain injury. We will now consider some of the more frequently encountered special popula-tions.

Children

Children, unfortunately, represent a particularly vulnerable group in society when it comes to traumatic brain injury. Traumatic brain injury can result in severe disruption of children's and adolescents' schooling, social development, eventual employment status, and physical development, among many other things. For example, Taylor and colleagues (2008) investigated some of the consequences of traumatic brain injury on children, including cognitive functioning. Moreover, it should be remembered that, for children, when compared to adults, the association between increased age and poorer outcome appears to be different, if not opposite, from that observed in adults with traumatic brain injury (Niedzwecki, 2008). Younger children may, thus, be particularly vulnerable. Even where children make a good physical recovery after traumatic brain injury, other impairments can result in significant disability. It should also be remembered that the disability children present with after traumatic brain injury will, in the majority of cases, be very long term. Bedell (2008) examined data on 176 children between the ages of five and eighteen years who had suffered a traumatic brain injury and who received inpatient rehabilitation. While these children achieved good gains with regard to mobility and self-care, their social function was poorer than the expected norm (Bedell, 2008). This finding could have significant implications for schooling and socialization later on for these children with traumatic brain injury, as social functioning is fundamental to many adulthood tasks and responsibilities and, thus, can prove to have a crippling effect in many areas.

Regrettably, there appears to be limited research on anxiety and mood disorders after traumatic brain injury sustained in childhood, but, from the data available, we know that children are vulnerable to the development of these mental disorders following traumatic brain injury. Grados and colleagues (2008) examined eighty children between the ages of six and eighteen years within one year of having suffered a severe traumatic brain injury and found that 29.2% had obsessive–compulsive symptoms. Furthermore, other anxiety disorders, including post traumatic stress disorder, and also manic episodes and depression were found to be strongly associated with the onset of obsessive–compulsive symptoms after traumatic brain injury in this group (*ibid.*). Finally, the nature of these obsessive–compulsive symptoms were related to worries about cleanliness and disease, whereas the actions or behaviours concerned ordering, mental rigidity, and excessive cleaning (*ibid.*). Depression also appeared to be common after childhood traumatic brain injury (Kirkwood et al., 2000; Bloom et al., 2001), as was post traumatic stress disorder in young children six to twelve months post-injury (Levi, Drotar, Yeates, & Taylor, 1999). With regard to slightly older patients, Viguier, Dellatolas, Gasquet, Martin, and

Choquet (2001) reported that, in their sample of young persons between fourteen and twenty-five years, depression and anxiety were common and that depression appeared to be related to impaired self-awareness as well as behavioural and cognitive difficulties.

Which factors influence the onset and specific clinical presentation of anxiety and depression in this clinical population? Age is one factor that appears to have an effect on the nature of symptomatology in childhood traumatic brain injury. Geraldina and colleagues (2003) assessed ninety-six traumatically brain-injured children of eighteen years or younger, one year after injury, and found that younger children showed internalization, including withdrawal or becoming more closed off, whereas older children or adolescents displayed more behavioural problems, including aggressiveness or hyperactivity. Barker-Collo (2007) reported that increased anxiety or depression was associated with older children. However, there are factors other than age to consider also. Luis and Mittenberg (2002) used *DSM-IV* (American Psychiatric Association, 1994) diagnostic criteria and assessed sixty-one children with traumatic brain injury, discovering that the severity of the injury and post-injury stress levels were the best predictors of new onset anxiety or mood disorders. Interestingly, the relation with cognitive impairment is not straightforward, and Kirkwood and colleagues (2000) reported that depressive symptoms were not related to cognitive impairment in their group of eighty-nine children with moderate to severe traumatic brain injury. This seems to suggest that factors other than cognitive impairment *per se* may be associated with emotional difficulties: for example, reduced skills for interpersonal functioning and subsequent isolation in the social domain.

It is not only cognitive impairment or reduced skills that can contribute to anxiety and depression in children who have suffered traumatic brain injury. Barker-Collo (2007) examined seventy-four children between the ages of four and thirteen years and compared these children to a control group consisting of children with severe orthopaedic injuries (but not traumatic brain injury). More significant anxiety was associated with increased age at the time of injury and a shorter period of inpatient rehabilitation (*ibid.*). Interestingly, the sub-group of children with moderate traumatic brain injury had higher levels of anxiety and depression compared to those with mild or severe injuries (*ibid.*). The author concluded that, with moderate traumatic brain injury, children may present with better preserved self-awareness and the potential implication might well be that psychological issues related to loss, grief, and mortality may need to be addressed in therapy (*ibid.*). Clearly, then, we need to be aware that children need more than physical rehabilitation and that psychological factors are important in the onset and evolution of anxiety and depression in this population also.

Ethnic minorities

Disappointingly, there are racial disparities in outcome after traumatic brain injury also. Bowman, Martin, Sharar, and Zimmerman (2007) reviewed 56,482 patients with moderate to severe traumatic brain injury admitted to trauma centres and found that Black and Asian persons experienced increased in-hospital mortality and, for survivors, Hispanic and Black persons were less likely to be discharged to post-acute rehabilitation centres. Shafi and colleagues (2007) also found that patients from ethnic minority groups were less likely to have access to neuro-rehabilitation services. Furthermore, Marquez de la Plata and colleagues (2007) investigated 476 patients with traumatic brain injury and found that, while health insurance, injury severity, and age had a significant influence on access to rehabilitation services, more severe disability was found among Hispanic persons and Spanish speakers compared to non-Hispanic White persons and non-Hispanic English speakers. What about longer-term outcome? Arango-Lasprilla and colleagues (2007) retrospectively reviewed 3065 persons with moderate to severe traumatic brain injury with regard to functional outcome at one year follow-up, and found that Hispanic persons had significantly poorer functional outcome, even after controlling for other factors. These racial disparities in mortality and access to neuro-rehabilitation, and, ultimately, outcome, clearly represent an extremely disappointing and unacceptable situation that is in dire need of addressing at a governmental public health and policy level.

What is the situation when other factors, such as age, are considered within minority groups? Rather predictably, the situation does not appear hopeful. While data from thirteen American states revealed that most (84%) hospitalizations related to traumatic brain injuries in older adults occurred among White persons, for those aged 65–74, the highest rate was among American Indian and Native Alaskan persons (Coronado, Thomas, Sattin, & Johnson, 2005). Moreover, Nelson and colleagues (2007) found that traumatic brain injury was present in 394 out of 2687 (nearly 15%) of their sample of American Indian persons, and that one year or later after injury, mood and anxiety disorders were common. What about rehabilitation and outcomes for older people from ethnic minorities? Chang, Ostir, Kuo, Granger, and Ottenbacher (2008) looked at 9240 older patients (sixty-five years or older) who received inpatient rehabilitation after traumatic brain injury. In this group, it was revealed that older Black and older Hispanic persons with traumatic brain injury were more likely to be discharged home compared to older White persons (*ibid.*). What about children from ethnic minorities? Haider and colleagues (2007) reviewed 41,122 children between the ages of two and sixteen who had suffered a traumatic brain injury and reported that Black children had worse clinical and functional outcome when they were discharged. These are particularly disturbing figures, and there is clearly a need for further research and service development initiatives to attempt to address some of these unacceptable disparities.

Refugees

Refugees often flee their countries of origin because of high levels of violence, torture by oppressive political regimes, or civil war, among other events. These events can, for obvious reasons, increase the likelihood of sustaining a traumatic brain injury in this population. And clearly, given the circumstances under which these persons leave their home countries, the potential for anxiety and mood disorders must be very high, perhaps especially so for disorders like post traumatic stress disorder and major depressive disorder. Refugees, or displaced persons, may find it difficult to adjust in their new countries and may find it almost impossible, at least initially, to navigate unfamiliar health and social care systems. Often, there may be language barriers further complicating the person's ability to secure appropriate healthcare. This may possibly result in refugees presenting somewhat later than the norm after sustaining a traumatic brain injury and, by implication, also sometimes after a considerable period of time has elapsed since exposure to traumatic life events. Finally, adjusting to life in a new country, the loss of friends and family, as well as the possible economical adversity they may face, can, of course, also affect this group's mental health. Hence, it is important not only to focus on the presence of a traumatic brain injury, but also to consider all the relevant social, cultural, and psychological factors.

There is, unfortunately, very limited research available about traumatic brain injury and co-morbid mental illness in refugee populations. One notable study is that reported by Mollica, Henderson, and Tor (2002), who investigated traumatic brain injury and mental illness in Cambodian survivors of mass violence under the Pol Pot regime, and who were displaced and living in Camp 2 for up to ten years at the time the study was conducted. Traumatic brain injury was associated with major depressive disorder and post traumatic stress disorder in this population, with the association slightly weaker for the latter (*ibid.*). There were a couple of limitations to this study, though, most notably the relatively modest number of identified persons with traumatic brain injury, as well as the fact that the presence of traumatic brain injury could, for unavoidable reasons (for example, no access to past medical records), be identified only by self-report. Nevertheless, this remains an extremely important study into mental illness and traumatic brain injury among displaced persons. These authors rightly conclude that it is surprising that traumatic brain injury in refugees has traditionally not been recognized as a potentially major public health concern, and advise that it is very important to identify symptoms of major depressive disorder and post traumatic stress disorder in refugees who have suffered traumatic brain injury (*ibid.*). Furthermore, MacDonald, Mummery, and Heaney (2001) reminded frontline practitioners working with refugees to be alert to the possibility of traumatic brain injury in patients who have been tortured, and to specifically examine these patients for frontal lobe symptoms, including cognitive impairment, so that these patients can be referred to appropriate rehabilitation services.

Rural populations

Persons living in rural areas often have less access to healthcare, especially specialist healthcare, including both acute and post-acute brain injury rehabilitation programmes. For example, Johnstone, Nossaman, Schopp, Holmquist, and Rupright (2002) report that, in rural Missouri, there was a lack of specialist rehabilitation services and clinicians providing treatment for persons with traumatic brain injury. Moreover, Schootman and Fuortes (1999) report that persons with a history of traumatic brain injury who were living in a rural area had poorer health outcomes and were more dependent than those living in urban areas. Furthermore, rural areas often lack social, recreational (tertiary), educational, and employment opportunities, among other things. Hence, functional outcomes, such as return to employment, may, in some cases, be poor (e.g., Coetzer, Hayes, & Du Toit, 2002). These authors found that, for sixty-five persons of an average age of approximately thirty-six years who were at least two years post-injury, only about twenty-five per cent were in employment, compared to eighty per cent being in employment pre-injury (*ibid.*). The young average age of persons in this group is particularly worrying.

Nevertheless, poor outcome after traumatic brain injury for people living in rural areas has not been universally reported. Indeed, some studies have found no differences between rural and urban populations' outcomes after traumatic brain injury (e.g., Gontkovsky, Sherer, Nick, Nakase-Thompson, & Yablon, 2006; Harradine et al., 2004). In fact, rural areas, because of the social support and potentially higher quality of life, might even be a moderator as regards outcome after traumatic brain injury, according to some researchers (e.g., Farmer, Clark, & Sherman, 2003). Nevertheless, while it remains unclear whether rural populations have poorer, or perhaps even better, outcomes after traumatic brain injury, it is likely that services for those who inevitably do present with anxiety or mood disorders will be more sparse or perhaps even absent in these remote areas. Even where appropriate services do exist, patients and their relatives would have to travel much further to access these services. Accordingly, there is a pressing need for innovative service development initiatives to ensure that more equitable rehabilitation services are available to residents of rural areas.

In very remote, isolated, and small communities, basic rehabilitation interventions or advice may be provided by means of tele-medicine. This, while obviously less than ideal, can sometimes be the only way to provide at least some input to these communities.

Socio-economic deprivation

We know that traumatic brain injury is one of the leading causes of death and disability, especially among younger people in the UK, the USA, and most other developed countries of the world. However, traumatic brain injury is a particularly serious and contentious public health problem in developing countries also. For example, Nantulya and Reich (2002) reported the staggering statistic that about ninety per cent of the disability resulting from road traffic collisions was to be found in developing countries. There is some evidence that acute outcome for traumatic brain injury is worse in developing countries (e.g., Harris et al., 2008). Developing countries most often have very high levels of socio-economic deprivation, making it less likely that disabled persons would be receiving adequate rehabilitation. This may, in part, be responsible for injury resulting in very high levels of disability in these countries. In addition, it is likely that the effects of traumatic brain injury in these countries or communities would tend to have a much wider impact on, for example, families. In these situations, relatives would inevitably have to look after those severely injured victims for whom there are not only no rehabilitation services, but also no appropriate facilities for long-term care.

People from the lower socio-economic strata (Bruns & Hauser, 2003) living in developing countries represented particularly vulnerable groups with a huge potential for poor psychosocial outcome. To add to the problem, economic and social characteristics of the survivors of traumatic brain injury's neighbourhood have been reported to have an effect on outcome additional to, for example, injury severity or patient demographics (Corrigan & Bogner, 2008). Furthermore, consideration must, of course, be given to the young age group in which the incidence peaks in order to understand the catastrophic economic consequences of traumatic brain injury on the potential future workforce of developing countries. Traumatic brain injury is not only disproportionately present in young people, most notably young males, it also has a tri-modal distribution affecting young children, young adults, and the elderly (Bruns & Hauser, 2003), with less post-acute services sometimes being available to the young and the elderly. Young adults represent the current workforce of a country; children, the future. Levin (2004) commented on the devastating effect of a high incidence of traumatic brain injury in children within the South African context, where socio-econic deprivation and limited rehabilitation resources pose serious difficulties. Developing countries can ill afford the substantial long-term economic consequences that inevitably follow traumatic brain injury.

What are the potential effects on patients' emotional wellbeing? While socio-economic deprivation may make people more vulnerable to sustaining a traumatic brain injury in the first place, it is important to remember that it may also be a potent independent factor contributing to anxiety and mood disorders after traumatic brain injury. Indeed, Grados and colleagues (2008), in their study, found that the new onset of anxiety and mood disorders, including obsessive–compulsive symptoms after severe traumatic brain injury, was associated with, among other things, psychosocial adversity. Furthermore, Kirkwood and colleagues (2000), in an earlier study, reported that socially disadvantaged children were more vulnerable to developing depression after traumatic brain injury. Regarding the rehabilitation of persons from developing countries, Judd (2003) proposes a community-based rehabilitation approach to address, in particular, the emotional difficulties resulting from traumatic brain injury in this population. Judd proposed that the training of community-based rehabilitation workers should include, among other neuro-rehabilitation principles, an understanding of emotional rehabilitation, by considering the patient's pre-injury personality, emotional reactions to the injury and disability, and, finally, the organic or biological factors associated with brain damage resulting in changes in emotional functioning.

Older adults

Older adults represent a group that is particularly vulnerable to sustaining traumatic brain injury, probably to some extent because of maintaining independence up to much later in life now, through driving, walking, and other activities that in turn may result in accidents. Traumatic brain injury rates for the elderly also appear to have increased over recent years, with falls resulting in traumatic brain injury becoming increasingly more frequent (Fletcher, Khalid, & Mallonee, 2007). Indeed, Bouras and colleagues (2007) also reported high incidences of falls resulting in traumatic brain injury in their group of elderly patients. Outcome after traumatic brain injury sustained in later life generally appears to be poorer for most persons (Thompson, McCormick, & Kagan, 2006). There are significant gaps in our knowledge with regard to outcomes in elderly persons who have suffered traumatic brain injury, and a "one size fits all" approach to the management of this group is likely to miss the special characteristics that define this group of persons (*ibid.*). For example, one of the factors to consider in this population is the issue of cognitive decline in old age. While there has been some suggestion that traumatic brain injury can accelerate cognitive decline in those older adults thought to be genetically vulnerable, this has not been a universal finding (Ashman et al., 2008). Hence, rehabilitation should perhaps not be assumed to be contra-indicated when older adults present after traumatic brain injury.

Unfortunately, most of the limited numbers of outcome studies looking at older adults have produced somewhat sombre results. With regard to acute care, persons over the age of seventy-four were found to be less likely to respond favourably to intensive care or to survive neuro-surgical intervention (Bouras et al., 2007). Post-acute outcome also appears to be worse for older adults. For example, Rapoport and colleagues (2006) studied sixty-nine persons aged fifty years or above who had sustained a traumatic brain injury and compared this group with a control group of seventy-nine persons. One year post-injury, the persons with traumatic brain injury experienced poorer psychosocial outcome, more cognitive impairment, and reported more psychological distress (*ibid.*). Moreover, Colantonio, Ratcliff, Chase, and Vernich (2004) reported increasing physical health problems as well as psychological difficulties in those persons who were aging and who had a history of traumatic brain injury. However, it has fortunately not been a universally bleak picture. Yap and Chua (2008), in a retrospective study of older patients in Singapore, reported that older persons do appear to benefit from rehabilitation. They found a significant improvement in outcome measures, and that ninety per cent of their patients were discharged home after rehabilitation. While these results were encouraging, there were a couple of limitations to Yap and Chua's study, including small sample size (fifty-two persons) and the relatively younger age of participants (patients were fifty-five years or older).

With regard to anxiety and mood disorders, it should be very likely for the elderly to experience difficulties in these areas after traumatic brain injury. As outlined above, this group appears to present with more physical difficulties, cognitive impairment, and generally poorer outcome. It is probable that these impairments would, in many cases, result in significant disability, including loss of independence, in persons who often, because of their age, may have been socially isolated already or at least not in employment any more. Clearly, there is significant potential for emotional difficulties, including depression, to be present in this population because of environmental and psychological factors, including isolation. Regarding research findings pertaining to anxiety or mood disorders in this population, Menzel (2008) recently reviewed the literature and reported that the prevalence of depression after traumatic brain injury was between twenty-one and thirty-seven per cent among older adults. Furthermore, Coronado, Thomas, Sattin, and Johnson (2005) reported a high incidence of depression among elderly persons who had sustained a traumatic brain injury through falling. These are rather sobering figures, especially when considering that it is unlikely that there will be as wide a range of specialist rehabilitation services available as, say, to young adults with traumatic brain injury. The next section contains a case report about an older adult who sustained a severe traumatic brain injury.

Case report

This case is intended to highlight some of the specific difficulties faced by older adults who sustain a serious traumatic brain injury. As reported by Menzel (2008), depression after traumatic brain injury is often present in older adults. Mr M was in his early sixties and in full-time employment when he was severely injured in a road traffic collision. He sustained multiple injuries, including internal injuries, fractures, and a severe traumatic brain injury. His Glasgow Coma Scale (Teasdale & Jennet, 1974) score at the scene of the accident was 6/15. By the time he arrived at hospital, his score had improved to 14/15. A computed tomography scan of the brain revealed a right-sided subdural haematoma, without any midline shift. No neurosurgery was performed. However, Mr M spent a considerable amount of time in hospital, initially in intensive care, and subsequently for repeated surgery related to his numerous orthopaedic injuries, before being discharged to a community hospital closer to home for a period of convalescence. Here, he received further physical rehabilitation, including physiotherapy and occupational therapy, before being discharged home. He was unable to return to employment. Mr M was referred for community-based brain injury rehabilitation and was seen initially for an assessment approximately one year after he was injured in the collision.

Mr M, predictably, given the very extensive injuries he sustained, presented with profound physical disability resulting from the numerous impairments in function associated with his injuries. Furthermore, clinical assessment also revealed that he was experiencing cognitive difficulties, most notably in the areas of information processing or attention and, in addition, short-term memory (new learning). However, most striking was his presentation with a depressed mood. The magnitude of this was severe, as borne out by several qualitative observations. For example, while not suicidal, he saw no real purpose in his further life, felt guilty about the effects his disability had on his family, felt worthless, and felt ashamed that he could not perform tasks that were simple to perform prior to his injury. The latter especially resulted in huge frustration for him. This was entirely understandable as he was professionally, intellectually, and recreationally very active and involved prior to his injury. Now he could not perform, for example, very simple DIY jobs, a state of affairs he found very difficult to reconcile with the person he was prior to the accident. He tended to mull over this, increasingly becoming more depressed.

Of further note was the fact that Mr M did not present with any of the somatic markers of depression. He did not, for example, have any problems with his sleep pattern or appetite. Finally, with regard to other clinical symptoms, his attentional problems and fatigue were thought to be clearly related to his traumatic brain injury. A diagnosis of a major depressive episode was made, based in the main on the significant qualitative indicators of a depressed mood, in the absence of most of the usual accompanying somatic symptoms. Mr M was provided with psychological therapy as part of his overall rehabilitation to try to help with his depressed mood. One of the main themes during psychotherapy concerned his role or identity following the injury, and how, at his age, coupled with his extensive disability, it was difficult to find new meaning and purpose in life. Part of the psychotherapy intervention, hence, focused on defining new purpose and meaning, coupled to defining personally relevant goals. With regard to the latter, Mr M reported deriving the most significant meaning from voluntary work. More generally, involvement in meaningful activities, besides helping him to define new purpose during this stage of his life, tended to have a potent effect on reducing the rumination that helped to maintain his depressed mood.

Implications for clinical practice

There are a few rather obvious implications for clinical practice and service development stemming from what we currently know about traumatic brain injury in special populations. The main points to be aware of are as follows. We do need to be more aware of, and sensitive to, minority groups' potential special needs resulting from traumatic brain injury. For example, in socio-economically deprived groups, return to employment initiatives (for those who can achieve this goal) should be prioritized, as this can be an ecologically very valid rehabilitation goal for some individuals, which may also serve to reduce the risk of the onset of anxiety and mood disorders. Regarding other special populations, sometimes clinicians may have a more important role than necessarily assumed in advocating for policy changes or service development initiatives, for example, where racial disparities in access to rehabilitation services persist. Similarly, this can apply to lack of rural service provision also.

An important point about the management of older adults who have sustained a traumatic brain injury relates to their perceived suitability for rehabilitation. Despite what research findings appear to tell us, never in the individual case assume that older adults will automatically have a poorer outcome. I have, on many occasions, been hugely surprised by excellent outcomes in this group. Remember that older adults may have their own unique strengths, for example, life experience, including, in many cases, the ability to overcome adversity. Consider also the following points about other special populations. Be sensitive to the needs of children, but equally so to the needs of their families when planning rehabilitation interventions. Remember to involve all the relevant agencies that can potentially contribute to children's rehabilitation and ongoing education. When working with refugees, always check for a possible history of traumatic brain injury. Finally, a sensitivity for cultural and language differences is essential to delivering effective clinical practice under all circumstances.

Summary points for this chapter

1. Not only young adults are vulnerable to suffering traumatic brain injury.
2. Some groups appear to be potentially more vulnerable to the development of anxiety and mood disorders post-injury: for example, those from lower socio-economic strata.
3. Racial disparities in outcome after traumatic brain injury are particularly worrying and are in urgent need of intervention at a more strategic level.
4. Minority groups tend to have less access to specialist rehabilitation services and there is a need to address these and other inequities at a service development level.
5. While older adults tend to have poorer outcome, many can and do achieve good outcomes following rehabilitation

CHAPTER THIRTEEN

Conclusions and future directions

Introduction

This book attempts to cover the assessment, identification, formulation, and psychological management of anxiety and mood disorders in persons with a history of traumatic brain injury. Perhaps, then, one of the fundamental questions in this book pertains to why practitioners need to be competent at performing a bedside mental status examination and cognitive screening. The simplistic answer here is that, within the context of a patient's biological, social, and psychological history, this clinical assessment helps to identify the potential presence of a mood or anxiety disorder after traumatic brain injury. However, the diagnosis, while essential as a starting point, is only that: a starting point for providing a biopsychosocial formulation that endeavours to explain not only what the clinical presentation is, but also to explain why. For example, a person who has sustained a traumatic brain injury may present with a depressed mood because of a combination of factors. Some of these may include increased self-awareness (perhaps as a function of time since injury), loss of identity and role, inability to return to work (possibly in the context of pre-existing perfectionistic personality traits and current cognitive impairment), and pre-injury biological vulnerability (history) to depression. Clearly, formulation further explains or refines the diagnosis and, as such, is an integral part of the overall diagnostic process. It also highlights why history is so important. We cannot hope to formulate and understand our patients without knowing their pre-injury histories.

In this book, psychotherapy as an approach to rehabilitation is emphasized. Psychotherapy should not, however, be seen as an intervention in isolation, since, for most persons, multi-professional rehabilitation plans are likely to be indicated. In fact, pharmacological, social, and occupational interventions in combination with other therapies often constitute the major components of many individuals' rehabilitation. Furthermore, cognitive rehabilitation has a very important role in brain injury rehabilitation. Nevertheless, psychotherapy, specifically where a person is presenting with anxiety or depression, has an important adjunctive role in the management of emotional difficulties after traumatic brain injury. Often, psychotherapy is one of the very few treatment options for persons with anxiety or mood disorders in the context of traumatic brain injury. Sadly, in many cases, there are limited resources to provide these patients with this potentially very important component of their rehabilitation. It is to be hoped that, in the future, commissioners and funders of post-acute brain injury rehabilitation services will consider this as well as other gaps in service delivery. This chapter concludes the book with brief overviews of three areas with potential implications for the future management of patients with anxiety and mood disorders after traumatic brain injury: diagnostic approaches, research, and training.

Diagnostic approaches

DSM-IV (American Psychiatric Association, 1994) is due to be updated and replaced in the near future. *DSM-V* is likely to be published by mid 2012. While *DSM-IV* (American Psychiatric Association, 1994) is probably viewed with suspicion by many, the fact remains that many more clinicians all over the world use it on a daily basis and this diagnostic system is likely to be here to stay. With regard to the updating, already there have been several suggestions on how to improve on the current version of this diagnostic system. For example, on how the debates have centred on diagnostic categories as opposed to dimensions (e.g., Brown & Barlow, 2005; Kraemer, 2007; Widiger & Samuel, 2005), and also specifically pertaining to, for example, how dimensions can improve our understanding and diagnosis of depression (e.g., Klein, 2008). Essentially, the point about the inclusion of dimensions alongside categories (or diagnostic labels) is that it has the potential to better reflect severity and chronicity of a specific disorder in a fashion that is less complex and, one hopes, provide clearer distinctions with co-morbidity than in the current system (*ibid.*). Do these suggestions have any potential implications for mood and anxiety disorders in the context of traumatic brain injury? Most probably they will, if ever implemented. To illustrate this point, we should, for example, consider the evolution over time of depression after traumatic brain injury: understanding the disorder's severity and chronicity in this population can only serve to improve the rehabilitation of patients.

Using dimensions to specify the nature of specific diagnoses may also help to reduce the possibly artificial overlap or co-morbidity observed, in particular, among the anxiety disorders associated with traumatic brain injury. Rather than specifying several different diagnoses, where possible a single anxiety disorder could be identified, and the dimensions such as chronicity and severity used as specifiers. Again, this could help clinicians to focus on rehabilitation efforts. The use of dimensions may also help us to routinely incorporate formulation into the overall diagnostic process. For example, being cued to think about chronicity, one would inevitably have to consider which biological, psychological, and social factors are likely to maintain the disorder, and which may serve to ameliorate its effects. Specifying more clearly the severity of disorders may also help us to consider the factors in each individual case that may explain the "why now, and why so severe under these circumstances" question that underpins many formulations. Finally, whatever modifications *DSM-V* may contain, the general concepts or diagnoses describing the emotional difficulties we define as anxiety and depression will remain in one form or another; they have been present in persons since the earliest times and are unlikely to be airbrushed out of history or, indeed, people's experience by a new diagnostic manual.

Future research

While there has been significant progress in the acute management of traumatic brain injury, especially related to neurosurgical interventions (see Chapter One), there has, unfortunately, been more limited progress in the pharmacological management of acute traumatic brain injury (e.g., Beauchamp, Mutlak, Smith, Shohami, & Stahel, 2008). These authors conclude that experimental findings from animal studies have not yet yielded significant success in everyday clinical environments, and suggest that one reason might be that, during research, the therapeutic window of opportunity may often be missed, and that future protocols should allow emergency personnel to administer drugs at the scene of the accident. With regard to post-acute pharmacological management of emotional, behavioural, and cognitive difficulties associated with traumatic brain injury, Fleminger (2008) points out that, as yet, there are no data from randomized controlled trials with patients with traumatic brain injury to guide clinical practice, but suggests several clinical guidelines that could be considered when prescribing for these patients. Clearly, there is a need for further research in this area also.

While there is now at least some (albeit limited in some areas) emerging systematic evidence for the effectiveness of cognitive rehabilitation (e.g., Cicerone et al., 2005; Rees et al., 2007), a great need still exists for research focused more specifically on the effectiveness of psychotherapy as an intervention after traumatic brain injury. Some indirect evidence is provided by Pepping and Prigatano (2003) for the cost-effectiveness of psychotherapy, as part of a holistic brain injury rehabilitation programme. Practitioners increasingly view cognitive–behaviour therapy as a useful psychotherapeutic intervention in this population also, but perhaps more general and larger scale studies of psychotherapy with brain-injured persons are now needed. There is also growing recognition that cognitive rehabilitation strategies should be integrated with interventions targeting emotional difficulties after traumatic brain injury (Mateer, Sira, & O'Connell, 2005). With regard to future psychotherapy research, one strategy to consider here might be the use of a generic model that would allow the researcher to investigate the contribution of more general psychotherapeutic factors to outcome (Coetzer, 2007). For example, the therapeutic alliance has been found to be a potentially important factor (also with regard to the relatives of patients) (e.g., Sherer et al., 2007) and perhaps should be investigated in this manner to determine its potential role in the overall psychotherapeutic process.

One of the perennial problems in brain injury treatment outcomes research relates to the difficulties associated with the almost exclusive practice of not using control groups when conducting research in this population. To improve the evidence base of interventions, this problem will have to be overcome. Hart, Fann, and Novack (2008), in a recent review, looked at a variety of designs to help researchers identify strategies to ensure control groups where treatment is not given. More generally, the identification of pre-injury as well as post-injury factors increasing the risk for mental health difficulties after traumatic brain injury has been the focus of recent research also, but further work is needed in this area to refine future treatments and preventative strategies (Warriner & Velikonja, 2006). Finally, research is desperately needed for some of the special populations with traumatic brain injury. While significant advances have been made over the past couple of decades regarding the rehabilitation of children with traumatic brain injury (e.g., Ylvisaker et al., 2005), more work needs to be done. For example, we need to understand more about environmental influences, the role of specific lesions, and also developmental changes in children who have sustained traumatic brain injury (Taylor, 2004), and specifically also in the context of children from ethnic minorities and poorer socio-economic groups (Martin & Falcone, 2008).

Implications for training

Inevitably, the development of new diagnostic systems and cutting edge research findings tend to generate substantial and ongoing training needs. One merely needs to look at the multitude of conferences with brain injury rehabilitation as the core theme being advertised each year to realize this. There is no doubt that, to ensure safe and effective clinical practice, the responsible clinician needs an updating of his or her clinical and academic skills on a regular basis. However, many practitioners report coming away from (at least some) conferences feeling somewhat disillusioned or even more uncertain than before. Could it be that our continual focus on the newest and latest techniques or research findings is possibly obscuring a potential truism related to our everyday provision of a clinical service in the here and now, today? Is it possibly true that to provide effective brain injury rehabilitation, practitioners must, in the first instance, learn and then repeatedly apply the more basic skills related to assessment and rehabilitation, before focusing on the very latest research findings in the field? Do we not need to revisit the fundamentals of brain injury rehabilitation practice more often? And what about those clinicians who are pursuing initial training in brain injury rehabilitation? How can training and professional development opportunities be developed to best meet their needs as well as those of experienced practitioners? These are questions that are relevant to all of us working in brain injury rehabilitation settings.

As we know, consolidating fundamental and basic brain injury rehabilitation skills can demand considerable effort. Take, for example, the skill of becoming proficient at using a diagnostic system in clinical practice. Not only would this include the in-depth study of a recognized diagnostic system, but also different methods of assessment and, of course, formulation skills, as outlined in earlier chapters of this book. Or neuroanantomy, where knowledge is very difficult to retain and internalize without at least some exposure to alternative teaching strategies such as dissection demonstrations. Achieving an acceptable level of knowledge and skill in these areas most probably requires substantially more time allocated to, for example, direct teaching, observation at ward rounds, supervised practice, and formal assessment of knowledge, than, for example, other training models of problem-based learning or assessment by essays and critique of a given topic. Each of these training methods, of course, has its own distinct benefits and limitations. Clearly, the latter is more cost effective and perhaps better stimulates debate and research. Conversely, the former is not always practical or even achievable. It remains unclear which training method produces more rounded and effective practitioners within brain injury rehabilitation. Perhaps, in brain injury rehabilitation, we initially need to be able to perform several more fundamental tasks effectively, rather than being highly proficient at a few overly complex tasks. It is here that the provision of both traditional methods of training, such as direct teaching and practical demonstration followed by a period of supervised practice, in combination with more innovative training methods, can potentially prove to be a useful training model for brain injury rehabilitation professionals.

There is a recognized need for more formalized and perhaps structured training in brain injury rehabilitation, and some authors have indeed commented on this (e.g., Jackson & Manchester, 2001). Most programmes currently available in most countries of the world tend to not have an exclusive focus on traumatic brain injury, or, indeed, rehabilitation of mental health difficulties after brain injury. Most programmes cover a vast range of topics and tend to be very full already. Generally speaking, in the UK, for example, excellent training and professional development opportunities in the field, including the topic of rehabilitation of persons with traumatic brain injury, are provided by the Division of Neuro-psychology of the British Psychological Society and also the Special Interest Group in Neuropsychiatry of the Royal College of Psychiatry. In the USA, the Association of Postdoctoral Programs in Clinical Neuropsychology, as well as Division 40 of the American Psychological Association, are involved in promoting professional training in neuropsychology. Other organizations in the USA that are involved in the promotion of opportunities for training and professional development include, for example, the American Neuropsychiatric Association, which was established during 1988. Similar organizations exist in many other countries of the world. Some of the existing training programmes of these and other organizations, institutions, and universities have been developed relatively recently and may be enhanced by further development of the curriculum content and teaching methods.

While there is limited research dealing specifically with methods of training rehabilitation professionals, some interesting findings have nevertheless been reported by the few existing studies. For example, Simpson, Winstanley, and Bertapelle (2003) report a significant increase in professionals' skills and knowledge pertaining to the assessment and management of persons with traumatic brain injury who present with suicidal behaviours. A particular strength of this research is the use of a control group and the fact that it investigated an area of significant clinical relevance. Furthermore, the authors also report that the use of a self-assessment skills and knowledge tool they developed showed some promise (*ibid.*). Another innovative approach to brain injury rehabilitation was reported by Pentland, Hutton, Macmillan, and Mayer (2003). These investigators engaged seventy-two professionals in a brain injury simulation exercise, and report that pre- and post-exercise questionnaires revealed that participants thought they had an increased understanding of the phenomenological experiences of persons with traumatic brain injury. Creative approaches to training such as these can enhance substantially more didactic teaching approaches as well as self-directed learning. Finally, we need to ensure that brain injury rehabilitation training programmes include training of skills necessary for developing cultural sensitivity and competencies. Niemeier, Burnett, and Whitaker (2003) provide an overview of some of the important areas that need to be covered in this regard, including issues pertaining to, for example, assessment tools and attitudes towards disability.

One of the most valuable insights I have ever experienced happened to come from a young man who sustained a traumatic brain injury several years earlier. After several sessions, he must have sensed that I did not quite understand exactly how frustrated and depressed he was feeling. Perhaps observing my use of metaphors to explain things, he remarked that, for him, sustaining a traumatic brain injury was like being transformed instantaneously to anther continent, without having a memory of this journey, and then his first memory being that of swimming and swimming without end. After this marathon swim over a period of two years, he arrives "home". But nobody speaks his language; it is a new continent, meaning that nobody understands the person who has returned from having sustained a traumatic brain injury. Perhaps this metaphor reminds us that we need to do the basics very well, such as listening to our patients when we assess them or when providing psychotherapy interventions. There are ways to incorporate this type of knowledge acquisition into teaching and training, by, for example, co-opting expert patients on to teaching sessions, the use of appropriate clinical placements, and accessing patient accounts of traumatic brain injury. Despite these strategies, unfortunately, these are the lessons and skills that, in general, do not easily lend themselves to formal training and that textbooks cannot provide, but, rather, are learnt in the daily school that is clinical practice.

REFERENCES

Al-Adawi, S., Dorvlo, A. S. S., Al-Naamani, A., Glenn, M. B., Karamouz, N., Chae, H., Zaidan, Z. A., & Burke, D. T. (2007). The ineffectiveness of the Hospital Anxiety and Depression Scale for diagnosis in an Omani traumatic brain injured population. *Brain Injury, 21*(4): 385–393.

Al-Adawi, S., Dorvlo, A. S. S., Burke, D. T., Huynh, C. C., Jacob, L., Knight, R., Shah, M. K., & Al-Hussaini, A. (2004). Apathy and depression in cross-cultural survivors of traumatic brain injury. *Journal of Psychiatry & Clinical Neurosciences, 16*(4): 435–438.

Alderfer, B. S., Arciniegas, D. B., & Silver, J. M. (2005). Treatment of depression following traumatic brain injury. *Journal of Head Trauma Rehabilitation, 20*(6): 544–562.

Aloia, M. S., Long, C. J., & Allen, J. B. (1995). Depression among the head-injured and non-head-injured: a discriminant analysis. *Brain Injury, 9*(6): 575–583.

American Psychiatric Association (1994). *Diagnostic and Statistical Manual of Mental Disorders* (4th edn). Washington, DC: American Psychiatric Association.

Andelic, N., Sigurdardottir, S., Brunborg, C., & Roe, C. (2008). Incidence of hospital-treated traumatic brain injury in the Oslo population. *Neuroepidemiology, 30*(2): 120–128.

Aniskiewicz, A. (2007). *Psychotherapy for Neuropsychological Challenges*. New York: Jason Aronson.

Anson, K., & Ponsford, J. (2006a). Coping and emotional adjustment following traumatic brain injury. *Journal of Head Trauma Rehabilitation, 21*(3): 248–259.

Anson, K., & Ponsford, J. (2006b). Who benefits? Outcome following a coping skills group intervention for traumatically brain injured individuals. *Brain Injury, 20*(1): 1–13.

Arango-Lasprilla, J. C., Rosenthal, M., Deluca, J., Cifu, D. X., Hanks, R., & Komaroff, E. (2007). Functional outcomes from inpatient rehabilitation after traumatic brain injury: how do Hispanics fare? *Archives of Physical & Medical Rehabilitation, 88*(1): 11–18.

Arco, L. (2008). Neurobehavioural treatment for obsessive–compulsive disorder in an adult with traumatic brain injury. *Neuropsychological Rehabilitation, 18*(1): 109–124.

Ashman, T. A., Cantor, J. B., Gordon, W. A., Sacks, A., Spielman, L., Egan, M., & Hibbard, M. R. (2008). A comparison of cognitive functioning in older adults with and without traumatic brain injury. *Journal of Head Trauma Rehabilitation, 23*(3): 139–148.

Ashman, T. A., Gordon, W. A., Cantor, J. B., & Hibbard, M. R. (2006). Neurobehavioural consequences of traumatic brain injury. *The Mount Sinai Journal of Medicine, 73*(7): 999–1005.

Ashman, T. A., Spielman, L. A., Hibbard, M. R., Silver, J. M., Chandna, T., & Gordon, W. A. (2004). Psychiatric challenges in the first 6 years after traumatic brain injury: cross-sequential analyses of Axis I disorders. *Archives of Physical Medicine & Rehabilitation, 84*(4 Suppl. 2): 36–42.

Babin, P. R. (2003). Diagnosing depression in persons with brain injuries: a look at theories, the *DSM-IV* and depression measures. *Brain Injury, 17*(10): 889–900.

Barker-Collo, S. L. (2007). Behavioural profiles and injury severity following childhood traumatic brain injury. *Brain Impairment, 8*(1): 22–30.

Battistone, M., Woltz, D., & Clark, E. (2008). Processing speed deficits associated with traumatic brain injury: processing inefficiency or cautiousness? *Applied Neuropsychology, 15*(1): 69–78.

Bay, E., & Donders, J. (2008). Risk factors for depressive symptoms after mild-to-moderate traumatic brain injury. *Brain Injury, 22*(3): 233–241.

Beauchamp, K., Mutlak, H., Smith, W. R., Shohami, E., & Stahel, P. F. (2008). Pharmacology of traumatic brain injury—where is the "golden bullet"? *Molecular Medicine, 14*(11–12): 731–740.

Beck, A. T., Steer, R. A., & Brown, G. K. (1996). *Beck Depression Inventory-II Manual.* London: The Psychological Corporation.

Bedell, G. M. (2008). Functional outcomes of school-age children with acquired brain injuries at discharge from inpatient rehabilitation (2008). *Brain Injury, 22*(4): 313–324.

Berthier, M. L., Kulisevsky, J., Gironell, A., & Heras, J. A. (1996). Obsessive–compulsive disorder associated with brain lesions: clinical phenomenology, cognitive function, and anatomic correlates. *Neurology, 47*: 353–361.

Berthier, M. L., Kulisevsky, J. J., Gironell, A., & Lopez, O. L. (2001). Obsessive–compulsive disorder and traumatic brain injury: behavioural, cognitive and neuroimaging findings. *Neuropsychiatry, Neuropsychology & Behavioural Neurology, 14*(1): 23–31.

Berthier, M. L., Posada, A., & Puentes, C. (2001). Dissociative flashbacks after right frontal injury in a Vietnam veteran with combat related posttraumatic stress disorder. *Journal of Neuropsychiatry and Clinical Neuroscience, 13*(1): 101–105.

Beutler, L. E., Moleiro, C., & Talebi, H. (2002). How practitioners can systematically use empirical evidence in treatment selection. *Journal of Clinical Psychology, 58*(10): 1199–1212.

Biegler, P. (2008). Autonomy, stress, and treatment of depression. *British Medical Journal, 336*: 1046–1048.

Bigler, E. D. (2001). The lesion(s) in traumatic brain injury: implications for clinical neuropsychology. *Archives of Clinical Neuropsychology, 16*: 95–131.

Bigler, E. D. (2007). Anterior and middle cranial fossa in traumatic brain injury: relevant neuroanatomy and neuropathology in the study of neuropsychological outcome. *Neuropsychology, 21*(5): 515–531.

Bisson, J., & Andrew, M. (2007). Psychological treatment of post-traumatic stress disorder (PTSD). *Cochrane Database of Systematic Reviews, 18*(3): CD003388.

Block, S. H. (1987). Psychotherapy of the individual with brain injury. *Brain Injury, 1*(2): 203–206.

Bloom, D. R., Levin, H. S., Ewing-Cobbs, L., Saunders, A. E., Song, J., Fletcher, J. M., & Kowatch, R. A. (2001). Lifetime and novel psychiatric disorders after pediatric traumatic brain injury. *Journal of the American Academy of Child & Adolescent Psychiatry, 40*(5): 572–579.

Bombardier, C. H., Fann, J. R., Temkin, N., Esselman, P. C., Pelzer, E., Keough, M., & Dikmen, S. (2006). Posttraumatic stress disorder symptoms during the first six months after traumatic brain injury. *Journal of Neuropsychiatry & Clinical Neurosciences, 18*(4): 501–508.

Borkovec, T. D., & Ruscio, A. M. (2001). Psychotherapy for generalised anxiety disorder. *Journal of Clinical Psychiatry*, *62*(Suppl. 11): 37–42.

Bouras, T., Stranjalis, G., Korfias, S., Andrianakis, I., Pitaridis, M., & Sakas, D. E. (2007). Head injury mortality in a geriatric population: differentiating an "edge" age group with better potential for benefit than older poor-prognosis patients. *Journal of Neurotrauma*, *24*(8): 1355–1361.

Bowen, A., Neumann, V., Conner, M., Tennant, A., & Chamberlain, M. A. (1998). Mood disorders following traumatic brain injury: identifying the extent of the problem and the people at risk. *Brain Injury*, *12*(3): 177–190.

Bowen, C. (2007). Family therapy and neuro-rehabilitation: forging a link. *International Journal of Therapy and Rehabilitation*, *14*(8): 344–349.

Bowman, S. M., Martin, D. P., Sharar, S. R., & Zimmerman, F. J. (2007). Racial disparities in outcomes of persons with moderate to severe traumatic brain injury. *Medical Care*, *45*(7); 686–690.

Boyle, M. (2007). The problem with diagnosis. *The Psychologist*, *20*(5): 290–292.

Bracy, O. L. (1994). Counselling and psychotherapy for those with brain injury. *Journal of Cognitive Rehabilitation*, *12*(1): 8–11.

Breen, J. (2004). Road safety advocacy. *British Medical Journal*, *328*: 888–890.

British Society of Rehabilitation Medicine (1998). *Rehabilitation after Traumatic Brain Injury. A Working Party Report of the British Society of Rehabilitation Medicine*. London: Royal College of Physicians.

Brown, T. A., & Barlow, D. H. (2005). Dimensional versus categorical classification of mental disorders in the fifth edition of the *Diagnostic and Statistical Manual of Mental Disorders* and beyond: comment on the special section. *Journal of Abnormal Psychology*, *114*(4): 551–556.

Bruns, J., & Hauser, W. A. (2003). The epidemiology of traumatic brain injury: a review. *Epilepsia*, *44*(Suppl. 10): 2–10.

Bryant, R. A. (2001). Posttraumatic stress disorder and traumatic brain injury: can they co-exist? *Clinical Psychology Review*, *21*(6): 931–948.

Butler, R. W., & Satz, P. (1999). Depression and its diagnosis and treatment. In: K. G. Langer, L. Laatsch, & L. Lewis (Eds.), *Psychotherapeutic Interventions for Adults with Brain Injury or Stroke: A Clinician's Treatment Resource* (pp. 97–112). Madison, CT: Psychosocial Press.

Cameron, C. M., Purdie, D. M., Kliever, E. V., & McClure, R. J. (2008). Ten-year outcomes following traumatic brain injury: a population-based cohort. *Brain Injury*, *22*(6): 437–449.

Cantor, J. B., Ashman, T. A., Schwartz, M. E., Gordon, W. A., Hibbard, M. R., Brown, M., Spielman, L., Charatz, H. J., & Cheng, Z. (2005). The role of self-discrepancy theory in understanding post-traumatic brain injury affective disorders: a pilot study. *Journal of Head Trauma Rehabilitation, 20*(6): 527–543.

Chambless, D. L., & Ollendick, T. H. (2001). Empirically supported psychological interventions: controversies and evidence. *Annual Review of Psychology, 52*: 685–716.

Chang, P. F., Ostir, G. V., Kuo, Y. F., Granger, C. V., & Ottenbacher, K. J. (2008). Ethnic differences in discharge destination among older patients with traumatic brain injury. *Archives of Physical & Medical Rehabilitation, 89*(2): 231–236.

Chaytor, N., Temkin, N., Machamer, J., & Dikmen, S. (2007). The ecological validity of neuropsychological assessment and the role of depressive symptoms in moderate to severe traumatic brain injury. *Journal of the International Neuropsychological Society, 13*(3): 377–385.

Childers, M. K., Holland, D., Ryan, M. G., & Rupright, J. (1998). Obsessional disorders during recovery from severe head injury: report of four cases. *Brain Injury, 12*(7): 613–616.

Cicerone, K. D., Dahlberg, C., Malec, J. F., Langenbahn, D. M., Felicetti, T., Kneipp, S., Ellmo, W., Kalmar, K., Giacino, J. T., Harley, J. P., Laatsch, L., Morse, P. A., & Catanese, J. (2005). Evidence-based cognitive rehabilitation: updated review of the literature from 1998 through 2002. *Archives of Physical & Medical Rehabilitation, 86*(8): 1681–1692.

Cicerone, K. D., Mott, T., Azulay, J., & Friel, J. C. (2004). Community integration and satisfaction with functioning after intensive cognitive rehabilitation for traumatic brain injury. *Archives of Physical Medicine & Rehabilitation, 85*(6): 943–950.

Coetzer, B. R. (2004). Grief, self-awareness and psychotherapy following brain injury. *Illness, Crisis & Loss, 12*(2): 171–186.

Coetzer, B. R. (2006). *Traumatic Brain Injury Rehabilitation: A Psychotherapeutic Approach to Loss and Grief.* New York: Nova Science.

Coetzer, B. R., & Blackwell, H. (2003). Traumatic brain injury: caseload of a rural community based brain injury service. *Texas Journal of Rural Health, 21*(1): 42–46.

Coetzer, B. R., & Stein, D. J. (2003). Obsessive–compulsive disorder following traumatic brain injury: clinical issues. *The Journal of Cognitive Rehabilitation, 21*(4): 4–8.

Coetzer, B. R., Hayes, N. M., & Du Toit, P. L. (2002). Long term employment outcomes following traumatic brain injury in a rural area. *The Australian Journal of Rural Health, 10*(4): 229–232.

Coetzer, B. R., Vaughan, F. L., Roberts, C. B., & Rafal, R. (2003). The development of a holistic, community based neurorehabilitation service in a rural area. *Journal of Cognitive Rehabilitation, 21*(2): 4–8.

Coetzer, R. (2007). Psychotherapy following traumatic brain injury: integrating theory and practice. *The Journal of Head Trauma Rehabilitation, 22*(1): 39–47.

Coetzer, R. (2008). Holistic neuro-rehabilitation in the community: is identity a key issue? *Neuropsychological Rehabilitation, 18*(5–6): 766–783.

Colantonio, A., Ratcliff, G., Chase, S., & Vernich, L. (2004). Aging with traumatic brain injury: long-term health conditions. *International Journal of Rehabilitation Research, 27*(3): 209–214.

Coronado, V. G., Thomas, K. E., Sattin, R. W., & Johnson, R. L. (2005). The CDC traumatic brain injury surveillance system: Characteristics of persons aged 65 years and older hospitalized with a TBI. *Journal of Head Trauma Rehabilitation, 20*(3): 215–218.

Corrigan, J. D., & Bogner, J. A. (2008). Neighborhood characteristics and outcome after traumatic brain injury. *Archives of Physical and Medical Rehabilitation, 89*(5): 912–921.

Crossman, A. R., & Neary, D. (2000). *Neuronanatomy. An Illustrated Colour Text* (2nd edn). Edinburgh: Churchill Livingstone.

Crowell, T. A., Kieffer, K. M., Siders, C. A., & Vanderploeg, R. D. (2002). Neuropsychological findings in combat-related posttraumatic stress disorder. *The Clinical Neuropsychologist, 16*(3): 310–321.

Cummings, J. L. (1993). Frontal-subcortical circuits and human behaviour. *Archives of Neurology, 50*: 873–880.

Curren, C. A., Ponsford, J. L., & Crowe, S. (2000). Coping strategies and emotional outcome following traumatic brain injury: a comparison with orthopaedic patients. *Journal of Head Trauma Rehabilitation, 15*(6): 1256–1274.

Damasio, A. R. (1994). *Descartes' Error*. London: Picador.

Dawkins, N., Cloherty, M., Gracey, F., & Evans, J. J. (2006). The factor structure of the Hospital Anxiety and Depression Scale in acquired brain injury. *Brain Injury, 20*(12): 1235–1239.

Deb, S., & Burns, J. (2007). Neuropsychiatric consequences of traumatic brain injury: a comparison between two age groups. *Brain Injury, 21*(3): 301–307.

Deb, S., Lyons, I., Koutzoukis, C., Ali, I., & McCarthy, G. (1999). Rate of psychiatric illness 1 year after traumatic brain injury. *American Journal of Psychiatry*, 156(3): 374–378.

Derogatis, L. R. (1975). *Brief Symptom Inventory*. Baltimore, MD: Clinical Psychometric Research.

Dikmen, S. S., Machamer, J. E., Powell, J. M., & Temkin, N. R. (2003). Outcome 3 to 5 years after moderate to severe traumatic brain injury. *Archives of Physical Medicine & Rehabilitation*, 84(10): 1449–1457.

Dombovy, M. L., & Olec, A. C. (1996). Recovery and rehabilitation following traumatic brain injury. *Brain Injury*, 11(5): 305–318.

Draper, K., & Ponsford, J. (2008). Cognitive functioning ten years following traumatic brain injury and rehabilitation. *Neuropsychology*, 22(5): 618–625.

Ehlers, A., & Clark, D. M. (2000). A cognitive model of posttraumatic stress disorder. *Behaviour Research and Therapy*, 38: 319–345.

Ekers, D., Richards, D., & Gilbody, S. (2008). A meta-analysis of randomized trials of behavioural treatment of depression. *Psychological Medicine*, 38(5): 611–623.

Elbaum, J. (2007). Counselling individuals post acquired brain injury: consideration and objectives. In: J. Elbaum & D. M. Benson (Eds.) *Acquired Brain Injury. An Integrative Neuro-rehabilitation Approach* (pp. 259–273). New York: Springer.

Epstein, R. S., & Ursano, R. J. (1994). Anxiety disorders. In: J. M. Silver, S. C. Yudofsky, and R. E. Hales (Eds.), *Neuropsychiatry of Traumatic Brain Injury* (pp. 285–311). Washington, DC: American Psychiatric Press.

Farmer, J., Clark, M., & Sherman, A. (2003). Rural versus urban social support seeking as a moderating variable in traumatic brain injury outcome. *Journal of Head Trauma Rehabilitation*, 18(2): 116–127.

Flashman, L. A., Amador, X., & McAllister, T. W. (1998). Lack of awareness of deficits in traumatic brain injury. *Seminars in Clinical Neuropsychiatry*, 3: 201–210.

Fleming, J. M., Strong, J., & Ashton, R. (1998). Cluster analysis of self-awareness levels in adults with traumatic brain injury and relationship to outcome. *Journal of Head Trauma Rehabilitation*, 13(5): 39–51.

Fleminger, S. (2008). Long-term psychiatric disorders after traumatic brain injury. *European Journal of Anaesthesiology*, 42(Suppl.): 123–130.

Fleminger, S., Oliver, D. L., Lovestone, S., Rabe-Hesketh, S., & Giora, A. (2003). Head injury as a risk factor for Alzheimer's disease: the evidence 10 years on; a partial replication. *Journal of Neurology, Neurosurgery & Psychiatry*, 74: 857–862.

Fleminger, S., Oliver, D. L., Williams, W. H., & Evans, J. (2003). The neuropsychiatry of depression after brain injury. *Neuropsychological Rehabilitation, 13*(1–2): 65–87.

Fletcher, A. E., Khalid, S., & Mallonee, S. (2007). The epidemiology of severe traumatic brain injury among persons 65 years of age and older in Oklahoma, 1992–2003. *Brain Injury, 21*(7): 691–699.

Foa, E. B., Cashman, L., Jaycox, L., & Perry, K. (1997). The validation of a self-report measure of posttraumatic stress disorder: The Post-traumatic Diagnostic Scale. *Psychological Assessment, 9*(4): 445–451.

Follette, W. C., & Greenberg, L. S. (2006). Technique factors in treating dysphoric disorders. In: L. G. Castonguay & L. E. Beutler (Eds.), *Principles of Therapeutic Change that Work* (pp. 83–109). New York: Oxford University Press.

Folstein, M. F., Folstein, S. E., & McHugh, P. R. (1975). Mini-mental state. *Journal of Psychiatric Research, 12*: 189–198.

Freed, P. (2002). Meeting of the minds: ego reintegration after traumatic brain injury. *Bulletin of the Menninger Clinic, 66*(1): 61–78.

Gabella, B., Hoffman, R. E., Marine, W. W., & Stallones, L. (1997). Urban and rural traumatic brain injuries in Colorado. *Annals of Epidemiology, 7*(3): 207–212.

Gaudiano, B. A., Weinstock, L. M., & Miller, I. W. (2008). Improving treatment adherence in bipolar disorder: a review of current psychosocial treatment efficacy and recommendations for future treatment development. *Behaviour Modification, 32*(3): 267–301.

Gava, I., Barbui, C., Aguglia, E., Carlino, D., Churchill, R., De Vanna, M., & McGuire, H. F. (2007). Psychological treatments versus treatment as usual for obsessive compulsive disorder (OCD). *Cochrane Database of Systematic Reviews, 18*(2): CD005333.

Geraldina, P., Mariarosaria, L., Annarita, A., Susanna G., Michela, S., Alessandro, D., Sandra, S., & Enrico, C. (2003). Neuropsychiatric sequelae in TBI: a comparison across different age groups. *Brain Injury, 17*(10); 835–846.

Giacino, J. T., & Cicerone, K. D. (1998). Varieties of deficit unawareness after brain injury. *Journal of Head Trauma Rehabilitation, 13*(5): 1–15.

Gibson, J. (2005). Letter to the Editor. *International Journal of Psychiatry in Medicine, 35*(4): 435.

Glenn, M. B. (2002). A differential diagnostic approach to the pharmacological treatment of cognitive, behavioural, and affective disorders after traumatic brain injury. *Journal of Head Trauma Rehabilitation, 17*(4): 273–283.

Glenn, M. B., & Wroblewski, B. (2005). Twenty years of pharmacology. *Journal of Head Trauma Rehabilitation, 20*(1): 51–61.

Glenn, M. B., O'Neil-Pirozzi, T., Goldstein, R., Burke, D., & Jacob, L. (2001). Depression amongst outpatients with traumatic brain injury. *Brain Injury, 15*(9): 811–818.

Goel, V., & Grafman, J. (1995). Are the frontal lobes implicated in "planning" functions? Interpreting data from the Tower of Hanoi. *Neuropsychologia, 33*: 623–642.

Gontkovsky, S. T., Sherer, M., Nick, T. G., Nakase-Thompson, R., & Yablon, S. A. (2006). Effect of urbanicity of residence on TBI outcome at one year post-injury. *Brain Injury, 20*(7); 701–709.

Goodman, W. K., Price, L. H., Rasmussen, S. A., Maczure, C., Fleischmann, R. L., Hill, C. L., Heninger, G. R., & Charney, D. S. (1989). The Yale–Brown Obsessive Compulsive Scale. I. Development, use, and reliability. *Archives of General Psychiatry, 46*(11): 1006–1011.

Gracey, F., Brentnall, S., & Megoran, R. (2009). Judith; learning to do things "at the drop of a hat": behavioural experiments to explore and change the "meaning" in meaningful functional activity. In: B. A. Wilson, F. Gracey, J. J. Evans, & A. Bateman (Eds.), *Neuropsychological Rehabilitation: Theory, Therapy and Outcomes* (Chapter 17, pp. 256–270). Cambridge: Cambridge University Press.

Grados, M. A. (2003). Obsessive–compulsive disorder after traumatic brain injury. *International Review of Psychiatry, 15*: 350–358.

Grados, M. A., Vasa, R. A., Riddle, M A., Slomine, B. S., Salorio, C., Christensen, J., & Gerring, J. (2008). New onset obsessive–compulsive symptoms in children and adolescents with severe traumatic brain injury. *Depression & Anxiety, 25*(5): 398–407.

Green, A., Felmingham, K., Baguley, I. J., Slewa-Younan, S., & Simpson, S. (2001). The clinical utility of the Beck Depression Inventory after traumatic brain injury. *Brain Injury, 15*(12): 1021–1028.

Grieger, T. A., Cozza, S. J., Ursano, R. J., Hoge, C., Martinez, P. E., Engel, C. C., & Wain, H. J. (2006). Posttraumatic stress disorder and depression in battle-injured soldiers. *American Journal of Psychiatry, 163*(10): 1777–1783.

Guilmette, T. J. (1997). *Pocket Guide to Brain Injury, Cognitive, and Neurobehavioural Rehabilitation.* London: Singular Publishing.

Haider, A. H., Efron, D. T., Haut, E. R., DiRusso, S. M., Sullivan, T., & Cornwell, E. E. (2007). Black children experience worse clinical and functional outcomes after traumatic brain injury: an analysis of the National Pediatric Trauma Registry. *Journal of Trauma, 62*(5): 1259–1262.

Handel, S. F., Ovitt, L., Spiro, J. R., & Rao, V. (2007). Affective disorder and personality change in a patient with traumatic brain injury. *Psychosomatics*, 48(1): 67–70.

Harradine, P. G., Winstanley, J. B., Tate, R., Cameron, I. D., Baguley, I. J., & Harris, R. D. (2004). Severe traumatic brain injury in New South Wales: comparable outcomes for rural and urban residents. *Medical Journal of Australia*, 181(3): 130–134.

Harris, O. A., Bruce, C. A., Reid, M., Cheeks, R., Easley, K., Surles, M. C., Pan, Y., Rhoden-Salmon, D., Webster, D., & Crandon, I. (2008). Examination of the management of traumatic brain injury in the developing and developed world: focus on resource utilization, protocols, and practices that alter outcome. *Journal of Neurosurgery*, 109(3): 433–438.

Hart, T., Fann, J. R., & Novack, T. A. (2008). The dilemma of the control condition in experience-based cognitive and behavioural treatment research. *Neuropsychological Rehabilitation*, 18(1): 1–21.

Hawley, C. A., & Joseph, S. (2008). Predictors of positive growth after traumatic brain injury: a longitudinal study. *Brain Injury*, 22(5): 427–435.

Hayes, S. C., Strosahl, K. D., & Wilson, K. G. (2004). *Acceptance and Commitment Therapy. An Experiential Approach to Behavior Change.* New York: Guilford Press.

Heaton, R. K. (1981). *Wisconsin Card Sorting Test (WCST).* Odessa, FL: Psychological Assessment Resources.

Hibbard, M. R., Bogdany, J., Uysal, S., Kepler, K., Silver, J. M., Gordon, W. A., & Haddad, L. (2000). Axis II psychopathology in individuals with traumatic brain injury. *Brain Injury*, 14(10): 45–61.

Hibbard, M. R., Uysal, S., Kepler, K., Bogdany, J., & Silver, J. (1998). Axis I psychopathology in individuals with traumatic brain injury. *Journal of Head Trauma Rehabilitation*, 13(4): 24–39.

Hillier, S. L., Hiller, J. E., & Metzer, J. (1997). Epidemiology of traumatic brain injury in South Australia. *Brain Injury*, 11(9): 649–659.

Hiott, W. D., & Labbate, L. (2002). Anxiety disorders associated with traumatic brain injuries. *NeuroRehabilitation*, 17: 1–11.

Hodges, J. R. (1994). *Cognitive Assessment for Clinicians.* Oxford: Oxford University Press.

Hodgson, J., McDonald, S., Tate, R., & Gertler, P. (2005). A randomised controlled trial of a cognitive–behavioural therapy programme for managing social anxiety after acquired brain injury. *Brain Impairment*, 6(3): 169–180.

Holsinger, T., Steffens, D. C., Philips, C., Helms, M.J., Havlik, R. J., Breitner, J. C. S., Guralnik, J. M., & Plassman, B. L. (2002). Head injury in early adulthood and the lifetime risk of depression. *Archives of General Psychiatry, 59*: 17–22.

Horner, M. D., Selassie, A. W., Lineberry, L., Ferguson, P. L., & Labbate, L. A. (2008). Predictors of psychological symptoms 1 year after traumatic brain injury: a population-based, epidemiological study. *The Journal of Head Trauma Rehabilitation, 23*(2): 74–83.

Huang, D. B., Spiga, R., & Koo, H. (2005). Use of the Zung depression scale in patients with traumatic brain injury: 1 year post-injury. *Brain Injury, 19*(11): 910–908.

Hunot, V., Churchill, R., Silva de Lima, M., & Teixaira, V. (2007). Psychological therapies for generalised anxiety disorder. *Cochrane Database of Systematic Reviews, 24*(1): CD001848.

Hutchinson, P. J., & Pickard, J. D. (2006). Deficiencies in rehabilitation after traumatic brain injury. *British Medical Journal, 332*: 118.

Jackson, H., & Manchester, D. (2001). Towards the development of brain injury specialists. *NeuroRehabilitation, 16*(1): 27–40.

Johnstone, B., Nossaman, L. D., Schopp, L. H., Holmquist, L., & Rupright, S. J. (2002). Distribution of services and supports for people with traumatic brain injury in rural and urban Missouri. *Journal of Rural Health, 18*(1): 109–117.

Jorge, R. E. (2005). Neuropsychiatric consequences of traumatic brain injury: a review of recent findings. *Current Opinion in Psychiatry, 18*(3); 289–299.

Jorge, R. E., & Starkstein, S. E. (2005). Pathophysiologic aspects of major depression following traumatic brain injury. *Journal of Head Trauma Rehabilitation, 20*(6): 475–487.

Jorge, R. E., Robinson, R. G., Moser, D., Tateno, A., Crespo-Facorro, B., & Arndt, S. (2004). Major depression following traumatic brain injury. *Archives of General Psychiatry, 61*(1); 42–50.

Jorge, R. E., Robinson, R. G., Starkstein, S. E., Arndt, S. V., Forrester, A. W., & Geisler, F. H. (1993). Secondary mania following traumatic brain injury. *American Journal of Psychiatry, 150*(6): 916–921.

Judd, D., & Wilson, S. L. (2005). Psychotherapy with brain injury survivors: an investigation of the challenges encountered by clinicians and their modifications to therapeutic practice. *Brain Injury, 19*(6): 437–449.

Judd, T. (2003). Rehabilitation of the emotional problems of brain disorders in developing countries. *Neuropsychological Rehabilitation, 13*(1–2): 307–325.

Kant, R., Smith-Seemiller, L., & Duffy, J. D. (1996). Obsessive–compulsive disorder after closed head injury: review of literature and report of four cases. *Brain Injury, 10*(1): 55–63.

Kaplan-Solms, K., & Solms, M. (2000). *Clinical Studies in Neuro-psychoanalysis. Introduction to a Depth Neuropsychology.* London: Karnac.

Keiski, M. A., Shore, D. L., & Hamilton, J. M. (2007). The role of depression in verbal memory following traumatic brain injury. *Clinical Neuropsychology, 21*(5): 744–761.

Keltner, N. L., & Cooke, B. B. (2007). Traumatic brain injury—war related. *Perspectives in Psychiatric Care, 43*(4): 223–226.

Khan-Bourne, N., & Brown, R. G. (2003). Cognitive behaviour therapy for the treatment of depression in individuals with brain injury. *Neuropsychological Rehabilitation, 13*(1–2): 89–107.

Kim, E., Lauterbach, E. C., Reeve, A., Arciniegas, D. B., Coburn, K. L., Mendez, M. F., Rummans, T. A., Coffey, E. C., & ANPA Committee on Research (2007). Neuropsychiatric complications of traumatic brain injury: a critical review of the literature (a report by the ANPA Committee on Research). *Journal of Neuropsychiatry and Clinical Neuroscience, 19*(2): 106–127.

Kim, H. J., Burke, D. T., Dowds, M. M., Boone, K. A., & Park, G. J. (2000). Electronic memory aids for outpatient brain injury: follow-up findings. *Brain Injury, 14*(2): 187–196.

King, N. S. (2008). Post-traumatic stress disorder and traumatic brain injury: folklore and fact? *Brain Injury, 22*(1): 1–5.

Kinney, A. (2002). Cognitive therapy and brain injury: theoretical and clinical issues. *Journal of Contemporary Psychotherapy, 31*(2): 89–102.

Kirkwood, M., Janusz, J., Yeates, K. O., Taylor, H. G., Wade, S. L., Stancin, T., & Drotar, D. (2000). *Child Neuropsychology, 6*(3): 195–208.

Klein, D. N. (2008). Classification of depressive disorders in the *DSM-V*: proposal for a two-dimension system. *Journal of Abnormal Psychology, 117*(3): 552–560.

Klonoff, P. S., Watt, L. M., Dawson, L. K., Henderson, S. W., Gehrels, J. A., & Wethe, J. V. (2006). Psychosocial outcomes 1–7 years after comprehensive milieu-orientated neurorehabilitation: the role of pre-injury status. *Brain Injury, 20*(6): 601–612.

Kneebone, I. I., & Al-Daftary, S. (2006). Flooding treatment of phobia to having her feet touched by physiotherapists, in a young woman with Down's syndrome and traumatic brain injury. *Neuropsychological Rehabilitation, 16*(2): 230–236.

Koenigs, M., Huey, E. D., Raymont, V., Cheon, B., Solomon, J., Wasserman, E. M., & Grafman, J. (2008). Focal brain damage protects against post-traumatic stress disorder in combat veterans. *Nature & Neuroscience, 11*(2): 232–237.

Koponen, S., Taiminen, T., Kurki, T., Portin, R., Isoniemi, H., Himanen, L., Hinkka, S., Salokangas, R. K., & Tenovuo, O. (2006). MRI findings and Axis I and II psychiatric disorders after traumatic brain injury: a 30-year retrospective follow-up study. *Psychiatry Research, 146*(3): 263–270.

Koponen, S., Taiminen, T., Portin, R., Himanen, L., Isoniemi, H., Heinonen, H., Hinkka, S., & Tenovuo, O. (2002). Axis I and II psychiatric disorders after traumatic brain injury: a 30-year follow-up study. *American Journal of Psychiatry, 159*(8): 1315–1321.

Kraemer, H. C. (2007). DSM categories and dimensions in clinical and research contexts. *International Journal of Methods in Psychiatry Research, 16*(Suppl. 1): 8–15.

Kreutzer, J. S., Seel, R. T., & Gourley, E. (2001). The prevalence and symptom rates of depression after traumatic brain injury: A comprehensive examination. *Brain Injury, 15*(7): 563–576.

Labbate, L. A., & Warden, D. L. (2000). Common psychiatric syndromes and pharmacologic treatments of traumatic brain injury. *Current Psychiatry Reports, 2*(3): 268–273.

Labbate, L. A., Warden, D., & Murray, G. B. (1997). Salutary change after frontal brain injury. *Annals of Clinical Psychiatry, 9*(1): 27–30.

Landon, T. M., & Barlow, D. H. (2004). Cognitive–behavioural treatment for panic disorder: current status. *Journal of Psychiatric Practice, 10*(4): 211–226.

Larson, E. B., Leahy, B., Duff, K. M., & Wilde, M. C. (2008). Assessing executive functions in traumatic brain injury: an exploratory study of the Executive Interview. *Perceptual & Motor Skills, 106*(3): 725–736.

Lee, H. B., Lyketsos, C. G., & Rao, V. (2003). Pharmacological management of the psychiatric aspects of traumatic brain injury. *International Review of Psychiatry, 15*(4): 359–370.

Lefebvre, H., Cloutier, G., & Josee Levert, M. (2008). Perspectives of survivors of traumatic brain injury and their caregivers on long-term social integration. *Brain Injury, 22*(7), 535–543.

Leon-Carrion, J. (1997). An approach to the treatment of affective disorders and suicide tendencies after traumatic brain injury. In: J. Leon Carrion (Ed.), *Neuropsychological Rehabilitation: Fundamentals, Innovations and Directions* (pp. 415–429). Delroy Beach, FL: GR/St Lucie Press.

Levi, R. B., Drotar, D., Yeates, K. O., & Taylor, H. G. (1999). Post-traumatic stress symptoms in children following orthopaedic or traumatic brain injury. *Journal of Clinical Child Psychology, 28*: 232–243.

Levin, K. (2004). Paediatric traumatic brain injury in South Africa: some thoughts and considerations. *Disability Rehabilitation, 26*(5): 306–314.

Lewis, G. (2001). Mental health after head injury. *Journal of Neurology, Neurosurgery & Psychiatry, 71*(4): 431.

Lewis, L., & Rosenberg, S. J. (1990). Psychoanalytic psychotherapy with brain-injured adult psychiatric patients. *Journal of Nervous & Mental Disorders, 178*(2): 69–77.

Lezak, M. D., Howieson, D. B., & Loring, D. W. (2004). *Neuropsychological Assessment* (4th edn). New York: Oxford University Press.

Linden, D. E. J. (2006). How psychotherapy changes the brain—the contribution of functional neuroimaging. *Molecular Psychiatry, 11*(6): 528–538.

Lishman, W. A. (1998). Organic psychiatry. *The Psychological Consequences of Cerebral Disorder* (3rd edn). Abingdon: Blackwell Science.

Luis, C. A., & Mittenberg, W. (2002). Mood and anxiety disorders following paediatric traumatic brain injury: a prospective study. *Journal of Clinical & Experimental Neuropsychology, 24*(3): 270–279.

MacDonald, B. K., Mummery, C. J., & Heaney, D. (2001). Health needs of asylum seekers and refugees. Head injury needs to be taken into consideration in survivors of torture. *British Medical Journal, 323*: 230.

Macmillan, M. (2008). Phineas Gage—unraveling the myth. *The Psychologist, 21*(9): 828–831.

Maegele, M., Engel, D., Bouillon, B., Lefering, R., Fach, H., Raum, M., Buchheister, B, Schaefer, U., Klug, N., & Neugebauer, E. (2007). Incidence and outcome of traumatic brain injury in an urban area in Western Europe over 10 years. *European Surgical Research, 39*(6): 372–379.

Mainio, A., Kyllonen, T., Viilo, K., Hakko, H., Sarkioja, T., & Rasanen, P. (2007). Traumatic brain injury, psychiatric disorders and suicide: a population-based study of suicide victims during the years 1988–2004 in Northern Finland. *Brain Injury, 21*(8): 851–855.

Malec, J. F., Brown, A. W., Leibson, C. L., Flaada, J. T., Mandrekar, J. N., Diehl, N. N., & Perkins, P. K. (2007). The Mayo classification system for traumatic brain injury severity. *Journal of Neurotrauma, 24*: 1417–1424.

Malec, J. F., Testa, J. A., Rush, B. K., Brown, A. W., & Moessner, A. M. (2007). Self-assessment of impairment, impaired self-awareness, and depression after traumatic brain injury. *Journal of Head Trauma Rehabilitation, 22*(3): 156–166.

Manchester, D., & Wood, R. Ll. (2001). Applying cognitive therapy in neurobehavioural rehabilitation. In: R. Ll. Wood & T. M. McMillan (Eds.), *Neurobehavioural Disability and Social Handicap Following Traumatic Brain Injury* (pp. 157–174). Hove: Psychology Press.

Marquez de la Plata, C. D., Hart, T., Hammond, F. M., Frol, A. B., Hudak, A., Harper, C. R., O'Neil-Pirozzi, T. M., Whyte, J., Carlile, M., & Diaz-Arrastia, R. (2008). Impact of age on long-term recovery from traumatic brain injury. *Archives of Physical & Medical Rehabilitation, 89*(5): 896–903.

Marquez de la Plata, C., Hewlitt, M., de Oliveira, A., Hudak, A., Harper, C., Shafi, S., & Diaz-Arrastia, R. (2007). Ethnic differences in rehabilitation placement and outcome after TBI. *Journal of Head Trauma Rehabilitation, 22*(2): 113–121.

Martin, C. D. (2006). Ernest Hemingway: a psychological autopsy of a suicide. *Psychiatry, 69*(4): 351–361.

Martin, C., & Falcone, R. A. (2008). Pediatric traumatic brain injury: an update of research to understand and improve outcomes. *Current Opinion in Pediatrics, 20*(3): 294–299.

Mateer, C. A., & Sira, C. S. (2006). Cognitive and emotional consequences of TBI: intervention strategies for vocational rehabilitation. *NeuroRehabilitation, 21*(4): 315–326.

Mateer, C. A., Sira, C. S., & O'Connell, M. E. (2005). Putting Humpty Dumpty together again: the importance of integrating cognitive and emotional interventions. *Journal of Head Trauma Rehabilitation, 20*(1): 62–75.

Maultsby, M. C. (1984). *Rational Behaviour Therapy*. Englewood Cliffs, NJ: Prentice Hall.

McAllister, T. W. (2008). Neurobehavioural sequelae of traumatic brain injury: evaluation and management. *World Psychiatry, 7*(1): 3–10.

McCrea, M., Pliskin, N., Barth, J., Cox, D., Fink, J., French, L., Hammeke, T., Hess, D., Hopewell, A., Orme, D., Powell, M., Ruff, R., Schrock, B., Terryberry-spohr, L., Vanderploeg, R., & Yoash-Gantz, R. (2008). Official position of the military TBI task force on the role of neuropsychology and rehabilitation psychology in the evaluation, management, and research of military veterans with traumatic brain injury. *The Clinical Neuropsychologist, 22*: 10–26.

McKeon, J., McGuffin, P., & Robinson, P. (1984). Obsessive–compulsive neurosis following head injury. A report of four cases. *British Journal of Psychiatry, 144*: 190–192.

McMillan, T. M. (1991). Post-traumatic stress disorder and severe head injury. *British Journal of Psychiatry, 159*: 431–433.

McMillan, T. M. (2001). Errors in diagnosing post-traumatic stress disorder after traumatic brain injury. *Brain Injury, 15*: 39–46.

McMillan, T. M., & Ledder, H. (2001). A survey of services provided by community neurorehabilitation teams in South East England. *Clinical Rehabilitation, 15*: 582–588.

McMillan, T. M., Williams, W. H., & Bryant, R. (2003). Post-traumatic stress disorder and traumatic brain injury: a review of causal mechanisms, assessment, and treatment. *Neuropsychological Rehabilitation, 13*(1–2): 149–164.

Meachen, S. J., Hanks, R. A., Millis, S. R., & Rapport, L. J. (2008). The reliability and validity of the Brief Symptom Inventory-18 in persons with traumatic brain injury. *Archives of Physical & Medical Rehabilitation, 89*(5): 958–965.

Menzel, J. C. (2008). Depression in the elderly after traumatic brain injury: a systematic review. *Brain Injury, 22*(5): 375–380.

Meyer, A. (1904). The anatomical facts and clinical varieties of traumatic insanity. *American Journal of Insanity, 60*: 373–441.

Miklowitz, D. J. (2006). A review of evidence-based psychosocial interventions for bipolar disorder. *Journal of Clinical Psychiatry, 67*(Suppl. 11): 28–33.

Miklowitz, D. J., Goodwin, G. M., Bauer, M. S., & Geddes, J. R. (2008). Common and specific elements of psychosocial treatments for bipolar disorder: a survey of clinicians participating in randomised trials. *Journal of Psychiatric Practice, 14*(2): 77–85.

Miller, L. (1993). *Psychotherapy of the Brain-injured Patient: Reclaiming the Shattered Self.* New York: W. W. Norton.

Milliken, C. S., Auchterlonie, J. L., & Hoge, C. W. (2007). Longitudinal assessment of mental health problems among active and reserve component soldiers returning from the Iraq war. *Journal of the American Medical Association, 298*(18): 2141–2148.

Minns, R. A., Jones, P. A., & Mok, J. Y. (2008). Incidence and demography of non-accidental head injury in Southeast Scotland from a national database. *American Journal of Preventative Medicine, 34*(4 Suppl.): 126–133.

Mollica, R. F., Henderson, D. C., & Tor, S. (2002). Psychiatric effects of traumatic brain injury in Cambodian survivors of mass violence. *British Journal of Psychiatry, 181*: 339–347.

Moncrieff, J. (2007). Diagnosis and drug treatment. *The Psychologist, 20*(5): 296–297.

Mortensen, P. B., Mors, O., Frydenberg, M., & Ewald, H. (2003). Head injury as a risk factor for bipolar affective disorder. *Journal of Affective Disorders, 76*: 79–83.

Mustafa, B., Evrim, O., & Sari, A. (2005). Secondary mania following traumatic brain injury. *Journal of Neuropsychiatry and Clinical Neuroscience, 17*(1): 122–124.

Nantulya, V. M., & Reich, M. R. (2002). The neglected epidemic: road traffic injuries in developing countries. *British Medical Journal, 324*: 1139–1141.

National Institutes of Health (1998). Rehabilitation of persons with traumatic brain injury. *NIH Consensus Statement, 16*(1): 1–41.

Nelson, L. A., Rhoades, D. A., Noonan, C., Manson, S. M., & AI-SUPERPFP Team (2007). Traumatic brain injury and mental health among two American Indian populations. *Journal of Head Trauma Rehabilitation, 22*(2): 105–112.

Neylan, T. C. (2000). Neuropsychiatric consequences of traumatic brain injury: observations from Adolf Meyer. *Journal of Psychiatry & Clinical Neurosciences, 12*(3): 406.

Niedzwecki, C. M., Marwitz, J. H., Ketchum, J. M., Cifu, D. X., Dillard, C. M., & Monasterio, E. A. (2008). Traumatic brain injury: a comparison of inpatient functional outcomes between children and adults. *Journal of Head Trauma Rehabilitation, 23*(4): 209–219.

Niemeier, J. P., Burnett, D. M., & Whitaker, D. A. (2003). Cultural competence in the multidisciplinary rehabilitation setting: are we falling short of meeting needs? *Archives of Physical & Medical Rehabilitation, 84*(8): 1240–1245.

Norton, P. J., & Price, E. C. (2007). A meta-analytic review of adult cognitive-behavioural treatment outcomes across the anxiety disorders. *Journal of Nervous & Mental Disorders, 195*(6): 521–531.

O'Callaghan, C., Powell, T., & Oyebode, J. (2006). An exploration of the experience of gaining awareness of deficit in people who have suffered a traumatic brain injury. *Neuropsychological Rehabilitation, 16*(5): 579–593.

O'Gorman, M. (2006). Two accidents—one survivor: neurological and narcissistic damage following traumatic brain injury. *Psychodynamic Practice, 12*(2): 133–148.

Orlinsky, D. E., & Howard, K. I. (1986). Process & outcome in psychotherapy. In: S. L. Garfield & A. E. Berglov (Eds.), *Handbook of Psychotherapy and Behaviour Change* (pp. 311–383). New York: Wiley.

Orlinsky, D. E., & Howard, K. I. (1995). Unity and diversity among psychotherapies: a comparative perspective. In: B. Bongar & L.E. Beutler (Eds.), *Comprehensive Textbook of Psychotherapy. Theory and Practice* (pp. 3–23). New York: Oxford University Press.

O'Shanick, G. J. (2006). Update on antidepressants. *Journal of Head Trauma Rehabilitation*, 21(3): 282–284.

Oster, T. J., Anderson, C. A., Filley, C. M., Wortzel, H. S., & Arciniegas, D. B. (2007). Quetiapine for mania due to traumatic brain injury. *CNS Spectrum*, 12(10): 764–769.

Ownsworth, T. (2005). The impact of defensive denial upon adjustment following traumatic brain injury. *Neuro-Psychoanalysis*, 7(1): 83–94.

Ownsworth, T. L., McFarland, K., & Young, R. M. (2002). The investigation of factors underlying deficits in self-awareness and self-regulation. *Brain Injury*, 16(4): 291–309.

Parcell, D. L., Ponsford, J. L., Redman, J. R., & Rajaratnam, S. M. (2008). Poor sleep quality and changes in objectively recorded sleep after traumatic brain injury: a preliminary study. *Archives of Physical & Medical Rehabilitation*, 89(5): 843–850.

Park, E., Bell, J. D., & Baker A. J. (2008). Traumatic brain injury: can the consequences be stopped? *Canadian Medical Association Journal*, 178(90): 1163–1170.

Parker, R. S. (2002). Recommendations for the revision of DSM-IV diagnostic criteria for co-morbid posttraumatic stress disorder and traumatic brain injury. *NeuroRehabilitation*, 17(2): 131–143.

Parkes, C. M. (2006). Guest Editor's conclusions. *Omega*, 52(1): 107–113.

Paterson, B., & Scott-Findlay, S. (2002). Critical issues in interviewing people with traumatic brain injury. *Qualitative Health Research*, 12(3): 399–409.

Pentland, B., Hutton, L., Macmillan, A., & Mayer, V. (2003). Training in brain injury rehabilitation. *Disability Rehabilitation*, 25(10): 544–548.

Pepping, M., & Prigatano, G. P. (2003). Psychotherapy after brain injury: costs and benefits. In G. P. Prigatano & N. H. Pliskin (Eds.), *Clinical Neuropsychology and Cost Outcome Research: A Beginning* (pp. 313–327). New York: Psychology Press.

Pollack, I. W. (2005). Psychotherapy. In: J. M. Silver, T. W. McAllister, & S. C. Yudofsky (Eds.), *Textbook of Traumatic Brain Injury* (pp. 641–654). Washington, DC: American Psychiatric Publishing.

Ponniah, K., & Hollon, S. D. (2008). Empirically supported psychological interventions for social phobia in adults: a qualitative review of randomized controlled trials. *Psychological Medicine*, 38(1): 3–14.

Ponsford, J. (1995). Dealing with the impact of traumatic brain injury on psychological adjustment and relationships. In: J. Ponsford, S. Sloan, & P. Snow (Eds.), *Traumatic Brain Injury: Rehabilitation for Everyday Adaptive Living* (pp. 231–264). Hove: Psychology Press.

Powell, J., Heslin, J., & Greenwood, R. (2002). Community based rehabilitation after severe traumatic brain injury: a randomised controlled trial. *Journal of Neurology Neurosurgery and Psychiatry, 72*(2): 193–202.

Prigatano, G. P. (1997). The problem of impaired self-awareness in neuropsychological rehabilitation. In: J. Leon-Carrion (Ed.) *Neuropsychological Rehabilitation. Fundamentals, Innovations and Directions* (pp. 301–311). Delray Beach, FL: GR/St. Lucie Press.

Prigatano, G. P. (1999). *Principles of Neuropsychological Rehabilitation.* New York: Oxford University Press.

Prigatano, G. P. (2005). Therapy for emotional and motivational disorders. In: W. M. High, A. M. Sander, M. A. Struchen, & K. A. Hart (Eds.), *Rehabilitation for Traumatic Brain Injury* (pp. 118–130). New York: Oxford University Press.

Prigatano, G. P., Borgaro, S. R., & Caples, H. S. (2003). Nonpharmacological management of psychiatric disturbances after traumatic brain injury. *International Review of Psychiatry, 15*: 371–379.

Randolph, C. (1998). *RBANS Manual.* San Antonio, TX: The Psychological Corporation.

Rao, V., & Lyketsos, C. G. (2002). Psychiatric aspects of traumatic brain injury. *Psychiatric Clinics of North America, 25*(1): 43–69.

Rao, V., Spiro, J. R., Handel, S., & Onyike, C. U. (2008). Clinical correlates of personality changes associated with traumatic brain injury. *Journal of Neuropsychiatry & Clinical Neuroscience, 20*(1): 118–119.

Rao, V., Spiro, J., Degoankar, M., Horska, A., Rosenberg, P. B., Yousem, D. M., & Barker, P. B. (2006). Lesion location in depression post traumatic brain injury using magnetic resonance spectroscopy: preliminary results from a pilot study. *European Journal of Psychiatry, 20*(2): 65–73.

Rao, V., Spiro, J., Vaishnavi, S., Rastogi, P., Mielke, M., Noll, K., Cornwell, E., Schretlen, D., & Makley, M. (2008). Prevalence and types of sleep disturbances acutely after traumatic brain injury. *Brain Injury, 22*(5): 381–386.

Rapoport, M. J., Herrmann, N., Shammi, P., Kiss, A., Phillips, A., & Feinstein, A. (2006). Outcome after traumatic brain injury sustained in older adulthood: a one-year longitudinal study. *American Journal of Geriatric Psychiatry, 14*(5): 456–465.

Rapport, L. J., Bryer, R. C., & Hanks, R. A. (2008). Driving and community integration after traumatic brain injury. *Archives of Physical & Medical Rehabilitation, 89*(5): 922–930.

Ratcliff, G., Colantonio, A., Escobar, M., Chase, S., & Vernich, L. (2005). Long-term survival following traumatic brain injury. *Disability Rehabilitation, 27*(6): 305–314.

Rees, L., Marshall, S., Hartridge, C., Mackie, D., Weiser, M., & Erabi Group (2007). Cognitive interventions post acquired brain injury. *Brain Injury, 21*(2): 161–200.

Reitan, R. M., & Wolfson, D. (1985). *The Halstead–Reitan Neuropsycholgical Test Battery: Therapy and Clinical Interpretation.* Tucson, AZ: Neuropsychological Press.

Riley, G. A., Brennan, A. J., & Powell, T. (2004). Threat appraisal and avoidance after traumatic brain injury: why and how often are activities avoided? *Brain Injury, 18*(9): 871–888.

Rivera, P. A., Elliott, T. R., Berry, J. W., & Grant, J. S. (2008). Problem solving training for family caregivers of persons with traumatic brain injuries: a randomised controlled trial. *Archives of Physical and Medical Rehabilitation, 89*(5): 931–941.

Roebuck-Spencer, T., & Sherer, M. (2008). Moderate and severe traumatic brain injury. In: J. E. Morgan & J. H. Ricker (Eds.), *Textbook of Clinical Neuropsychology* (pp. 411–429). New York: Taylor & Francis.

Rogers, J. M., & Read, C. A. (2007). Psychiatric comorbidity following traumatic brain injury. *Brain Injury, 21*(13–14): 1321–1333.

Rose, F. D., & Johnson, D. A. (Eds.). (1996). *Brain Injury and After. Towards Improved Outcome.* Chichester: Wiley.

Rosen, G. M., Spitzer, R. L., & McHugh, P. R. (2008). Problems with the post-traumatic disorder diagnosis and its future in DSM-V. *British Journal of Psychiatry, 192*: 3–4.

Royal College of Physicians and British Society of Rehabilitation Medicine (2003). *Rehabilitation Following Acquired Brain Injury: National Clinical Guidelines,* L. Turner-Stokes (Ed.). London: Royal College of Physicians, British Society of Rehabilitation Medicine.

Royall, D. R., Lauterbach, E. C., Cummings, J. L., Reeve, A., Rummans, T. A., Kaufer, D. I., LaFrance, W. C. Jr., & Coffey, E. C. (2002). Executive control function: a review of its promise and challenges for clinical research. A report from the Committee on Research of the American Neuropsychiatric Association. *Journal of Neuropsychiatry & Clinical Neuroscience, 14*(4): 377–405.

Royall, D. R., Mahurin, R. K., & Gray, K. F. (1992). Bedside assessment of executive cognitive impairment: the executive interview. *Journal of the American Geriatric Society*, 40(12): 1221–1226.

Runyan, D. K., Berger, R. P., & Barr, R. G. (2008). Defining an ideal system to establish the incidence of inflicted traumatic brain injury: summary of the consensus conference. *American Journal of Preventative Medicine*, 34(4 Suppl.): 163–168.

Sadock, B. J., & Sadock, V. A. (2007). *Kaplan and Sadock's Synopsis of Psychiatry* (10th edn). London: Wolters Cluver/Lippincott Williams & Wilkins.

Safaz, I., Alaca, R., Yasar, E., Tok, F., & Yilmaz, B. (2008). Medical complications, physical function and communication skills in patients with traumatic brain injury: a single centre 5-year experience. *Brain Injury*, 22(10): 733–739.

Salvarani, C. P., Colli, B. O., & Júnior, C. G. C. (2009). Impact of a programme for the prevention of traffic accidents in a Southern Brazilian city: a model for implementation in a developing country. *Surgical Neurology*, 72(1): 6–13.

Sarajuuri, J. M., & Koskinen, S. K. (2006). Holistic neuropsychological rehabilitation in Finland: The INSURE programme—a transcultural outgrowth of perspectives from Israel to Europe via the USA. *International Journal of Psychology*, 41(5): 362–370.

Sarmiento, K., Langlois, J. A., & Mitchko, J. (2008). "Help seniors live better, longer: prevent brain injury": an overview of CDC's education initiative to prevent fall-related TBI among older adults. *Journal of Head Trauma Rehabilitation*, 23(3): 164–167.

Sayal, K., Ford, T., & Pipe, R. (2000). Case study: bipolar disorder after head injury. *Journal of the American Academy of Child and Adolescent Psychiatry*, 39(4): 525–528.

Scheutzow, M. H., & Wiercisiewski, D. R. (1999). Panic disorder in a patient with traumatic brain injury: a case report and discussion. *Brain Injury*, 13(9): 705–714.

Schootman, M., & Fuortes, L. (1999). Functional status following traumatic brain injuries: population-based rural-urban differences. *Brain Injury*, 13(12): 995–1004.

Scicutella, A. (2007). Neuropsychiatry and traumatic brain injury. In: J. Elbaum & D. M. Benson (Eds.), *Acquired Brain Injury. An Integrative Neuro-rehabilitation Approach* (pp. 81–121). New York: Springer.

Selassie, A. W., Zaloshnja, E., Langlois, J. A., Miller, T., Jones, P., & Stener, C. (2008). Incidence of long-term disability following traumatic brain injury hospitalization, United States, 2003. *Journal of Head Trauma Rehabilitation, 23*(2): 123–131.

Shafi, S., de la Plata, C. M., Dïaz-Arrastia, R., Bransky, A., Frankel, H., Elliott, A. C., Parks, J., & Gentilello, L. M. (2007). Ethnic disparities exist in trauma care. *Journal of Trauma, 63*(5): 1138–1142.

Shapiro, E. D. (2008). Using case-control studies to assess the prevention of inflicted traumatic brain injury. *American Journal of Preventative Medicine, 34*(4 Suppl.): 153–156.

Sherer, M., Evans, C. C., Leverenz, J., Stouter, J., Irby, J. W. Jr, Lee, J. E., & Yablon, S. A. (2007). Therapeutic alliance in post-acute brain injury rehabilitation: predictors of strength of alliance and impact on outcome. *Brain Injury, 21*(7): 663–672.

Sherer, M., Hart, T., Whyte, J., Nick, T. G., & Yablon, S. A. (2005). Neuroanatomic basis of impaired self-awareness after traumatic brain injury. *Journal of Head Trauma Rehabilitation, 20*(4): 287–300.

Sherer, M., Oden, K., Bergloff, P., Levin, E., & High, W. M. (1998). Assessment and treatment of impaired awareness after brain injury: implications for community re-integration. *NeuroRehabilitation, 10*:25–37.

Shukla, S., Cook, B. L., Mukherjee, S., Godwin, C., & Miller, M. (1987). Mania following head trauma. *American Journal of Psychiatry, 144*: 93–96.

Silver, J. M., Kramer, R., Greenwald, S., & Weissman, M. A. (2001). The association between head injuries and psychiatric disorders: findings from the New Haven NIMH Epidemiologic Catchment Area Study. *Brain Injury, 15*(11): 935–945.

Simpson, G. K., & Tate, R. L. (2005). Clinical features of suicide attempts after traumatic brain injury. *Journal of Nervous and Mental Disorders, 193*(10): 680–685.

Simpson, G. K., & Tate, R. L. (2007). Preventing suicide after traumatic brain injury: implications for general practice. *Medical Journal of Australia, 187*(4): 229–232.

Simpson, G., Winstanley, J., & Bertapelle, T. (2003). Suicide prevention training after traumatic brain injury: evaluation of a staff training workshop. *Journal of Head Trauma Rehabilitation, 18*(5): 445–456.

Smith, T. C., Ryan, M. A. K., Wingard, D. L., Slymen, D. J., Sallis, J. F., Kritz-Silverstein, D., for the Millennium Cohort Study Team (2008). New onset and persistent symptoms of post-traumatic stress disorder self reported after deployment and combat exposure: prospective population based US military cohort study. *British Medical Journal, 336*: 366–370.

Spitzer, R. C., Williams, J. B., Gibbon, M., & First, M. B. (1992). The Structured Clinical Interview for DSM III-R (SCID). I: History, rationale and description. *Archives of General Psychiatry, 49*(8): 624–629.

Sprenkle, D. H., & Blow, A. J. (2004). Common factors and our sacred models. *Journal of Marital and Family Therapy, 30*(2): 113–129.

Stallones, L., Gibbs-Long, J., Gabella, B., & Kakefuda, I. (2008). Community readiness and prevention of traumatic brain injury. *Brain Injury, 22*(7): 555–564.

Starkstein, S. E., & Lischinsky, A. (2002). The phenomenology of depression. *NeuroRehabilitation, 17*(2): 105–113.

Stengler-Wenzke, K., Muller, U., & Matthes-von-Cramon, G. (2003). Compulsive–obsessive disorder after severe head trauma: diagnosis and treatment. [Article in German]. *Psychiatrie Praxis, 1*: 37–39.

Storch, E. A., Kaufman, D. A. S., Bagner, D., Merlo, L. J., Shapira, N. A., Geffken, G. R., Murphy, T. K., & Goodman, W. K. (2007). The Florida Obsessive–Compulsive Inventory: development, reliability and validity. *Journal of Clinical Psychology, 63*(9): 851–859.

Strub, R. L., & Black, F. W. (1993). *The Mental Status Examination in Neurology* (3rd edn). Philadelphia, PA: F. A. Davis.

Struchen, M. A., Clark, A. N., Sander, A. M., Mills, M. R., Evans, G., & Kurtz, D. (2008). Relation of executive functioning and social communication measures to functional outcomes following traumatic brain injury. *NeuroRehabilitation, 23*(2): 185–198.

Sumpter, R. E., & McMillan, T. M. (2005). Misdiagnosis of post-traumatic stress disorder following severe TBI. *British Journal of Psychiatry, 186*: 423–426.

Svendsen, H. A., & Teasdale, T. W. (2006). The influence of neuropsychological rehabilitation on symptomatology and quality of life following brain injury: a controlled long-term follow-up. *Brain Injury, 20*(12): 1295–1306.

Taber, K. K., Warden, D. L., & Hurley, R. A. (2006). Blast-related traumatic brain injury: what is known? *Journal of Neuropsychiatry and Clinical Neuroscience, 18*(2): 141–145.

Tate, R. L., McDonald, S., & Lulham, J. M. (1998). Incidence of hospital-treated traumatic brain injury in an Australian community. *Australian & New Zealand Journal of Public Health, 22*(4): 419–423.

Tawil, I., Stein, D. M., Mirvis, S. E., & Scalea, T. M. (2008). Posttraumatic cerebral infarction: incidence, outcome, and risk factors. *Journal of Trauma, 64*(4): 849–853.

Taylor, C. A., & Price, T. R. P. (1994). Neuropsychiatric assessment. In: J. M. Silver, S. C. Yudofsky, and R. E. Hales (Eds.), *Neuropsychiatry of Traumatic Brain Injury* (pp. 81–132). Washington, DC: American Psychiatric Press.

Taylor, H. G. (2004). Research on outcomes of pediatric brain injury: current advances and future directions. *Developmental Neuropsychology, 25*(1–2): 199–225.

Taylor, H. G., Swartwout, M. D., Yeates, K. O., Walz, N. C., Stancin, T., & Wade, S. L. (2008). Traumatic brain injury in young children: postacute effects on cognitive and school readiness skills. *Journal of the International Neuropsychological Society, 14*(5): 734–745.

Teasdale, G., & Jennett, B. (1974). Assessment of coma and impaired consciousness: a practical scale. *Lancet, 2*: 81–84.

Teasdale, T. W., Christensen, A.-L., Willmes, K., Deloche, G., Braga, L., Stachowiak, F., Vendrell, J., Castro-Caldas, A., Laaksonen, R. K., & Leclercq, M. (1997). Subjective experience in brain-injured patients and their close relatives: a European Brain Injury Questionnaire study. *Brain Injury, 11*(8): 543–563.

Teasdale, W., & Engberg, A. W. (2001). Suicide after traumatic brain injury: a population study. *Journal of Neurology, Neurosurgery & Psychiatry, 71* (4): 436–440.

Tenovuo, O. (2006). Pharmacological enhancement of cognitive and behavioural deficits after traumatic brain injury. *Current Opinion in Neurology, 19*(6): 528–533.

Thomas, K. E., Stevens, J. A., Sarmiento, K., & Wald, M. M. (2008). Fall-related traumatic brain injury deaths and hospitalizations among older adults—United States, 2005. *Journal of Safety Research, 39*(3): 269–272.

Thompson, H. J., McCormick, W. C., & Kagan, S. H. (2006). Traumatic brain injury in older adults: epidemiology, outcomes, and future implications *Journal of the American Geriatric Society, 54*(10): 1590–1595.

Tian, H. L., Geng, Z., Cui, Y. H., Hu, J., Xu, T., Cao, H. L., Chen, S. W., & Chen, H. (2008). Risk factors for posttraumatic cerebral infarction in patients with moderate or severe head trauma. *Neurosurgery Review, 31*(4): 431–436.

Tobe, E. H., Schneider, J. S., Mrozik, T., & Lidsky, T. I. (1999). Persisting insomnia following traumatic brain injury. *The Journal of Neuropsychiatry and Clinical Neurosciences, 11*(4): 504–506.

Trexler, L. E., Eberle, R., & Zappala, G. (2000). Models and programmes of the Center for Neuropsychological Rehabilitation: fifteen years experience. In: A.-L. Christensen & B. P. Uzzell (Eds.) *International Handbook of Neuropsychological Rehabilitation* (pp. 215–229). Dordrecht, Netherlands: Kluwer Academic Publishers.

Turner-Stokes, L., Kalmus, M., Hirani, D., & Clegg, F. (2005). The Depression Intensity Scale Circles (DISCs): a first evaluation of a simple assessment tool for depression in the context of brain injury. *Journal of Neurology, Neurosurgery & Psychiatry, 76*: 1273–1278.

Turner-Stokes, L., MacWalter, R., Guideline Development Group of the British Society of Rehabilitation Medicine, British Geriatrics Society, & Royal College of Physicians London (2005). Use of antidepressant medication following acquired brain injury: concise guidance. *Clinical Medicine, 5*(3): 268–274.

Van Reekum, R., Bolago, I., Finlayson, M. A., & Garner, S. (1996). Psychiatric disorders after traumatic brain injury. *Brain Injury, 10*(5): 319–327.

Van Reekum, R., Cohen, T., & Wong, J. (2000). Can traumatic brain injury cause psychiatric disorders? *Journal of Neuropsychiatry and Clinical Neurosciences, 12*(3): 316–327.

Veale, D. (2008). Behavioural activation for depression. *Advances in Psychiatric Treatment, 14*(1): 29–36.

Viguier, D., Dellatolas, G., Gasquet, I., Martin, C., & Choquet, M. (2001). A psychological assessment of adolescent and young adult inpatients after traumatic brain injury. *Brain Injury, 15*(3): 263–271.

Votruba, K. L., Rapport, L. J., Vangel, S. J., Hanks, R. A., Lequerica, A., Whitman, R. D., & Langenecker, S. (2008). Impulsivity and traumatic brain injury: the relations among behavioural observation, performance measures, and rating scales. *The Journal of Head Trauma Rehabilitation, 23*(2): 65–73.

Warden, D. (2006). Military TBI during the Iraq and Afghanistan wars. *Journal of Head Trauma Rehabilitation, 21*(5): 398–402.

Warnell, P. (1997). Injury prevention programs: do they really make a difference? *AXON, 19*(1): 6–9.

Warriner, E. M., & Velikonja, D. (2006). Psychiatric disturbances after traumatic brain injury: neurobehavioral and personality changes. *Current Psychiatry Reports, 8*(1): 73–80.

Whelan-Goodinson, R., Ponsford, J., & Schonberger, M. (2009). Validity of the Hospital Anxiety and Depression Scale to assess depression and anxiety following traumatic brain injury as compared with the Structured Clinical Interview for DSM-IV. *Journal of Affective Disorders, 114*(1–3): 94–102.

Whitnall, L., McMillan, T. M., Murray, G. D., & Teasdale, G. M. (2006). Disability in young people and adults after head injury: 5–7 year follow up of a prospective cohort study. *Journal of Neurology, Neurosurgery & Psychiatry*, 77(5): 640–645.

Widiger, T. A., & Samuel, D. B. (2005). Diagnostic categories or dimensions? A question for the *Diagnostic and Statistical Manual of Mental Disorders* (5th edition). *Journal of Abnormal Psychology*, 114(4): 494–504.

Williams, W. H. (2003). Neuro-rehabilitation and cognitive therapy for emotional disorders in acquired brain injury. In: B. A. Wilson (Ed.), *Neuropsychological Rehabilitation: Theory and Practice* (pp. 115–136). Lisse, Netherlands: Swets & Zeitlinger.

Williams, W. H., Evans, J. J., & Fleminger, S. (2003). Neurorehabilitation and cognitive–behaviour therapy of anxiety disorders after brain injury: an overview and case illustration of obsessive–compulsive disorder. *Neuropsychological Rehabilitation*, 13(1–2): 133–148.

Williams, W. H., Evans, J. J., & Wilson, B. A. (2003). Neurorehabilitation for two cases of post-traumatic stress disorder following traumatic brain injury. *Cognitive Neuropsychiatry*, 8(1): 1–18.

Williams, W. H., Evans, J. J., Wilson, B. A., & Needham, P. (2002). Brief report: prevalence of post-traumatic stress disorder symptoms after severe traumatic brain injury in a representative community sample. *Brain Injury*, 16(8): 673–679.

Wilson, B. A., Evans, J., Brentnall, S., Bremner, S., Keohane, C., & Williams, H. (2000). The Oliver Zangwill Center for Neuropsychological Rehabilitation: A partnership between health care and rehabilitation research. In A-L. Christensen & B. P. Uzzell (Eds.) *International Handbook of Neuropsychological Rehabilitation* (pp. 231–246). Dordrecht, Netherlands: Kluwer Academic.

Wood, R. Ll. (2008). Long-term outcome of serious traumatic brain injury. *European Journal of Anaesthesiology*, 42(Suppl.): 115–122.

Wood, R. Ll., & Rutterford, N. A. (2006). Psychosocial adjustment 17 years after severe traumatic brain injury. *Journal of Neurology, Neurosurgery & Psychiatry*, 77(1): 71–73.

Woody, S. R., & Ollendick, T. H. (2006). Technique factors in treating anxiety disorders. In: L. G. Castonguay & L. E. Beutler (Eds.), *Principles of Therapeutic Change that Work* (pp. 167–186). New York: Oxford University Press.

World Health Organization (1992). *The ICD-10 Classification System of Mental and Behavioural Disorders*. Geneva: WHO.

Yap, S. G., & Chua, K. S. (2008). Rehabilitation outcomes in elderly patients with traumatic brain injury in Singapore. *Journal of Head Trauma Rehabilitation*, 23(3): 158–163.

Yeates, G. N., Gracey, F., & McGrath, J. C. (2008). Biopsychosocial deconstruction of "personality change" following acquired brain injury. *Neuropsychological Rehabilitation*, 18(5–6): 566–589.

Yeates, G. N., Henwood, K., Gracey, F., & Evans, J. (2007). Awareness of disability after acquired brain injury and the family context. *Neuropsychological Rehabilitation*, 17(2): 151–173.

Ylvisaker, M., Adelson, P. D., Braga, L. W., Burnett, S. M., Glang, A., Feeney, T., Moore, W., Rumney, P., & Todis, B. (2005). Rehabilitation and ongoing support after pediatric TBI: twenty years of progress. *Journal of Head Trauma Rehabilitation*, 20(1): 95–109.

Ylvisaker, M., McPherson, K., Kayes, N., & Pellett, E. (2008). Metaphoric identity mapping: facilitating goal setting and engagement in rehabilitation after traumatic brain injury. *Neuropsychological Rehabilitation*, 18(5–6): 713–741.

Zigmond, A. S., & Snaith, R. P. (1983). The hospital anxiety and depression scale. *Acta Psychiatrica Scandinavia*, 67(6): 361–370.

Zung, W. W. K. (1965). A self-rating depression scale. *Archives of General Psychiatry*, 12: 63–70.

Zygun, D. A., Laupland, K. B., Hader, W. J., Kortbeek, J. B., Findlay, C., Doig, C. J., & Hammeed, S. M. (2005). Severe traumatic brain injury in a large Canadian health region. *Canadian Journal of Neurological Science*, 32(1): 87–92.